Gateways to Knowledge

Gateways to Knowledge
The Role of Academic Libraries in
Teaching, Learning, and Research

edited by
Lawrence Dowler

The MIT Press
Cambridge, Massachusetts
London, England

Second printing, 1998

© 1997 Massachusetts Institute of Technology

This book was set in Sabon by Wellington Graphics and was printed and bound in the United States of America.

Library of Congress Cataloging-in-Publication Data

Gateways to knowledge: the role of academic libraries in teaching, learning, and research / edited by Lawrence Dowler.
  p. cm.
Includes bibliographical references and index.
ISBN 0–262–04159–6 (hb: alk. paper)
  1. Academic libraries—Aims and objectives—United States. I. Dowler, Lawrence.
Z675.U5G39 1997
027.7—dc20   96-31423
                                                        CIP

Contents

Foreword

Richard De Gennaro

Gateways to Knowledge is an important and timely book because it examines the changing role of research libraries in supporting research and learning in the information age. Information technology is perhaps the defining issue for libraries today as everyone in higher education struggles to understand the challenges and opportunities it provides in an era of diminishing resources.

Although there have been many changes in the Harvard College Library over the years, in some important ways the library still operates much as it has in the past. The collection is, as it has always been, paramount, and services to readers are tailored to the particular constituencies in the eleven libraries of the Harvard College Library and several dozen departmental libraries in the Faculty of Arts and Sciences (FAS). This system has been highly successful in the past, but now it needs to become more responsive to the changes occurring in higher education. New technologies, increasing multidisciplinary research, rapid expansion in the quantity and variety of evidence needed for research, rising costs and finite resources, and the complexities of navigating an expanding system of research sources are among the elements of change that prompted the Harvard College Library to prepare a strategic plan that establishes priorities and charts a course for the last decade of this century and the opening of the next.

One of the goals of the library's strategic plan is to "help students and faculty to achieve maximum benefit from library services and resources by making use of the Library more convenient and efficient." To do this, the library proposes that it will provide more resources, especially staff and space, to help students and faculty locate, retrieve, and use the materials they need. Predicated on the notion that research ought to inform instruction and that interdisciplinary studies and information technologies are transforming the ways of knowing, the strategic plan proposes that learning how to use electronic information effectively in a variety of formats and on networks is an increasingly important part of undergraduate education. The library therefore plans to supplement books and journals with information technology to introduce students to the plethora of sources at Harvard and beyond. This aspect of the strategic plan was the beginning of the idea of a gateway.

For Harvard, a gateway library does not replace the book collection with technology. Rather, the gateway, like Janus, looks to the documentary sources of the past, even as it looks in the direction of electronic sources that will be increasingly available in the future. If the primary function of Widener Library is to build a preeminent research collection, the purpose of the gateway is to provide the services that will enable readers at all levels to locate and efficiently use these resources. Three interrelated ideas emerged from these discussions of the gateway: first, the gateway is a point of access, an intellectual portal to other library and research resources at Harvard and, electronically, beyond; second, the gateway is a place for teaching; and, finally, the gateway is a source for the services and support needed by students and faculty to locate and use the information they need in the form in which they need it.

Several related issues and events contributed to the evolving idea of the gateway as a bridge to the library of the future for the community at Harvard. First, the beginning of Harvard's capital campaign in May 1994 created an opportunity to renovate Lamont Library, the principal undergraduate library at Harvard. Nearly fifty years old, Lamont needed to be refurbished; but planners questioned whether the renovation should replicate the structure and programs of the past or whether it should reconsider them in light of changing needs and uses. From the groundwork laid by the strategic planning process grew a particular interest in reexamining the role of the undergraduate library and a discussion of the metaphor of a gateway as a new paradigm for the role of Lamont within the College Library.

Another circumstance that contributed to the concept of the gateway was Harvard's decentralization. How could the library deliver services efficiently in a highly decentralized system of libraries? There are eleven libraries in the Harvard College Library, in addition to nine professional school libraries and the Schlesinger Library at Radcliffe College. Each serves its own segment of the Harvard community and operates independently, setting policies for collection development, access, and use. Harvard's libraries adhere to the University's custom of "every tub on its own bottom"; decentralization and autonomy are at the core of our history. As a result of the strategic planning effort, however, it became clear that it was simply no longer feasible or logical to duplicate services in all eleven of the libraries in the Harvard College Library. Centralization of some services and greater coordination of reference, instructional, and access services would help overcome the inefficiencies, excessive costs, and inadequate reference support, especially for electronic resources.

The decisive impetus to the idea of the gateway, however, was electronic information technology. Determining the Library's response to changes that follow in the wake of an information technology explosion involves discussions much broader than those limited to the undergraduate library. But the immediate need to renovate Lamont provided an opportunity not only to consider the relationship of information technology to undergraduate education but also to discuss how the library might best carry out its mission to support teaching and research in Harvard College. Initial discussions about technology focused on Lamont and library support for undergraduate learning, but the discussion of technology and research quickly shifted to include the research collections in Widener and in the rest of the College and FAS libraries. Task forces were created to explore issues such as networking numerical data, improving access to research materials through document delivery, and providing reference and instructional services in a gateway environment. Over several months, the groups assessed the possibilities and problems of each topic, and the libraries have acted on their recommendations— from establishing a position to coordinate resources for environmental studies to developing a coordinated research publication program. More recently, groups have been formed to address the challenges of supporting the use of electronic texts by students and faculty and finding an appropriate (and affordable) strategy for providing access to databases in a variety of formats.

Thanks to a grant from the Council on Library Resources, the Harvard College Library was able to host a conference that drew together librarians, administrators, and scholars to explore in depth the idea of the gateway and the future of research libraries. As Billy E. Frye, interim president and provost of Emory University, observes in part I of this book, the title of this book and the conference on which it is based, *Gateways to Knowledge,* is particularly apt

because it emphasizes one of the traditional functions of the library—access to information. In the context of electronic technologies, the gateway concept causes us to suspend our usual notions of boundaries, whether library walls or book covers. More than that, it offers the portent—indeed, in considerable degree the actuality—that the melding of information with the powers of electronic technologies will bring about basic changes in the ways we teach and learn, the sorts of research questions we ask, and the ways we synthesize knowledge.

Patrick Manning from Northeastern University and Anthony Appiah from Harvard provide in part II an interesting perspective on one of the least reported phenomena in academia today—how changes in research are affecting library resources. For those curious about what a scientist, a social scientist, and humanist might think about the influence of information technology on research and scholarly communication, Paul Ginsparg, Richard C. Rockwell, and John Unsworth explore in part III how electronic information technology is affecting these three areas of scholarship and research.

Part IV presents the ideas of some of the leading proponents and practitioners of the gateway concept. Lawrence Dowler argues for centralizing some library services within the physically distributed library system at Harvard, while Richard C. Rockwell portrays the library of the future in terms of networks. Jan Olsen, who directs the Mann Library at Cornell, provides one model of a gateway library, and Peter Lyman's new gateway library at the University of Southern California incorporates the latest in technology for student workstations. Both are being studied by librarians throughout the country. In part V three of the most thoughtful scholars on the issue of teaching and learning—Richard A. Lanham from UCLA, Karen Price from the Graduate School of Education at Harvard, and James Wilkinson, director of the Derek Bok Center for Teaching and Learning at Harvard—examine the influence of technology on learning and the role of the library in these activities.

Part VI introduces still another version of the gateway concept—the Information Arcade at the University of Iowa, which is directed by another of our authors, Anita Lowry—and an educational software package—an electronic book—called *Who Built America? From the Centennial Celebration to the Great War of 1914,* which was produced by Roy Rosenzweig and Steve Brier, that is one of the most interesting, from a pedagogical perspective. Finally, in the postscript Lawrence Dowler tries to explicate the influence of information technology on the mission and goals of research libraries.

This is a distinguished group of scholars, academic administrators, and librarians, and their ideas, assembled in this volume, make an important contribution to the national discussion of the role of research libraries in the emerging information age.

Preface

Gateways to Knowledge is about change; it is about suspending old ideas without rejecting them and thinking anew about the purpose of the university and the library. It examines three basic and interrelated areas—teaching, learning, and research—exploring how concepts in each are changing. The point is not just to pay homage to what everyone readily acknowledges—that the purpose of the library is to support teaching, learning, and research—but to understand what the transformation of these basic concepts of higher education means for libraries. Since old terms and definitions no longer fit comfortably the emerging reality of the university, they cannot determine the role of the library within it. This collection of essays examines the influence of digital technology on teaching, learning, and scholarly communication and suggests some ways the library might respond.

The conference at which these articles first were presented posed a set of questions that aimed at curbing the participants' inevitable tendency to stray across what is still an open landscape. I have organized these papers into six parts and a postscript and have supplied headnotes to each part that introduce the principal themes suggested by the title of each part—a structure that reflects the different parts of the discussion about higher education and the library. But readers, like the authors of these essays, may find their attention wandering across these boundaries to compare what is being said with a parallel or contrary opinion suggested in an essay in another part. This suggests, of course, the connectedness and complexity of the cultural forces—the hypertextual connectedness—that are reshaping higher education. Writing these headnotes helped to clarify and deepen my own understanding of these essays, and I hope readers will find them useful.

The first essay, by Billy E. Frye, provides a helpful overview of the forces affecting universities and libraries today. He sets the stage for succeeding chapters by asking the question, Whither libraries? within the context of the larger question, Whither universities and higher education?

In the second part, "Changing Scholarship: Influences on Teaching and Research," Patrick Manning and Anthony Appiah look, albeit briefly, at an issue too little appreciated in terms of its impact on teaching and research and therefore on libraries: the changing patterns of research and the variety of resources now needed to support it. In a sense, changes in the nature of scholarship and research anticipated and created a climate for accepting many of the changes we now attribute to information technology. How, for example, have changes in research expanded the sources now needed for research? What effect does the expansion of these sources have on the basic mission of the library? How can the library improve access to these sources regardless of form, genre, or location? What is the library's role in managing and providing access to these varied sources?

The third part is entitled "The Gateway in Research and Scholarly Communication." What emerges from these essays by physicist Paul Ginsparg, social scientist Richard C. Rockwell, and humanist John Unsworth is a striking set of parallels and subtle differences in understanding the influences of information technology on three areas of intellectual inquiry. A fundamental question is, How does information technology alter the process of scholarly communication? How should the gateway library increase access to research data and information in each academic area? What are the implications for doing so? What are the advantages of library participation in the development of scholarly databases, electronic texts, and other sources for scholarship and instruction? How can the library provide a locus for experimentation and a collaborative environment for scholars, students, and librarians?

The fourth section, "Concepts of the Gateway: Libraries and Technology," contains themes that recur in nearly all of the essays in this book. But these four essays by Lawrence Dowler, Richard C. Rockwell, Jan Olsen, and Peter Lyman envision the library as gateway from different perspectives: What is the rationale for a gateway library, and what are the reasons for developing gateway services and facilities? What factors combine to produce the need for such an array of services? How does information technology affect the basic mission of the library, and does the gateway provide an appropriate response?

In the fifth section, "Technology and Education: The Role of Libraries in Teaching and Learning," Richard A. Lanham, Karen Price, and James Wilkinson also look at the future of libraries but primarily from the perspective of how libraries can affect teaching and learning during the transition from a culture of print to the digital age. What is the role of the library in teaching students and scholars in an information-rich environment? Are there ways the library can improve the information literacy of students? Are there fundamental differences between electronic information and traditional print sources that require different services for teaching and learning? Can information technology, especially interactive multimedia, improve learning?

The sixth section, "Tools for Learning," also focuses on teaching and learning but with an eye toward creating a particular kind of library environment or designing specific tools for learning. In it, Anita Lowry,* Roy Rosenzweig, and Steve Brier consider questions such as: What should be the role of librarians in evaluating electronic information? How can or should the library support faculty in developing courseware or information sources for courses? Is this an appropriate role for the library, and if not, who should do it?

The boundaries provided by these six groupings are, like those of the conference, somewhat artificial and certainly malleable. Readers may question the placement of a chapter in a particular part. The breadth of Lanham's and Lyman's essays, for example, defies easy categorization; Lyman might just as easily been grouped with the essays on "Technology and Education," and Lanham's chapter would not have been out of place in part IV on "Concepts of the Gateway." Anita Lowry and Jan Olsen could easily swap places, and Karen Price's essay would have been equally at home in part VI on "Tools for Learning" or part IV on "Concepts of the Gateway." This was true for many of the chapters included in this volume. The problem seemed particularly acute in Richard C. Rockwell's original essay, and so he graciously agreed to split it in two essays, which explains why he appears in two different parts.

Of the four underlying concerns of this book, only information technology is addressed explicitly either in the chapters or in the framework used for organizing them. These four themes merit further discussion: the first two are the subject of the remainder of this preface, and the last two are discussed in the postscript. First, the original focus on how the library ought to respond to the continued growth of information technology has broadened to an exploration of higher education and the potential role of the library within it. Second, information technology, a powerful force for change, is unsettling traditional arrangements and old agendas. Gauging its effect and locating the new opportunities that it may offer for universities and libraries are recurring themes in this book. This attention to technology takes two forms: how technology creates opportunities for dramatically increasing access to information and enhancing scholarly communication and how digital information affects what people learn and the ways they learn. Third, the centrality of the library within the academic community is a recurring theme in many of these essays. This was not an idea I expected to encounter in a discussion of emerging networked information and distributed computing. What this may suggest is a heartfelt plea for someone, somewhere, to order the volatile world of electronic information and provide a way to turn information into knowledge. A final theme implicit in many of these essays is the nature and locus of problems facing universities and research libraries. It is striking that many problems do not result simply from deficiencies in technology but more complicatedly from institutional and organizational structures that cannot respond to changes—some brought on by technology—in academia. Problems can result from lack of strategic vision or planning, from uncertainty about the kind of personnel needed in the new information environment, from lack of clarity about who should be responsible for adding value to information to make it more useful, and from failure to understand the kind of instruction that students and scholars need to engage the new information structures. Technological change and its pace have cast an unforgiving light on the areas of the university where a shadowy rigidity has held sway.

It is appropriate, indeed essential, to begin a conversation about the future role of research libraries by looking first at higher education and universities. Although scholarship and libraries are interrelated, they tend to be regarded organizationally as separate and distinct; the library is all too often seen as ancillary to the institution, a handmaiden to scholars that passively reflects current research interests. Scholarship is what one does; the library provides the resources that are consumed by scholars. This view of the library as separate, even an end unto itself, is understandable; it is partly a corollary to the development of librarianship as a profession separate from scholarship. It also is connected to the vision of research libraries as national institutions with national and even international scholarly clientele. In fact, the great research libraries are national resources and are dedicated to the support of a scholarship that knows no bounds; they dwell in the future as well as the past and depend on a community of scholars who reside everywhere. But there is a conceit here that belies the local purpose and the local financial support on which American research libraries depend.

Because many of the authors represented in this volume are scholars who view the library through an academic lens, they have important differences in their perceptions of the library. Most surprising is a tendency to define the library's role not as a passive agent within the university but as an active partner in contributing to the educational mission of the university. The questions they raise are not just about providing access to information, but about teaching students and scholars how to use it, and adding value to information to make it more useful for research and learning. Several writers also recognize that in the emerging digital environment, process and product, author and reader, even distinctions among forms of information—audio, text, visual—are becoming less clear, and institutional relationships less certain. From this perspective, the library and university are seen as part of the same intellectual frame, and changes to one directly implicate the other. The question is no longer how the library supports existing programs; rather, the question is how the purpose and role of the library can change to enable it to participate in new forms of learning and the educational mission of the university. To do this we must shift our attention to these basic elements of education and begin to consider the library from within this larger framework.

No examination of libraries or education can ignore the influence of information technology. The nature of its impact—a pervasive theme in these essays—is still scarcely understood, although there is little doubt that it will continue to change the face of higher education. Although few of these essays display the technodeterminism that characterizes much writing about technology today, a prevailing mood of optimism is displayed in nearly all of the chapters in this volume. There is certainly very little of the doubt and pessimism about the dire consequences that some fear technology will bring to learning and little of the reaction to technology that is now beginning to surface, ironically, in print. Perhaps this optimism is a function of the idea of the gateway and the promise of new beginnings. In any case, nearly all of the essays reveal a hopefulness about the possibilities that information technology might bring to teaching, learning, and research. What is striking, however, is the distinction between those who see technology as a solution to the problem of scholarly communication and those who are more concerned with how technology affects how and what we know and teaching and learning. These are not mutually exclusive categories, of course, and several authors are concerned with both themes. Both perspectives—technology as the means to greater access to information and enhanced communication versus the epistemological implications of digital information for education and learning—have implications for universities and libraries.

Finally, I have written a postscript that draws on and is informed by the preceding essays but represents my own opinions about the direction libraries are headed. It is becoming increasingly clear that we are now embarked on a national discussion about higher education, a discussion that everyone represented in this volume agrees ought to include libraries. I can best serve this purpose by being opinionated, perhaps even provocative—not so much to have the final say but to promote and contribute to this discussion. Without holding any of the authors represented here responsible for these opinions, this is what I have tried to do.

Note

*It is with great sadness that I must report that Anita Lowry died last summer following heart surgery. Ms. Lowry was one of the pioneers in implementing many of the concepts discussed in this volume. The Information Arcade at the University of Iowa, described in her essay, is one of the models librarians throughout the country are watching with interest and great expectations.

Acknowledgments

In addition to the authors represented here, many people contributed to this publication and to the conference on which it is based. The Council on Library Resources generously supported the conference as part of the Harvard College Library's strategic planning initiative. Sidney Verba, the Carl H. Pforzheimer University Professor and director of the University Library, and Richard De Gennaro, the Roy E. Larsen Librarian of Harvard College, were active participants in the conference. Jeremy R. Knowles, dean of the Faculty of Arts and Sciences, and Neil Rudenstine, president of Harvard University, gave their support and the president also addressed the presenters. My thanks to Geoffrey Freeman, principal, Shepley Bulfinch Richardson and Abbott Architects, for his stimulating presentation on "Designing the Gateway: Issues and Ideas." Special thanks are also due to William Kirby, professor of history, James Engell, professor of English and comparative literature, Richard Thomas, professor of Greek and Latin, and James Wilkinson, director of the Derek Bok Center for Teaching and Learning, each of whom chaired a panel and provided thoughtful analysis of the presentations on their panels and on the proceedings of the conference as a whole. In addition, Dr. Wilkinson wrote an essay for this book.

More than one hundred Harvard librarians participated in eleven task forces and working groups that contributed many of the ideas reflected in my own comments and observations. But I would like particularly to note the work and support of the Gateway Project Steering Committee: Heather Cole, Arlyne Jackson, Carrie Kent, Diane Garner, Donald Frank, Tommy Holton, Michael Fitzgerald, Jeffery Horrell, and Laura Farwell, the project coordinator. Elizabeth Johnson, Dennis Marnon, Jan Weiner, and, again, Laura Farwell and Jeffrey Horrell were instrumental in planning and arranging the conference, and Elizabeth Johnson provided unfailing administrative support in preparing this book. Jan Weiner keyed and rekeyed portions of chapters, converted a variety of text files into a single format, regularized the headings and layout of the various papers, and did all of the tasks that make turning conference presentations into a publication such a challenge. Cheryl LaGuardia, newly arrived at Harvard, exercised her considerable persuasive powers to encourage this book, and Doug Sery, my editor at the MIT Press, has been unfailingly helpful and has shown a level of composure and equanimity beyond his years. Deborah Cantor-Adams, my production editor, also at the MIT Press, introduced a measure of consistency among the disparate chapters.

My wife, Barbara Pine, who teaches graduate students in social work, was especially helpful in casting a critical, nonlibrarian's eye over the preface and made a number of suggestions that brought a measure of order to what was becoming an unwieldy introduction. Carrie Kent was the principal author of the idea that the nature of an inquiry, rather than a person's status within the university, ought to determine the kind of service provided by the library. Carrie also wrote portions of an earlier version of a chapter concerning the renovations of Lamont Library, which was incorporated into my own discussion chapter, published here in part IV on "Concepts of the Gateway: Libraries and Technology." I am also indebted to Carrie, Michael Blake, Terry Martin, and Diane Garner for contributions to the several scenarios that were used in this chapter. Finally, I would like to acknowledge and thank Laura Farwell, who not only served as project coordinator for the conference but who has been steadfast in her commitment to furthering discussion of the concept of the gateway. Laura sees "the big picture," and she has the uncommon ability to help authors say what they mean to say, generally with greater clarity than they could achieve on their own. Laura not only critiqued the preface, postscript, and all of the headnotes, but she provided insightful analysis and ideas that sharpened the focus of these essays. To Laura, to everyone who has contributed their ideas and work to this project, and, most of all, to all of the authors represented in this volume, my thanks for contributing to an important, national conversation about the future of research libraries in the emerging information age.

Contributors

Anthony Appiah is professor of Afro-American studies and philosophy in the Faculty of Arts and Sciences, Harvard University.

Steve Brier is director of the American Social History Project and the Center for Media and Learning at Hunter College at the City University of New York.

Richard De Gennaro, retired, was Roy E. Larsen Librarian of Harvard College.

Lawrence Dowler is associate librarian of Harvard College for public services at Harvard University.

Billy E. Frye is provost of Emory University, Atlanta, Georgia. He has long been involved in libraries and is one of the leading advocates of a national approach to library issues.

Paul Ginsparg is a theoretical high-energy physicist at Los Alamos National Laboratory. He is the founder and operator of the e-print archive for physics.

Richard A. Lanham is professor of English at the University of California at Los Angeles.

Anita Lowry was head of the Information Arcade in the Main Library at the University of Iowa.

Peter Lyman was the university librarian and dean of university libraries at the University of Southern California. Currently, he is director of libraries at the University of California at Berkeley.

Patrick Manning is distinguished professor of history and African-American studies at Northeastern University.

Jan Olsen is director of the Albert R. Mann Library at Cornell University.

Karen Price teaches in the Graduate School of Education at Harvard University and also is an independent consultant.

Richard C. Rockwell is executive director of the Inter-university Consortium for Political and Social Resarch at the University of Michigan.

Roy Rosenzweig is professor of history at George Mason University.

John Unsworth is director of the Institute for Advanced Technology in the Humanities at the University of Virginia.

James Wilkinson is director of the Derek Bok Center for Teaching and Learning at Harvard University.

Gateways to Knowledge

I

The Academy in Transition

By examining the library within the framework of the university, Billy E. Frye provides a much needed perspective on a national problem that is too often portrayed in local terms. Moreover, by focusing on the dramatic increase in research as a key component in the growth and spiraling cost of universities, he also points to the underlying reason libraries are struggling to assemble the resources needed by changing academic programs. New disciplines and interfaculty initiatives are launched leaving librarians, with library resources already overextended by current demands, wondering how to respond.

At one level, the problem for both universities and their libraries is financial, and cost containment is their most pressing need. Frye provides graphic evidence of the financial crisis now affecting universities. Equally important, however, he provides stunning proof of the enormous national commitment to building library resources and proffers a solution to our local needs. The challenge is to harness this system of resources. But the competitive model of American higher education, while it does not entirely preclude the idea that library resources are a common good, nevertheless tends to associate the benefit of the library with each university. Scholars understand, of course, that research depends on the contributions of many institutions, but the notion of a common good is too abstract to garner much public support, and universities simply cannot continue to sustain research collections at the same level as they have in the past.

Technology, says Frye, provides the tools for increasing access to and sharing information; what is lacking is the institutional will and collaborative organizational structures that would enable universities and their research libraries to share resources. But failure to achieve collaborative solutions undermines all universities' ability to support research, thereby undermining the principal ingredient in the success of American higher education and the engine of our economic prosperity.

1

Universities in Transition: Implications for Libraries

Billy E. Frye

Introduction

Many institutions are groping with the issues arising from the changing role and character of the university library, and it seems especially significant that Harvard University—the site of our nation's first and greatest academic libraries—should be engaged in an effort to fathom the full implications of emergent technologies for the future of information management.

Harvard, among all American universities, has the longest and most successful tradition of building and maintaining in-depth collections of books, monographs, journals, and archives across a wide spectrum of fields. These great collections provide Harvard libraries with the opportunity to exploit the benefits of new technologies by expanding access to them but also increase the risk that commitment to the collection may seem compromised by these technologies.

In some ways the status quo must seem both safer and more comfortable than the electronic future of libraries. But the choices presented by emergent information technologies *must* be faced by all of us. I suggest that the process is not one of turning away from our traditional approaches to information management but of looking beyond them. Without great collections the new technologies can have only limited significance for scholarship.

Although I have no expertise in digital technology, it is my thesis that a marriage between paper and electronic technologies is both necessary and serendipitous given the changing conditions of academic life. In the future the dominant feature of the information environment will not be scarcity of information but the need to make order of its abundance so that it is meaningfully accessible.

Thus, the metaphor of the library as the gateway to knowledge is very apt because it emphasizes one of the traditional functions of the library—access to information. In the context of electronic technologies, the gateway concept causes us to suspend our usual notions of boundaries, whether library walls or book covers. More than that, it offers the portent—indeed, in considerable degree the actuality—that the melding of information with the powers of electronic technologies will bring about basic changes in the ways we teach and learn, the sorts of research questions we ask, and the ways we synthesize knowledge.

Contemporary Challenges Faced by the Research University

When considering the higher education environment within which the new era of information access is evolving, I think it important to examine some of the prevailing challenges that American universities now face and will face into the foreseeable future and also to reflect on the predicament of research libraries. Together these perspectives point to the necessity, indeed the imperative, to look beyond the present to new approaches to information acquisition, storage, and access that can more adequately address our needs in light of the new realities of our operating environment.

A friend of mine, a prominent faculty member in the Emory Business School, recently gave a lecture to a group of businesspeople about the future of higher education. His central thesis was "change." The thrust of his speech was that "if the American system of higher education is going to retain its position as the greatest in the world, our universities have got to change the way they conduct the business of teaching and research."

This, of course, is essentially what all higher education soothsayers are saying. Indeed, it's about all they are saying with any degree of certainty. To be sure, some of the more imaginative speculate about new paradigms of teaching and research, and those with the courage to do so suggest what the nature of socially responsible changes *ought* to be. But considering the destabilizing tensions and imbalances that have built up over the years and are now pressing insistently for resolution, no one can say just what our future *will* be.

Most of the current concerns of research universities have their principal roots in two historical trends that have taken place over the last fifty years: (1) the great increase in the size and complexity of universities and (2) the increasing involvement of universities in broader social agendas. The latter trend includes especially the push for greater access to our universities by underrepresented social classes and a growing partnership between universities, government, and industry in pursuing the practical benefits of research.

The end of World War II brought a rapid influx of students into our colleges and universities. At the same time, the nation's appetite was whetted for more technology and a better-educated citizenry to cope with a world increasingly reliant on technology and knowledge. Driven by these developments, American colleges and universities grew enormously. Between 1949 and the present,

· The number of colleges and universities increased from 1,800 to over 3,000,
· Enrollments grew from 2,250,000 to over 12,500,000,
· Annual expenditures rose from about $1.7 billion to over $70 billion,
· The aggregate size and value of the physical plant increased more than fiftyfold, and
· Federal sponsorship of research grew from around $100 million to over $11 billion.

In the single decade of the 1960s, American higher education grew more than in the previous three centuries, and despite current complaints about downsizing and budget reduction, many of these figures continue to increase significantly each year.

This growth, extraordinary in its own right, fueled an even more fundamental change in the structure and organization of universities. It led to an enormous proliferation in the depth, variety, and scope of programs under the university's administrative umbrella and a corresponding multiplication of the missions and purposes of the university. To the core function of instruction in the liberal arts was added a vast array of professional education programs, auxiliary services, and institutes for research and application of knowledge.

For example, between 1945 and 1991, the number of faculty at Emory University, my own institution, grew from 126 to almost 1,900; the number of academic departments increased from 46 to 83; the number of degree programs increased from 14 to 70; and the number of centers, institutes, and other special programs increased from essentially none to several dozen.

In the now famous words of Clark Kerr, the American university has been transformed from a more or less "unified community of masters and students with a single 'soul' or purpose" into the "multiversity, a city of infinite variety." In short, while we have continued to think of ourselves in much the same terms as in the past, universities have in fact become vastly different places than they were before the war.

This transformation came about largely because growing enrollments generated revenues that enabled colleges and universities to add more faculty, which made the addition of new programs and fields much easier. This, in turn, led to increased emphasis on graduate education to supply the growing demand for new faculty. This greater emphasis on graduate education, combined with a new national appreciation for the practical benefits of research and scholarship, resulted in a great surge of public and government support for research and publication. Thus was ignited an explosion of knowledge that has been accompanied by the fragmentation of academe into new scholarly specialties and, of course, by a great increase in the variety and volume of scholarly publications.

Although this transformation began in the sciences, it was so powerful that it eventually spread to the social sciences and even to the humanities. While these disciplines had a smaller utilitarian claim on federal research funds than the sciences, the effect on the spirit of the faculty became almost as great as in the sciences, and so the rush was on to make research and publication the *sine qua non* of academic achievement and recognition.

This telescopic characterization of the metamorphosis of academia is not to be taken as a criticism. The rise in the importance of research and scholarship and the emergence of the academic disciplines as semiautonomous professions were accompanied by many highly desirable changes.

The pace of generating and applying new knowledge quickened in an autocatalytic cycle of expansion. Methodologies with greater power and reliability emerged. The intellectual standards of scholarship became higher and more consistent. And the ability of academic disciplines to serve both their professions and the public interest increased to the point that in some the junction became almost seamless.

Perhaps most significantly, the tie between teaching and scholarship became less the established canon around which intellectual life was centered and more the very process of search for objective knowledge. It is this, I believe, that has contributed most to the success of modern universities, not only because it created a great expansion of knowledge but because it has engendered a spirit of inquiry in place of dogma.

But if these developments invigorated American higher education, they also had their unfortunate effects—internal tensions and conflicts that to this day have not been resolved. Two of these, it seems to me, have particular pertinence to understanding the challenges that we are facing today.

In the first place, the growth that began in the 1950s and 1960s became habitual. Even in the decade of the 1980s, when the increase in enrollments declined and when many institutions began to experience difficulty balancing their budgets, expenditures for higher education in America grew by five or six points above inflation. Thus, an expansion that began as a necessary response to social need became a way of life that permeated the attitudes of faculty and administration alike. Growth continues to govern policy decisions long after the public has begun to doubt the worth of so much expansion and to question its own ability or willingness to pay the price of it. More faculty to develop new and emerging fields, larger and better laboratories and libraries, and other such things came to be viewed almost as entitlements. Growth that had been enabled by a rapid increase in revenues, driven largely by enrollment growth, became instead an upward cost spiral that drove institutions to increase revenues as fast as possible by whatever means available.

Thus was planted the seed of the biggest problem now confronting American higher education—*the need for cost containment*. As the provost at Cornell University put it in a letter to his faculty colleagues, "Each term I meet with the provosts of Stanford, Princeton, Columbia, Harvard,

Yale, MIT, and Chicago. Despite enormous differences between the institutions, we all find ourselves in similar financial situations—expenses outpace revenue by 1 to 3 percent a year." In my own case, the most persistent question I hear from Emory faculty is, "Why is our annual budget growing by only 9 to 10 percent a year, when our endowment has doubled in the last five years, and as recently as three years ago we were enjoying annual increases of 15 to 20 percent?" Learning to live within earned income rather than prospective income has proven to be enormously difficult after so many years of dependable growth.

But every sign indicates that the era of endlessly expanding budgets really is over—and has been for many institutions for over a decade. Under these circumstances building academic budgets each year becomes more and more characterized by the search for ways to cut costs, avoid costly redundancies, achieve greater selectivity and focus in the programs we support, and increase the "productivity" of the faculty (a phrase that for most of us has connotations that are about as pleasant as scratching one's fingernails across a chalkboard). We may be able to preserve the old values under these new circumstances, but we surely will have to relinquish our old ideas about *how* we do things.

In the second place, as has already been suggested, the period of growth was accompanied by significant shifts in institutional emphasis and culture. There were many such shifts, but it seems particularly significant to me that the undergraduate curriculum, which had been the major organizing force among college and university faculties, was displaced from center stage by a new emphasis on graduate and professional education and research. In any case, the era of growth and professionalization led to a real, if uneasy, shift in values within the higher education community. Research and publication came to be perceived as having greater value than teaching. This was understandable, since research and publication rather than teaching in large degree actually became the principal bases for academic promotion, salary increases, individual recognition, institutional prestige, and other rewards. Concurrently, as I've noted, the academic professions, including the professionalized liberal arts departments, became increasingly dominant centers of academic life, while the role of the university diminished in relative importance. In short, the faculty came to serve two masters, and a sort of conflict of commitment arose between them. Research vied with teaching, and external scholarly associations and agencies vied with the university for the faculty's time, loyalty, and affection. In some institutions, this conflict remained more latent than real, so long as growth in resources and in number of faculty enabled individual faculty members to reduce teaching loads and restrict teaching largely to their area of special interest and expertise. But the conflict was there, nonetheless, and forms the basis of much of the reform that is now brewing in American higher education.

To these shifts in the economic and social organization of higher education must be added other major transforming pressures, including the push for greater ethnic and cultural diversity in the faculty and student body and the growing dependence of large sectors of academe on the federal government and industry for support for their programs. Together these four factors probably account for 90 percent of our current concerns.

The best exposition of the current instability or unease that I have seen—distinctive because it points beyond the familiar economic exigencies that we all face to the underlying values conflicts within the academic community—is an essay by Jonathan Cole in the Fall 1993 issue of *Dædalus*. He describes four dilemmas of choice faced by research universities: (1) the dilemma of governance, or how to decide priorities in the face of an expanding knowledge base and diminishing resources; (2) the dilemma of balancing traditional views of university structure and process, built around notions of rationality, objective truth, and meritocracy, against the recently emergent view that all knowledge is subjective, situational, inherently political, and biased to preserve the traditional power base; (3) the familiar dilemma of striking a proper balance between teaching and research; and finally (4) the Faustian dilemma that derives from the partnership between universities and the federal government.

Whether one comes at the contemporary challenges of higher education from the vantage point of economic exigency or educational philosophy, change is the order of the day. This seems to be as true of rich institutions as poor ones, of large ones as much as small ones. Change will surely involve shrinkage or consolidation of programs as resources get tighter, but it will almost certainly involve much more than that:

revision of the curriculum, new approaches to and a greater emphasis on teaching, more focus and selectivity in the range of academic programs, new ways of publishing and evaluating scholarly work. All of these and more are hinted at. While the tensions and imbalances have to be relieved, exactly how that will happen depends on the choices we make.

Whither the Research Library

What does all of the foregoing have to do with libraries? Before I answer that, let's consider a few rather astonishing facts about the aggregate magnitude of our nation's research libraries.

Collectively, the research and teaching libraries of the country—including the major national, state, and public libraries (such as the Library of Congress and the New York Public Library) as well as all college and university libraries—probably contain between 450 and 500 million volumes. These 500 million books would occupy on the order of 50 million linear feet or almost 9,500 miles of shelf space—enough to reach across the nation three times! Library budgets typically comprise about 3 percent of an institution's operating funds or 8 to 10 percent of the instructional and research budget. The physical plant of the library usually comprises on the order of 5 percent of a university's capital assets.

These figures extrapolate into very large sums, but when one considers the replacement value of the books, journals, and archival materials housed in the library, its real value starts to be understood. Consider, for example, the average Association of Research Libraries (ARL) library of 2 million volumes (small by Harvard's standard). At a replacement cost of between $75 and $100 per volume (including the full costs of purchasing, cataloging, and shelving), the value of the collections is on the order of $150 to $200 million. Nationally this extrapolates to $35 to $45 billion.

Moreover, these numbers take no account of incremental *future* costs of owning and building major paper-based collections: the quickly expanding base of publications to be acquired; building maintenance, renovation, or construction to house ever-expanding collections; preservation of the 80 percent or so that, ironically, are printed on acidic paper and are in the process of self-destruction.

The point of reciting these figures is not merely to make the obvious point that the library is a great asset, but to emphasize that it is also a potential liability of enormous proportions, when one considers the future costs of continuing to grow, house, manage, and preserve these great collections in the same proportion as in the past.

To return to the earlier question about the relationship between the contemporary circumstances of universities and libraries, in a general way it is obvious that the developmental cycles of libraries over the past four or five decades reflect those of the institutions of which they are a part. Thus, libraries, like universities, experienced a period of intense growth and diversification followed by a period of increasingly severe resource constraint relative to need, while high expectations continued almost unabated. It is widely acknowledged that basic changes in the way information services are provided are inevitable, even though there is not yet complete consensus about what the nature of those changes can or should be.

Some specific connections can be made between the general lives of universities and of their libraries that are important in our progress toward the new era of information access. It is obvious that the restrained growth of revenues that American universities are experiencing will sig-nificantly limit the funding available to libraries to meet the information needs of students and faculty. Furthermore, libraries are the victims of a "double whammy." That is, while coping with a reduced rate of resource growth, libraries also have been experiencing a severe upward cost spiral of their own. Journal prices have soared 400 percent in the past twenty years, while books and monographs have increased 40 percent in just the past five. At the same time, the amount of published material to be acquired seems to be increasing almost geometrically. Thus, in recent years the acquisition of books, monographs, and journals has actually declined, even as the *number* of available books and journals and non-paper formats has grown at an accelerating pace, because inflation of costs has far outstripped the growth of acquisitions budgets. Into this economic dilemma must be factored the cost of renovating or expanding physical facilities that have generally become both inadequate and out-moded. In addition, between 25 and 50 percent of the books contained in those facilities are embrittled (up to 80 percent are endangered) because they are printed on acidic, self-destructing paper. Together these two problems of inadequate facilities and endangered books involve maintenance costs in the hundreds of millions of dollars for individual institutions and tens of billions for the nation as a whole, if we continue to do business as we have in the past and if there were any realistic prospect that expansion and preservation could actually be funded.

It is equally obvious that the explosion of information and fragmentation of the disciplines over the past fifty years that I described earlier led directly to an explosion of the volume and variety of books, journals, and monographs that libraries were expected—and needed—to acquire. Since 1945, the number of new book titles published each year has increased two- to threefold, from fewer than 300,000 to around 850,000, depending on what you count. The number of journals has increased during this period from around 7,500 to 140,000, a level of proliferation that I find absolutely astonishing. Just since 1991, a period in which many libraries have been canceling journal subscriptions on a significant scale, the number of new journals being published appears to have increased by 5,000. Even a casual scan of the titles of these new journals would provide ample evidence of the fragmentation of the scholarly disciplines into smaller specialties.

Moreover, as university faculties and students have become more and more diversified in their interests, background, and skills, they have brought to the library an increasingly diverse set of information needs. This in turn has meant—at least for the present—that librarians have had to cope with increasingly divergent levels of preparation and expectations among users, ranging from pressure to maintain the traditional card catalog at one extreme, to the desire for key-word access to the content of texts and the imminent expectancy of online electronic text retrieval at the other.

This cultural gap in our expectations has created a situation in which libraries today are in a very real sense struggling to be three different institutions concurrently: the library of the past, with all of its traditional expectations about building comprehensive collections and providing direct access to printed materials; the library of the present, with the extraordinary added costs of inflation, automation, and preservation of decaying print; and the library of the future, with all the attendant costs of developing and implementing new concepts, prototypes, and technologies for publishing, acquiring, storing, and providing access to information through digital technology. The fact that the costs and the expertise required to envision and support expectations and planning at all three levels are often directly competitive with one another surely makes academic librarianship one of the most politically challenging jobs in American higher education today. Such diverse interests and needs are served at the expense of considerable strain on both the library staff and the library's budget and simply cannot be sustained into the indefinite future.

Finally, prevailing attitudes and expectations in the academic community are affecting the evolution of information management and access. In large, diversified universities with a strong tradition of faculty independence and individuality, prevailing attitudes can have a profound effect on the capacity of libraries and universities to evolve. Two aspects of this have particular pertinence to this discussion.

First, despite the fact that what I have said about rising costs and the information explosion is generally known, many of our faculty and administrators continue to hold traditional ideas about the role of the library. The strength of the library as a provider of information services continues to be measured largely by the locally held and owned collection. This attitude has persisted despite the increasing evidence that a more appropriate measure of its effectiveness is its ability to provide *access* to the rich information resources of the world rather than the quantity of locally owned materials. Our reluctance to let go of tradition has a serious opportunity cost in the form of delayed development of new and more powerful approaches to information access through shared collection development and other forms of collaboration among universities and libraries.

The resistance to change that stems from traditional faculty autonomy and independence is reinforced by a similar tradition of *institutional* independence and individuality. To be sure, American colleges and universities have much in common. They form a kind of loose higher education system through the effects of common purposes, common sources of faculty renewal, the forces of the academic marketplace, and mutually accepted standards of accreditation. But within this system, the most dominant characteristic is a powerful culture of institutional autonomy and even competition.

This culture has contributed immeasurably to the richness of American higher education, but it also has some unfortunate consequences. It contributes to an almost paradoxical conservatism, as aspiring institutions often define their goals in terms of the path set by those few institutions perceived to be the best, and it has provided limited opportunity for and experience with cooperation and collaboration. This has become a particularly significant liability in the arena of information access, for it is in this arena above all others that cooperation offers the greatest benefit for universities.

One hundred twenty-five or so years ago Harvard Librarian John Langdon Sibley wrote, "It would be well if it were generally known that there is nothing printed of which the Harvard libraries is not desirous of obtaining a copy." This ambition was pursued with a wondrous degree of success for many decades, even centuries. But one may ask whether even Harvard can realistically hope to continue meeting the needs of its libraries entirely in the traditional way. The creation of the Harvard Depository several years ago, a less than ideal solution from the traditional point of view, was undoubtedly a response to the excessive cost of constructing and maintaining new space on the campus. More recently, Harvard's science libraries have had to cancel up to half of their journal subscriptions, and the Serials Review Project anticipates just such a contingency at Widener Library. It is urgent that these symptoms be recognized as the beginning of a curtailed ability to sustain the strength of collections through traditional acquisitions policy.

Conclusions

I can sum up this discussion in two points. First, it has become untenable for college and university libraries to plan to meet the future information needs of their faculty and students solely through the traditional avenue of growing their collections. The combination of continued high inflation in operating costs (especially for acquisitions), the explosion in the amount of published material, the emergence of numerous kinds of nonprint information (such as images, databases, and musical performances) in electronic format, and the decay of acidic paper on which the major part of most collections is printed makes it impossible today for institutions to maintain or build comprehensive collections as they did in the past.

Second, new digital and telecommunication technologies offer possibilities for resource sharing and collaborative collection development and management that were unimaginable a generation ago. Thus, both necessity and opportunity have led to the recognition that cooperation is the only realistic way for institutions of higher learning to assure their faculty and students that they will have access to a comprehensive storehouse of published knowledge.

The positive view of this realization has come to be expressed as the vision of "the virtual library": the dream that through the powers of computer and telecommunication technologies, the libraries of the nation (and eventually the world) will be linked to one another, enabling users to have access to any information in any format quickly and at reasonable cost, without regard to *where* the information is located physically. Notwithstanding the power—and even urgency—of this idea, it has not yet happened on a significant scale. In the words of James Govan, the recently retired librarian of the University of North Carolina,

The different and intriguing quality of this concept is that it acknowledges the fundamental shift in learning and investigation that information technology has introduced. This [digital] technology has the potential of liberating the academic library to become the proactive instrument in education and scholarship that it has struggled to become with printed tools. But so far no one has focused on the issues involved, the approaches to be used, or the structural changes required. No one has examined, in a formal setting, the kinds and organization of personnel, combining systems and library skills, to lead students and researchers to exploit this dual world of information. No one has investigated systematically the interaction of printed and electronic collections or identified the gaps in the infrastructure that prevent these collections from becoming an organic, unified tool. No one has delineated the kinds of instruction necessary to equip apprentice investigators to approach, engage, and advance this new informational structure. Partial and uncoordinated efforts have been made . . . but no effort that directly addresses [these] issues.

What is interesting about Govan's statement is that he points primarily not to deficiencies in technology—for indeed the technology is here now—but to the deficiencies in planning, education, organization, and commitment that are necessary to release the transforming power of digital technology. The gateway concept promises to develop that potential. The wonderful thing about this technology is, as Richard Lanham says in chapter 11, that it enables us to eat our cake and have it, too. For me, it's more like the parable of the loaves and fishes: as each of us develops the full capacity of digital technology on our own campuses, we are also creating the capability to act synergistically, and to build collectively a vastly greater capability for capturing and providing access to information than any of us could achieve alone.

I am convinced that continuing business as usual in the new environment of higher education is futile and is, paradoxically, the surest way to see the value of the great libraries that we have built over the centuries erode.

Note

1. This chapter is based in part on a paper entitled "University Priorities and Policies Affecting Library and Information Services" given by the author in 1991 at the Kanazawa Institute of Technology Library Center conference on "Information Access in the New Era" and published in abbreviated form in *Library Hi-Tech* 10, no. 4 (1991): 27–37.

II

Changing Scholarship: Influences on Teaching and Research

Research has changed significantly over the past three or four decades. The shift has been away from interpreting canonical texts and scholarship for the sake of erudition and toward examining the context or frame of reference within which a text, idea, or activity may be understood. There is, too, greater emphasis on novelty and general theories that very often are focused on the present or recent past. These changing patterns of research reflect developments in Western intellectual thought that have created new academic disciplines and areas of research. Several additional factors have accelerated these intellectual trends, resulting in significant changes in research after World War II. Quantitative methods gave new life to the social sciences, and increased federal funding tended to make research more result oriented. Social and demographic changes encouraged scholars to emphasize expressions of everyday life—social and cultural history, studies of women and families, popular culture, and public perceptions and beliefs about a variety of issues.

One of the consequences of these changes has been the broadening of the definition of information and the sources useful for research. The sources for documenting these activities have become more varied, and scholars are now more inclined to seek a range of nonprint materials that are only partially represented in most library collections: images, including photographs and motion pictures; popular literature; ephemera; spatial data; personal papers and archives; and virtually anything that might reflect the attitudes, activities, and culture of a society. Thus, scholars and librarians are overwhelmed not just by the quantity of information but also by the variety of forms of sources that are increasingly important for teaching and research.

The following two chapters approach these several issues from different perspectives, but both agree that universities and libraries must abandon old conceptual frameworks and agendas that arise from these changing patterns of research. Patrick Manning describes these changes and their impact on the study of history, and his analysis illustrates the kinds of changes that also are occurring in other disciplines. He explores the demands of these changes on curriculum and instruction and describes how the Northeastern University History Department is responding with a new curriculum. Anthony Appiah applauds the ways in which technology is improving research by making it more convenient and therefore more efficient. Not only is access improved, but technology has the potential to connect disparate bits and pieces of information, especially in the comparative and interdisciplinary areas of research that concern him. But he also points to some of the problems in these changes, including insufficient sources and the danger that old disciplinary agendas may blind librarians to the particular kinds of resources that are needed in these emerging areas of research.

2
History in the Era of Theory, Methodology, and Multiculturalism: New Configurations for the Discipline

Patrick Manning

The Revolution in Historical Studies since 1960

The discipline of history is broad in scope by any definition and unique in its concentration on the factor of time, which itself can be seen to have many dimensions. During the past generation, the study of history has expanded dramatically in its scope and in the range of its approaches to time. This revolution in historical studies has taken place quietly, but it is nonetheless pervasive and significant.

Peter Novick, in a 1988 book entitled *That Noble Dream: The "Objectivity Question" and the American Historical Profession,* made innovative use of the traditional techniques of the historian—leafing through documentary archives—to reveal some unheralded patterns of change in historical studies. He studied the letters, speeches, book reviews, and notes of historians working in the United States since 1886, when the American Historical Association was founded. He focused on the twists and turns in the debate about whether history could be an objective science or whether it was dominated by the subjective impressions of historical authors. In the concluding chapters to that study, Novick noted the collapse, in recent years, of an apparent consensus among historians that had been dominated by agreement on the main lines of political history. Instead, as he noted in a chapter entitled "There Was No King in Israel," the contending perspectives of women's history, black history, and social history led to an impression of the fragmentation of historical studies. (Novick 1988, 573–629).

Novick's detailed and subtle analysis is a great contribution to the history of history. Through it, for instance, entering graduate students can learn where they fit into the range of debates and specializations in historical studies. But I prefer to interpret the last thirty years of historical studies not in terms of fragmentation of a consensus but as a methodological and theoretical revolution accompanied by rapid expansion of the scope (geographical, thematic, and temporal) of historical studies. Biology had its revolution with the breaking of the DNA code; physics and chemistry had earlier revolutions with the development of quantum mechanics; economics had its revolution with the development of macroeconomics. History has had not one but several such innovations concurrently: here I present them as five overlapping dimensions of the revolution in historical studies.

One dimension of the revolution stemmed from the establishment of federally supported area-studies programs after World War II. These centers set history in the context of interdisciplinary study of Latin America, Russia and Eastern Europe, Asia, the Middle East, and Africa. New courses, new journals, and substantially expanded literatures grew for each of these areas. There were to be no more "people without history."[1]

A second dimension came with the rise of interdisciplinary, social science approaches to history. This included work inspired by the late E. P. Thompson's 1963 *The Making of the English Working Class,* a sort of "history from the bottom up" that privileged the viewpoint of artisans and wage workers and, in the hands of other authors, of the crowd and peasants (Rudé 1964; Tilly 1964). Works in African-American history gained wider attention in the era of the civil rights movement. The new economic history arose based on neoclassical economic theory and quantitative testing of hypotheses. The new social history arose, equally quantitative and sometimes equally theoretical. Feminism brought a new critique to history and an expanded literature on women's history. Political history too became more theoretical and more quantitative (Blassingame 1972; Conrad 1957; Thernstrom 1969; Tilly and Scott 1978; Formisano 1971). Overall, the social science dimension to history brought adoption into history of formal methodology (especially quantitative techniques), formal theory (neoclassical and Marxian economics, Parsonian and Marxian sociology, psychoanalysis, and feminism), and explicit identification of standpoints: working-class history, feminist outlooks, African-American outlooks, third world viewpoints.

A third dimension to the revolution in historical studies centered on advances in cultural studies. American studies arose as an interdisciplinary linking of history and literature; the rise of deconstructionism and other developments in literary theory soon had new impact on historical studies. Studies in popular culture were reinforced by the new social history.[2] Anthropology, with its foci on kinship, culture, and social structure, provided a framework utilized first by historians of third world areas; then Clifford Geertz became a guru to the historical profession in general, and echoes of his Balinese cock-fight showed up in analyses of the American heartland (Vansina 1966; Geertz 1973). Art history, long centered on Europe, especially in Renaissance and early modern times, began to extend its scope to other regions and times. Ethnomusicology, developed earlier for study of areas beyond the limits of European cultural dominance (in contrast to the studies of elite European musical traditions), came to provide a framework for study of music in general.[3] Studies in several subfields of cultural history are still gaining momentum and are moving toward linkages and recognition of each other's advances.

Yet another dimension of the change in historical studies centered on biological and environmental history. The field of historical demography expanded sharply, first with work on Europe, then on the United States, and then on regions throughout the world. Studies in nutrition, disease, and other aspects of biological history began to be conducted in greater numbers. Beyond human biology, historians also undertook study of other elements of the environment—plants, animals, land, and the atmosphere.[4]

The fifth and encompassing dimension of the revolution in historical studies came with the elaboration of global frameworks. Most history is still done in the national framework. The area-studies movement and its extension of historical studies to all corners of the world, while in one sense extending the national framework, still served to set the groundwork for interpretation at the global level. With William McNeill's 1963 *The Rise of the West: A History of the Human Community*, professional historians began to involve themselves in world history.[5] In an analogous but distinct trend, historical sociologists began more comparisons of national and regional units, responding in part to the growing impact of Max Weber on sociology (Moore 1966). In addition, certain issues—war, environment, and disease—commonly spilled over national limits and readily elicited global approaches to their analysis. In the United States, domestic social pressures by minority communities led eventually to what we now know as a multicultural approach in United States history. Similarly, and beyond our North American island, strife and debate over decolonization, the cold war and then its end gave impetus to a global approach to history (Nordquist 1992; Bradley Commission 1988). It has not proved easy, however, to develop a global conceptualization of historical change rather than one based on the summation of separate national histories. Global analysis is more than the comparison of separate national units, and it is more than the impact of General Motors, McDonald's, and Elvis Presley on the world. It is instead the interaction of all regions of the world in a single system—so that it may be helpful to think in automobiles of Hyundai, in food of the spread of Thai cuisine, and in music of Nigerian-born Sade, who sings her songs in cabaret style with American themes to a cosmopolitan British audience of European, African, and Asian ancestry.

I have made some effort to order these developments, but one may equally say that they came all on top of one another. The recent Nobel prizes awarded to Robert Fogel and Douglass North are based on their theory-based work in quantitative economic history conducted in the 1960s and 1970s. Andre Gunder Frank—who, in the same period, set forth a thesis of Latin American underdevelopment that sparked an important debate on interaction in modern world history—criticized, in a recent talk at Northeastern University, the work of both Fogel and North for interpreting economic history narrowly within the limits of the United States or Western Europe (Frank 1968; Frank and Gillis 1993). That is, we still have much to do in working out the mutual implications of the many new developments in historical studies.[6]

Constraints on the Study of History

So far, this is the story of a wonderful expansion and deepening in historical research—in documents, methods, theories, standpoints, and interpretations. Debate and dispute necessarily result from the range of new work.

But these remarkable developments took place within a set of severe constraints. The profession of history was in demographic decline during most of this time—among students and faculty members both. And while the research was changing dramatically, the institutions for the study and the teaching of history changed very little. An equally severe constraint was that the philosophy of historical studies changed rather little.

Demographically, historical studies underwent a boom during the 1960s during a period of rapid construction of colleges and universities. Undergraduate student enrollment peaked in about 1970 and then declined—partly because the baby boomers passed through college age but also because greater flexibility in the curriculum led to relaxation of the traditional requirements for U.S. history and Western civilization courses that had employed so many college history teachers. Many new doctoral programs opened up in the 1960s, and new Ph.D.s focused particularly in social history. But the market for history Ph.D.s collapsed suddenly in 1975, so that 600 a year were employed rather than the previous 1,200.[7]

Ironically, then, at the moment of greatest creativity and advance in historical research, demoralization came to dominate graduate education. Faculty members, seeking to avoid the prospect of training students who would never find work and exhausted by the strain of reading 200 dossiers for each replacement of a retiring colleague, put little energy into doctoral programs. Undergraduate programs suffered less, but in an era when book publishers focused mainly on competing versions of shiny textbooks, the logic of product differentiation dominated: moving the chrome strips was a safer tactic than marketing a whole new design, much less introducing an Edsel. The emphasis in teaching remained centered on synthesis of established facts rather than on presentation of new research results.

Under these conditions, some basic assumptions of historical studies continued to govern, even though they were contradicted by most of the good new work. History remained organized at the national level or within continental regions. Political history still retained its hegemony in the informal hierarchy of historical fields. Historians dabbled in adjoining disciplines but without taking formal training in their method or theory. Historians of Europe were assumed to take the lead in interpretive and theoretical work; historians of the United States were assumed to do the most thorough and critical empirical studies; historians of other regions were assumed to be filling in local gaps for their region.

Historians of the United States met among themselves and not with historians of other regions; the Americanists met by time period and subdiscipline. The American Historical Association, the big meeting designed to attract all historians, remained dominated first by historians of Europe (meaning Western Europe) and then by historians of the United States.[8] The numerous historians of Africa and the various regions of Asia went instead to their respective area-studies meetings, so that their work appeared quite marginal from the perspective of one attending the AHA. When historians of Europe began to learn the relevance of anthropology to history, they went straight to the anthropologists for coaching, thus bypassing the work of a generation of historians of Africa who had built up substantial experience in using anthropological approaches and materials in studies of history (Sabean 1984; Vansina 1978).

The old rigidities are now challenged, but they are not gone. Hiring of historians is still done by nation or region. Book reviews are still organized in the same way: thus, the *American Historical Review,* which gives the most comprehensive set of reviews of any historical journal, still does not have a section on world history.

New Directions: Consolidating the Advances in Historical Studies

Having discussed on one hand the strengths and innovations of recent work in history, and on the other hand the weaknesses and rigidities in the discipline, let me offer some comments on current directions in historical studies and attempt to tie these comments to library resources so that we may link the study of history to the discussion of the gateway library. My examples will be based on activities at Northeastern University, and I do hope that they will have some generality.

First, Northeastern University has just approved a new doctoral program in history, with a focus on methodology and global history. Candidates will specialize in world history, United States history, and European history, and all will include global dimensions in their studies and their dissertations.[9]

In methodology, we emphasize formal interdisciplinary training. Each doctoral candidate must identify a methodological specialization, a set of courses to develop skills in that area, and a faculty committee to oversee his or her methodological training (of the three faculty committee members, one is likely to be outside the history department). Thus, an economic historian would take a year of graduate courses in economics, a social historian would take graduate courses in sociology, and a cultural historian would take graduate study in such disciplines as literary theory, anthropology, art history, or musicology. In addition to developing these specializations, doctoral candidates will participate in a multidisciplinary seminar intended to develop both their strength in their own field and their basic literacy in a wide range of historical methodologies.

This approach is a direct challenge to the established tradition among historians of entering interdisciplinary work by doing a smattering of reading in adjoining disciplines rather than by taking formal training in new methodologies. The Northeastern history department had steadily increased its emphasis on methodology in recent years, and this program was the logical next step. My own commitment to this relatively rigorous approach to methodology comes from having spent half a career as an economic historian of Africa and observing the rudimentary level of that literature, since the great majority of scholars who call themselves economic historians of Africa have no training in economics.

Our focus on global history has both global and national dimensions. First and most boldly, we seek to provide comprehensive training in world history for specialists in that growing field. These doctoral students will perform analysis and interpretation of global patterns in history. Our intention is to involve young scholars in world history at the beginning of their career rather than restrict them to national history until mid-career. This means that we must establish the character of a dissertation in world history—a study that is monographic and based on primary research but that centers on interactive or comparative study of at least two regions. Our program will produce graduates who are prepared to teach world history, both because they have taken world history courses and because they have been supervised in the teaching of world history.

In addition, doctoral students who center on national history in the United States, in Europe, and in other regions will include a significant global dimension to their studies. Thus, a study in French social history would address interactions of French social structure with global economic trends and comparisons of social change in France and in other countries.

In a second major area of activity, the Northeastern history department launched a major project in revising the undergraduate history curriculum during the 1994–1995 academic year. This project was undertaken with the support of the National Endowment for the Humanities and with the collaboration of six other Boston-area institutions of higher education.[10] In a set of twelve lectures and workshops, we focused on introducing new research results into undergraduate teaching, with an emphasis on new trends in methodology and world history. We wrote a comprehensive history curricula for each of our seven institutions. In so doing, we focused not just on revising the introductory survey course but on upper-division courses and the full range of courses for history majors.

The preparations for this program include a daunting but stimulating project: surveying recent research advances in many areas of history. We are finding, for instance, that the field of cultural history includes numerous subfields organized around distinct regional and disciplinary viewpoints: cultural studies focused on recent England, cultural history centered on eighteenth- and nineteenth-century France, popular culture studies in the United States, plus studies in cultural anthropology, in folklore, in art history, in architectural history, in ethnomusicology, and in literary theory. Considering the contributions and the linkages of these subfields should lead to the discovery of some exciting opportunities for undergraduate learning. The focus on new research results has the potential for giving students the impression of being at the cutting edge of historical research and debate rather than of struggling to assimilate a backlog of established fact.

Both of these projects require heavy and imaginative use of library resources. We at Northeastern are fortunate to have benefitted from a recent and dramatic expansion in the scale and quantity of our library resources, which has given substantial encouragement to our new ventures in graduate and undergraduate education. In 1991 the new Snell Library opened, providing us with the largest physical plant among university libraries in Boston; a major and permanent increase in the library budget provided us with the basis for building a strong collection in history.

It was impressive to see how, within two years, student habits of library usage changed and improved. Quiet study in a roomy and sound-absorbing atmosphere replaced the din of the overcrowded old facility. Rates of book circulation easily doubled, and student papers became more densely documented. Students learned the online catalog system rapidly. Reference librarians, stationed prominently in the foyer between the catalog terminals and the circulation desk, are now kept very active. In the second-floor media library, students readily view assigned videos held on reserve for their classes.

At least one library modification had an unexpectedly positive effect. To simplify shelving, journals were consolidated over wide topical areas and given simplified call numbers.[11] Thus, for history, all history journals—with Library of Congress call numbers beginning with C, D, E, and F—were given the simple call number C and shelved alphabetically within that category, both in the Periodical Room and in the stacks. I well remember my initial reaction to this innovation, which was irritation—a typical historian's response to any change in the organization of familiar documents. Rapidly, however, I warmed to the modification because it was consistent with the growing trend to connections across fields of history. Journals on U.S. history were no longer isolated from those on Latin America, Africa, and Europe. Journals on political history might be shelved next to those on cultural history; journals on local history might be shelved next to those on global history. Now I saw linkages across regional and topical fields that had previously escaped my notice, and I could send students to browse through journals in the expectation that they would find similar connections.[12]

For the undergraduate curriculum project, we turned for help to the library staff. My initial hope was to create a separate collection, including books and journals containing a broad selection of major recent research advances, through which participants in the project could browse for inspiration during the year of our deliberations.[13] But it was impractical to pull so many volumes off the regular shelves during the academic year, and in any case library technology had developed greatly. Our solution is to prepare an annotated, online bibliography of recent advances in historical research, which may be accessed directly at Northeastern or by modem from remote locations. Users will consult the works either at Northeastern or at other libraries in the Boston Library Consortium. Preparation of this bibliography requires the energies of both historians and librarians—the former to select the entries and write the annotations, and the latter to assist in searches and to format and implement the bibliography.

At both graduate and undergraduate levels, our initiatives in the teaching of history will lead us to explore new possibilities in the library. Even as the frontiers among the disciplines are eroding, our students will have to learn the disciplinary map in sufficient detail to locate the methodological and empirical segments of the literature. Students will have to learn to read across the disciplines and to locate materials in a range of related disciplines.

The frontiers of historical research and interpretation have spread far beyond the nineteenth-century focus on political history and official texts. "Evidence" now includes many categories beyond written text—oral testimony, music, archaeological remains. The final product of historical research now also goes beyond written text—film, video, audio. As part of this change, theorists have generalized the terms *text* and *document* so that they may include any sort of evidence. One notable index of changing approaches of historians is that the *American Historical Review* now includes film reviews as a regular feature.

Training history students to use the new library technology presents itself with increasing insistency as we attempt to bring them to the frontiers of current research. Graduate students, by long tradition, have been required to master traditional library skills and to learn foreign language skills as part of their training. More recently, we have begun to require that graduate students develop a range of computer skills—word processing, databases, graphics, and in some cases statistics. By the same logic we should require students to become adept at a range of new library techniques. So far, we have instructed our students simply to go and learn: to utilize library databases in association with citation indices, to collect newspaper citations through CD-ROM indexes, and to utilize the Research Libraries Information Network (RLIN), a national bibliographic database, to search for archival holdings. The problem with this hands-on, self-help approach is that the students may not use these tools to best advantage. Our library has short courses to introduce its resources, and we will clearly have to move to ensure that all our graduate students and our more energetic undergraduates benefit from these courses.[14]

The Place of History in a Redrawn Disciplinary Map

The discipline of history has a dynamic of its own—as seen recently in the ups and downs of demand for courses, the rise of public history, and the interactions among fields (for example, quantitative social history and popular culture). But historical scholarship also reflects the dynamics of the disciplines with which it is closely associated—social science and humanities disciplines, as well as environmental and biological studies. Each of these show a development, in recent times, toward broader and more interconnected styles of inquiry, highlighted by a rising importance of theory and databases.

History, as it used to be, threatens to be swallowed up in the transformations of the disciplines surrounding it. My guess, however, is that in the wake of this ongoing reorganization of intellectual and academic life, the discipline of history will reemerge with a recognizable approach and character. I was trained in the 1960s both as an Africanist and as a cliometrician, a new economic historian. I watched as the field of economic history moved from history departments to economics departments. For a time it seemed that hypothesis testing would be the only way to do economic history. Indeed, hypothesis testing remains central in that field. But I watched as the economists who stayed with the subject gradually became more like historians: their writing style improved; they began to season their bold and decisive analyses and to tarry with nuances, with the specificities of one situation or another, with the ironies of timing (Wright 1978). Consider again the case of Douglass North, who began his career with hypothesis testing on American materials in which institutions were only constraints at the edge of his system. He then moved to a study of European development in which institutions became the key to growth and then to a study that is really philosophy of history (North 1966, 1981, 1990; North and Thomas 1973). His Nobel Prize was awarded really for the first stage of his career.

The new disciplinary frontiers will be different and more permeable than the old: we will read journals across what were once disciplinary lines, use each others' research techniques, and apply each others' theories. But I think that when the dust settles from this particular set of transformations, the study of history will still be, recognizably, the offspring of historical studies today.

One side of the historian's task will be a continuation of the traditional role of guardian and synthesizer of the evidence and teller of nuanced tales of the past. There will still be narrative history, and historians will remain the specialists at combining diverse categories of evidence into stories constructed with a focus on the passage of time.

The new side to the historian's role will be that of synthesizer of methodology. Historians taking on this new function will address their topics by mediating among the theoretical and methodological alternatives and by combining them or alternating among them artfully in interpreting the historical record to provide a comprehensive and, hopefully, realistic view of the past. Historians may be masters of few of the academic trades they will ply but journeymen at many of them. And as history in the past was tied closely to the traditional library, so will history in the future be tied to many dimensions of the transformed library.

Notes

1. In the United States, federally funded area-studies centers were established beginning in the 1950s. Major area-studies journals were founded during and after World War II, such as *Slavic Review* (1941), *Journal of Asian Studies* (1941), and *Middle East Journal* (1947). The main journal in Latin American history, *Hispanic American Historical Review,* was launched at the end of World War I, in 1921, while the *Journal of African History* was founded late, in 1960. The "people without a history" form part of the title of Eric Wolf's (1982) interpretive overview of modern world history.

2. The leading journal in American studies, the *American Quarterly,* was founded in 1949. On literary theory, studies in popular culture, and their combination in the historical literature, see Eagleton (1983), Gans (1974), and Sabean (1984).

3. The main impact of new methodology in art history and ethnomusicology came some years later than for the fields discussed above. See Vansina (1984), Johnson (1988), Blum, Bohlman, and Neuman (1991). In the last few years the *Musical Quarterly,* founded in 1915, has published a substantial number of articles written from an ethnomusicological perspective.

4. For historical demography in Europe see Laslett (1966); in the United States see Gordon (1973). For other areas, work proceeded more slowly: see Manning (1990). On biological history see Kiple and Himmelsteib King (1981). On environmental history see Cronon (1983) and Crosby (1986).

5. Philip Curtin (1964) is perhaps the best example of a scholar working in area studies (on Africa) who saw his work explicitly as a contribution to world history.

6. Peter Burke has written a book-length assessment of the interaction of history and other social sciences, focusing not only on recent and dramatic changes in historical studies but also on two centuries of change in the relations between history, sociology, and other fields. Burke's 1980 edition focuses on sociology; his 1992 edition addresses social sciences and culture studies more broadly.

Other reflections on interactions among the disciplines have appeared recently, especially for studies beyond Europe and North America. See, for instance, Bates (1993) and Cooper et al. (1993).

7. Figures as reported by the American Historical Association. Contractions in various subfields of history proceeded at different paces: African and Middle East history had tightened up in earlier years, but new and replacement positions continued to be offered in African-American history.

8. A summary categorization, by panel, of papers presented at the American Historical Association meetings of 1983 and 1991 showed that, in each case, about 75 percent of the panels and papers were focused on the United States and Western Europe (modern and medieval), while some 25 percent were focused on other areas of the world. More than half the latter group consisted of presentations on Eastern Europe and on Latin America. Africa, Oceania, the ancient world, and Asia (East, Southeast, South, Central, and West) were thus almost totally absent from sessions of the AHA.

9. This new program builds on the university's well-established M.A. program, which has particular strength in public history.

10. "Mainstreaming Methodology and World History for Undergraduates in History," supported by the Higher Education Division of the National Endowment for the Humanities (September 1994–June 1995; grant no. EH21745). Participating institutions, in addition to Northeastern, are Roxbury Community College, Wheelock College, Simmons College, Boston College, Tufts University, and University of Massachusetts at Lowell.

11. In the previous facility, all bound journals were held on closed stacks. It was a thrill to find them on open stacks—and also to find that they were relatively undamaged precisely because they had been held on closed stacks.

12. The enlarged category of history journals could not, however, be all-inclusive: journals in economic, social, and demographic history are classified under "H."

The old historians' technique of searching far afield for relevant materials thus retains their relevance.

13. My notion was inspired directly by the browsing library set up each summer for more than a decade in the Newberry Library Summer Institute in Quantitative History: this collection in social and quantitative history had introduced me and scores of other historians to the expanding social history literature.

14. The university is setting up short courses in computer skills. Library short courses are equivalent to these.

References

Bates, Robert H., ed. 1993. *Africa and the Disciplines*. Chicago: University of Chicago Press.

Blassingame, John. 1972. *The Slave Community*. New York: Oxford University Press.

Blum, Stephen, Philip V. Bohlman, and Daniel Neuman, eds. 1991. *Ethnomusicology and Modern Music History*. Urbana, IL: University of Illinois Press.

Bradley Commission on History in Schools. 1988. *Building a History Curriculum: Guidelines for Teaching History in Schools*. Washington, DC: Educational Excellence Network.

Burke, Peter. 1980. *Sociology and History*. London: Allen & Unwin.

Burke, Peter. 1993. *History and Social Theory*. Ithaca, NY: Cornell University Press.

Conrad, Alfred H., and John R. Meyer. 1958. "The Economics of Slavery in the Antebellum South," *Journal of Political Economy* 66, no. 2 (April): 95–130.

Cooper, Frederick, et al. 1993. *Confronting Historical Paradigms: Peasants, Labor, and the Capitalist World System in Africa and Latin America*. Madison: University of Wisconsin Press.

Cronon, William. 1983. *Changes in the Land: Indians, Colonists, and the Ecology of New England*. New York: Hill & Wang.

Crosby, Alfred W. 1986. *Ecological Imperialism: The Biological Expansion of Europe, 900–1900*. Cambridge: Cambridge University Press.

Curtin, Philip. 1964. *The Image of Africa: British Ideas and Action, 1780–1840*. Madison: University of Wisconsin Press.

Eagleton, Terry. 1983. *Literary Theory: An Introduction*. Oxford: Oxford University Press.

Formisano, Ronald P. 1971. *The Birth of Mass Political Parties, Michigan, 1827–1861*. Princeton, NJ: Princeton University Press.

Frank, Andre Gunder. 1969. *Capitalism and Underdevelopment in Latin America*. New York: Monthly Review Press.

Frank, Andre Gunder, and Barry K. Gillis, eds. 1993. *The World System: Five Hundred Years or Five Thousand?* London: Routledge.

Gans, Herbert. 1974. *Popular Culture and High Culture: An Analysis and Evaluation of Taste.* New York: Basic Books.

Geertz, Clifford. 1973. *The Interpretation of Cultures: Selected Essays.* New York: Basic Books.

Gordon, Michael, ed. 1973. *The American Family in Social-Historical Perspective.* New York: St. Martin's Press.

Johnson, W. McAllister. 1988. *Art History, Its Use and Abuse.* Toronto: University of Toronto Press.

Kiple, Kenneth F., and Virginia Himmelsteib King. 1981. *Another Dimension to the Black Diaspora: Diet, Disease, and Racism.* Cambridge: Cambridge University Press.

Laslett, Peter. 1966. *The World We Have Lost.* New York: Scribners.

Manning, Patrick. 1990. *Slavery and African Life: Occidental, Oriental and African Slave Trades.* Cambridge: Cambridge University Press.

McNeill, William H. 1991. *The Rise of the West: A History of the Human Community.* Chicago: University of Chicago Press.

Moore, Barrington. 1966. *Social Origins of Dictatorship and Democracy: Lord and Peasant in the Making of the Modern World.* Boston: Beacon Press.

Nordquist, Joan, compiler. 1992. *The Multicultural Education Debate in the University: A Bibliography.* Contemporary Social Issues: A Bibliographical Series, No. 25. Santa Cruz, Calif.

North, Douglass C. 1966. *Growth and Welfare in the American Past: A New Economic History.* Englewood Cliffs, NJ: Prentice-Hall.

North, Douglass C. 1981. *Structure and Change in Economic History.* New York: Norton.

North, Douglass C. 1990. *Institutions, Institutional Change and Economic Performance.* Cambridge: Cambridge University Press.

North, Douglass C., and Robert Paul Thomas. 1973. *The Rise of the Western World: A New Economic History.* Cambridge: Cambridge University Press.

Novick, Peter. 1988. *That Noble Dream: The "Objectivity Question" and the American Historical Profession.* Cambridge: Cambridge University Press.

Rudé, George. 1964. *The Crowd in History: A Study of Popular Disturbances in France and England, 1730–1848.* New York: Wiley.

Sabean, David. 1984. *Power in the Blood: Popular Culture and Village Discourse in Early Modern Germany.* Cambridge: Cambridge University Press.

Thernstrom, Stephan. 1969. *Poverty and Progress: Social Mobility in a Nineteenth Century City.* New York: Athenaeum.

Thompson, E.P. 1963. *The Making of the English Working Class.* New York: Pantheon Books.

Tilly, Charles. 1964. *The Vendée.* Cambridge, MA: Harvard University Press.

Tilly, Louise, and Joan Scott. 1978. *Women, Work and Family.* New York: Holt, Rinehart & Winston.

Vansina, Jan. 1966. *Kingdoms of the Savanna.* Madison: University of Wisconsin Press.

Vansina, Jan. 1978. *The Children of Woot: A History of the Kuba Peoples.* Madison: University of Wisconsin Press.

Vansina, Jan. 1984. *Art History in Africa: An Introduction to Method.* New York: Longman.

Wolf, Eric R. 1982. *Europe and the People without History.* Berkeley: University of California Press.

Wright, Gavin. 1978. *The Political Economy of the Cotton South.* New York: Norton.

3

Realizing the Virtual Library

Anthony Appiah

I hardly ever go to a library. But the libraries at Harvard University are among the major resources for my work as a teacher and researcher. I access them sitting at home or in the office, connected by modem, at all hours of the day or night. I can use them the way I do for a simple reason: the HOLLIS databases contain most of the books I use, organized in ways that make it possible for me to find them. The real books can be delivered to me and returned by my research assistants: what I need, when I am deciding what to read, is the virtual trace of the book in the database. If the system also made available online the *Philosopher's Index* and the MLA bibliographies, I could do almost all the journal searches I wanted, too: and if I could take the articles off the system (with a reasonable copyright charge), I would. I am delighted that the library makes possible what it does, in as transparent a way as possible for this user and look forward to more of the same: using even more of the resources of Widener Library while hardly ever going there.

One thing more I would like to see is online access to journal articles— not abstracts alone, but the articles themselves. This would add enormously to the utility of the library as a support for my research: I could read more of them, browse more (and not randomly as I now do on paper but using searches for key words), and could quickly follow up references. The difference in the quantity of time spent on research would make possible a qualitative difference in the kind of work I could do. It used to be a serious scholarly project to collect all the recent literature on a subject. To do it one needed the help of expert reference librarians or a great knowledge of the field. Now, with the bibliographic resources available and the fact that they are stored in machine-readable and thus searchable formats, the work of months or years can be done in a few hours.

It is not just that time is saved in locating the material: because texts can be searched online, I can actually handle the text in ways that were never before possible. I can ask questions—about the way in which an author uses language, for example—that I simply wouldn't have bothered to ask using traditional research methods.

Some years ago I wrote a piece about race as a literary theme (Appiah 1989). At one point I said, "Forty years after *Ivanhoe,* in *Salammbo,* published in 1862, the French novelist Gustave Flaubert created a similar racial romance, set in ancient Carthage. While the central contrast in the work is between civilized and barbarous peoples—the French word *barbares* (which is both noun and adjective) occurs 238 times, more often than any other noun or adjective." I was able to say this because I had come across a computer-generated analysis of the text. But if I had the text on my machine, stored on a Flaubert CD (along with the complete works of dozens of other French writers of the nineteenth century), I could have found this out for myself. I could have asked other questions, as well. I also wrote, for example, that "the novel is replete with references to Campanians, Garamantes, Gauls, Greeks, Iberians, Lusitanians, Libyans, Negroes, Numidians, Phoenicians, and Syssites; and these types are often identified with certain physical and moral characteristics." I would have liked to follow each of these terms through the text, looking at the contexts in which they were used and to do it in *Ivanhoe,* as well, for Norman, Anglo-Saxon, and Jew. I would think it worth investing the time to explore these issues in this way if I could do it with the help of a machine.

My connection to essentially traditional bibliographic information about the books I use in my work is made more productive not only because I can explore it quickly and efficiently without physical movement around the card catalog, but because the new catalog can store more information about the work. In principle, a faculty member who recommends a book for the library to acquire now also could add to its entry his or her annotations. In principle, in association with a class, I can pull together a bibliography and annotate it and make it available to students on a network, allowing them and my teaching assistants to add to it constantly, share the results of our reading, and pool some of our knowledge. Connecting with this information, then, is only half of what the new technology makes possible: it also allows us to connect pieces of information with each other. In the online catalog we do this in a relatively stable and permanent way, but we can make available online temporary collections of this information for particular teaching or research purposes.

To make the best use of these new possibilities, we need to work together as librarians and as users of the library to define the interfaces between user and data, the front ends, that would make this information most useful for our work. That means communicating with each other about what our needs are and what the potentialities and limitations and costs of the technology are. The *Philosopher's Index* had to be designed by philosophers: software to create bulletin boards of bibliographic and other information for classes needs to be responsive to what teachers and students are doing. In the end, however, most of us don't want to know how it is all done; we want an interface that's both transparent and responsive to exactly our particular needs.

It seems to me natural that these sorts of possibilities should be seen as an extension of the old work of the library with texts. The librarian is now our information manager and not just the person who knows how to acquire and preserve our books and journals and how to guide us to finding the ones we need. In the spirit, therefore, of communicating some of these needs, I'd like to mention two kinds of issues about what information is stored and made available to me in the new virtual catalog, and I'd like to sketch something that I'd like to see the library do.

First of all then, two kinds of inadequacies appear in the data that's there, especially if you work, as I do, in African and African-American studies. The first inadequacy is a reflection both of the historical exclusion of black culture from the center of Western scholarly work and the current economic crises in African publishing: most collections simply don't have the texts that would be most useful for us to use to do our work.

Sometimes they don't have a book because it wasn't thought worth collecting at the time it was produced or because, since no one was interested in it, the bibliographical information currently available is minimal. For more than a decade, the Black Periodical Literature Project, under the direction of Henry Louis Gates, Jr., has sought out material in African-American periodicals published in the nineteenth and early twentieth centuries. Thousands of poems, hundreds of reviews and short stories, scores of serial novels—all of which had largely disappeared from scholarly view—are now available once more on microfilm. But what really makes the collection useful—all of the material was available, in principle, through interlibrary loan or in Widener Library—is that it comes with a database that records for each entry some of the key publication data: place and date of publication, author (if known), genre (Appiah, Gates, and Bond 1988).

Sometimes material isn't available in a collection because collecting contemporary African ephemeral publications—the bulletins and pamphlets surrounding the return to constitutional government in Ghana over the last year, for example—hasn't seemed important to U.S. researchers. This is often not an insoluble problem. With infinite resources one could go looking for and find these ephemera, but we do not have infinite resources.

I mention these problems because in making current collections more accessible, enriching the data that surrounds them, and connecting them together and then to the user, we can end up perpetuating the blindness that shaped collections (to put it at its most political) and (more generally) we can be trapped in old scholarly agendas. In the *House of the Seven Gables,* Hawthorne writes that a "dead man sits in all our judgment seats." Perhaps a dead librarian sits in all our bibliographic databases.

Another way of being trapped in old scholarly agendas is to restrict ourselves to the book. In cultural studies we use film, advertising, video, and popular music. We read not just the *Journal of Philosophy* but also *Vogue* and *Women's Wear,* and we send our students to see not just the BBC Shakespeare but the movies of Ousmane Sembene and Sylvester Stallone. Access to these new sources, especially to still and moving pictures, is woefully behind access to text, in part because the technology for searching and storing images is so much harder to construct than that for searching words. Because of the relative simplicity of the mapping between syntax and semantics, looking through a text for ideas is a manageable task. But what software would you design to search *Termi-*

nator II for images of violent death? Annotating movies and photographs in useful ways and making that information available is a great need for current work.

So too is ease of access to these images. It is enormously expensive in terms of data to store a film, as any of you who have stored quicktime clips in a Mac will know. But making film clips easily available for use in teaching would be tremendously helpful. Imagine if I could use a video HOLLIS to find the movie I want (I am looking for one that explores drought in the Sahel in the context of a historical romance) and issue a request that it be made available on line. Then I would like to be able to mark and store on a server the two-minute sequence that I want my students to see for their preparation for class. I'd like to be able to put on the same bulletin board a clip from a Senegalese newspaper movie review, an interview with the director in *Der Spiegal* for those who read French and German (adding a rough and ready translation of each produced by me and my German-speaking teaching assistant), and a photograph of the director pulled from an online encyclopedia of African film.

This is what the new reserve librarian will be helping me to do. I am willing to work with her or him to make it possible. But in the end, once the work is done, I would like to be able to browse the library of texts and images without thinking about how it is done. That is what I do now when I log on to HOLLIS, and that is why the library I never go to is already one of the most important places in my life.

References

Appiah, Anthony. 1989. "Race." In *Critical Terms for Literary Study,* edited by Frank Lentricchia and Tom McLaughlin, pp. 274–287. Chicago: University of Chicago Press.

Gates, Henry Louis, Jr., Anthony Appiah, and Cynthia D. Bond. 1988. "Computer Applications at the Black Periodical Literature Project." *Literary Research* 13 (Winter): 31–37.

III

The Gateway in Research and Scholarly Communication

In this part, three authors explore the impact of information technology on research and scholarly communication in the sciences, social sciences, and humanities. Paul Ginsparg, a physicist, writes on scholarly communication in the sciences. Richard C. Rockwell, a social scientist, examines the use of social science data in a networked environment. John Unsworth discusses the effects of technology on research in the humanities. Are any influences of technology common to all three academic areas? Do any significant differences appear in the responses of the sciences, social sciences, and humanities to information technology?

Although three chapters cannot adequately represent the range of possible responses to these questions, they do point to intriguing parallels as well as differences among the sciences, social sciences, and humanities. In the humanities, Unsworth thinks linking texts to sources—that is, a shift to a distinctively archival character of information—is not the radical break with the culture of print commonly portrayed. Ginsparg, in contrast, sees a revolution in scholarly communication in the sciences and democratization of scholarship as well. Taking a slightly different tack, Rockwell thinks that the breaking down of artificial distinctions among kinds of information—graphical, textual, and numeric—has necessitated the rethinking of traditional organizational distinctions among libraries, museums, archives, research institutes, and computer centers. For Rockwell, the idea of a gateway indicates a need to rethink institutional structures for supporting research.

The terms and conditions of publication change in an electronic environment. For Unsworth, traditional publishing is fast becoming a mere footnote in the emerging world of telecommunications conglomerates, while Ginsparg thinks print publishing is scarcely relevant to scholarly communication in the sciences. For Rockwell, the issue is not so much about publishing but about access to data that are already in the public domain. Publication, in the traditional sense, is no longer an issue, and the acquisition of data is becoming less so. What matters is access to data archives maintained by consortia like the Inter-university Consortium for Political and Social Research (ICPSR).

Despite these variations, there is a telling convergence among the three approaches to adding value to information to make it useful for research. For Ginsparg there is a need to add intellectual value to information and an opportunity for any agency willing to take it on; the question is, Will it be done by publishers, academic associations, or libraries? For Unsworth, on the other hand, adding value to electronic information is a matter of survival for the humanities in the face of burgeoning commercial interests. Rockwell, too, wants value added to information, and he sees the gateway as providing the interface between users and resources. Librarians, he argues, are the experts or consultants who can and should support the use of raw data for the social sciences as well as other disciplines. Here, then, is the agenda for the library of the future: how to organize information to make it accessible and provide the expertise, both systemic and personal, that enables students and scholars to use it effectively.

4

First Steps toward Electronic Research Communication

Paul Ginsparg

hep-th@xxx.lanl.gov, the e-mail address for the first of a series of auto-mated archives for electronic communication of research information, went online in August 1991. This "e-print archive" began as an experi-mental means of circumventing recognized inadequacies of research jour-nals but unexpectedly became within a very short period the primary means of communicating ongoing research information in formal areas of high-energy particle theory. Its rapid acceptance within this community depended critically both on recent technological advances and on behav-ioral aspects of this research community, as described below. There are now more than 4,000 regular users of hep-th worldwide, and the archiv-ing software has also been expanded to serve over twenty-five other research disciplines, including not only other areas of high-energy physics such as astrophysics, lattice computations, and experiment but also other areas of physics such as astrophysics, condensed matter theory, materials theory, general relativity and quantum cosmology, nuclear theory and experiment, quantum physics, accelerator physics, superconductivity, and plasma physics. The software also serves fields such as nonlinear dynam-ics and Bayesian analysis and certain fields of mathematics including algebraic geometry, functional analysis, quantum algebra, differential geometry, automorphic forms, and complex dynamics. It even has ex-panded to disciplines such as economics, computation and linguistics, and atmosphere and oceanic sciences. World Wide Web access to these archives is available at http://xxx.lanl.gov/. The extended automatically maintained database and distribution system serves over 40,000 users from more than 70 countries, and processes over 100,000 electronic transactions per day: it is already one of the largest and most active databases on the Internet. This system provides a paradigm for recent changes in worldwide, disciplinewide scientific information exchange. It also serves as a model for how the next generation of electronic data highways can provide for electronic transmission of research and other information as access to high-speed computer networks becomes universally available.

Background

The rapid acceptance of electronic communication of research information in my own community of high-energy physics was facilitated by a preexisting "preprint culture" in which the irrelevance of refereed journals to ongoing research has long been recognized. At least since the mid-1970s, the primary means of communication of new research ideas and results had been a preprint distribution system in which printed copies of papers were sent via ordinary mail to large distribution lists at the same time that they were submitted to journals for publication. (Larger high-energy physics groups typically spent between $15,000 and $20,000 per year on photocopy, postage, and labor costs for their preprint distribution.) These papers could then typically take six months to a year to be published and appear in a journal. In this community, therefore, we have learned to determine from the title and abstract (and occasionally the authors) whether we wish to read a paper and to verify necessary results rather than rely on the alleged verification of overworked or otherwise careless referees. The small amount of filtering provided by refereed journals plays no effective role in our research.

This community, by the mid-1980s, had already begun highly informal but regular electronic information exchanges, which in turn were enabled by concurrent advances in computer software and hardware. The first such advance was the widespread standardization during this period on TeX (written by Donald E. Knuth of Stanford) as our scientific word processor. For the first time we could produce for ourselves a printed version equal or superior in quality to the ultimate published version. TeX has in addition the virtue of being ASCII based, which makes it straightforward to transmit TeX files between different computer systems. Collaborations at a distance became extraordinarily efficient, since we no longer had to express-mail multiple versions of a paper back and forth and could instead see one another's revisions essentially in real time. Figures as well can be generated within a TeX-oriented picture environment or more generally can be transmitted as standardized PostScript files produced by a variety of graphics programs.

A second technological advance was the exponential increase in computer network connectivity achieved during the same period. By the end of the 1980s, virtually all researchers in this community were plugged into one or another of the interconnected worldwide networks and were using e-mail on a daily basis. (It is conceivable that earlier attempts to set up "electronic journals" in other communities failed not due to any intrinsic flaw in implementation but rather due to the insufficiently mature state of computer networking itself—leaving an underconnected userbase.) Finally, the existence of on-line archives which allow access to large amounts of information has been enabled by the widespread availability of low-cost but high-powered workstations with high-capacity storage media. An average paper (with figures and after compression) requires 40 kilobytes to store. Hence one of the current generation of rapid-access 1 gigabyte disk drives costing under $500 can hold 25,000 papers at an average cost of 2 cents per paper. Slower-access media for archival storage cost even less: a digital audio tape cartridge, available from discount electronics dealers for under $15, can hold over 4 gigabytes—that is, over 100,000 such papers. The data equivalents of multiple years of most journals constitute a small fraction of what many experimentalists routinely handle on a daily basis, and the costs of data storage will only continue to diminish.

Since the storage is so inexpensive, it can be duplicated at several distribution points, minimizing the risk of loss due to accident or catastrophe and facilitating worldwide network access. The Internet runs twenty-four hours a day with virtually no interruptions, and transfers data at rates up to 45 megabit per second—less than .01 second per paper. Currently projected backbone upgrades to a few gigabits per second within a few years should be adequate to accommodate increased usage for the academic community. Commercial networks currently envisioned to comprise the nation's electronic data highway will have even greater capacity.

The above technological advances—combined with a remarkable lack of initiative on the part of conventional journals in response to the electronic revolution—rendered the development of e-print archives an accident waiting to happen. Perhaps more surprising has been the readiness of scientific communities to adopt this new tool of information exchange and to explore its implications for traditional review and publication processes. The exponential growth in archive usage suggests that scientific researchers are not only eager but indeed impatient for completion of the proposed information superhighways (though not necessarily the "information turnpikes").

Implementation

Having concluded that an electronic preprint archive was possible in principle, in the summer of 1991 I spent a few afternoons writing the software to assess the feasibility of *fully automating* such a system. At issue was whether an automated information exchange could permit its users to construct, maintain, and revise a comprehensive database and distribution network without outside supervision or intervention. The software was rudimentary and allowed users with minimal computer literacy to communicate e-mail requests to the Internet address hep-th@xxx.lanl.gov ("hep-th" stands for high-energy physics theory). Remote users submit and replace papers, obtain papers and listings, receive help on available commands, search the listings for author names, and so on. The system allows ongoing corrections and addenda and is implemented to ensure that only those who so desire are kept up to date.

It is important to distinguish the formal communication of such an e-print archive (which meets the standards and needs of the scientific community for research promulgation and circulation) from the informal (and unarchived) communication provided by electronic bulletin boards and network news. In the former case, researchers are deliberately restricted to communication via their abstracts and research papers which are in principle equally suitable for publication in conventional research journals, whereas the latter case is more akin to ordinary conversation or written correspondence—that is, neither indexed for retrieval nor stored indefinitely. The e-print archives, designed as a tool for the electronic communication of research results, include features such as the ability of a submitter to replace his or her submission, checks on database integrity (to ensure, for example, that the individual replacing a submission is indeed the original submitter), permanent records of submissions together with dates submitted; and records of number of user requests for each paper.

Users can subscribe to the system and thereby receive a daily listing of titles and abstracts of new papers received. This primitive e-mail interface provides a necessary lowest common denominator that ensures the widest possible access to users, independent of their network connection and local operating system. The initial user base for hep-th was assembled from preexisting e-mail distribution lists in the subject of two-dimensional gravity and conformal field theory. Starting from a subscriber list of 160 addresses in mid-August 1991, hep-th grew quickly within six months to encompass most of formal quantum field theory and string theory and as mentioned above currently has over 4,000 subscribers (it is the largest individual archive although still a small percentage of the over 40,000 subscribers aggregated over all of the archives). Its smooth operation has transformed it from its initial incarnation as a feasibility assessment experiment for a small subcommunity into an essential research tool for its users, many of whom have reported their dependence on receiving multiple fixes per day. The original hep-th archive alone now receives over 200 new submissions per month, and the archives as a whole process over 350 new submissions per week. Internet e-mail access time is typically a few seconds. The system originally ran as a background job on a small Unix workstation (a 25 MHz NeXTstation with a 68040 processor purchased for roughly $5,000 in 1991) that was primarily used for other purposes by another member of my research group, and placed no noticeable drain on Cpu resources. The system has since been moved to an HP 9000/735 that sits exiled on the floor under a table in a corner. A photo of the setup and related figures illustrating the growth in usage and current access rates are available via the World Wide Web at http://xxx.lanl.gov/blurb/.

The system also allows anonymous ftp (file transfer protocol) access to the papers and the listings directories, and World Wide Web access provides an even more sophisticated and convenient network access for those with the required (public domain) client software. This allows local menu-driven interfaces, automatically connected to the nearest central server, to transparently pipe selected papers through test formatters directly to a screen previewer or printer. Such software has moreover been set up to cache and redistribute papers on many local networks. The World Wide Web interface alone on http://xxx.lanl.gov currently processes roughly 45,000 requests per day on weekdays and has been growing each month by an additional 30,000 requests (as of September 1996).

An active archive such as hep-th requires about 70 megabytes per year (that is, $40 per year) for storing papers, including figures. Because network usage is less than 10^{-4} of the lanl.gov backbone capacity, it places a negligible drain on local network resources. In principle it requires little intervention and has run entirely unattended for extended periods while I have traveled. It is difficult to estimate the potential for dedicated systems of the future only because the resources of the current experimental one (run free of charge) are so far from saturation. In the meantime, additional e-print archives have been established for the more than twenty-five other disciplines of physics, mathematics, and other fields mentioned at the outset here.

Storage and retrieval of figures have not been a problem. While software for figures has not yet been standardized, the vast majority of networked physics institutions have screen previewers and laser printers that display and print PostScript files created by a wide variety of graphics programs. Figure files are typically submitted as compressed PostScript, and papers can be printed with the figures embedded directly in the text. High-resolution digital scanners will soon become as commonplace as fax machines and permit inclusion of figures of arbitrary origin. (It is already, of course, possible to fax arbitrary figures to a machine equipped with a fax modem, convert to bitmapped PostScript, and append them.) With appropriate data compression and PostScript conversion, figures typically increase paper storage requirements by an inconsequential factor of 2.

The success of e-print archives can be assessed by several measures. First, there are widespread testaments from users that they find it an indispensable research tool—effectively eliminating their reliance on conventional print journals. Some report no longer submitting to journals, either because they have forgotten to do so because they have already communicated the information, or because they have consciously chosen not to deal with a tedious and seemingly unnecessary process. Second, numerous institutions have decided to discontinue their preprint mailings in recognition of the superior service provided by e-print archives. Finally, it has now become customary in some of the fields served by e-print archives to provide as reference a paper's e-print archives index number rather than a local report number or a published reference.

Prospects and Concerns

The e-print archive system in its present form was intended not to replace journals but only to organize a haphazard and unequal distribution of electronic preprints. It is increasingly used as an electronic journal, however, because it is evidently more convenient to retrieve electronically a computer file of a paper than to retrieve physically a paper from a file cabinet. Besides minimizing geographic inequalities by eliminating the boat-mail gap between continents, the system institutes a form of democracy in research wherein access to new results is granted equally to beginning graduate students and seasoned operators. No longer is it crucial to have the correct connections or to be on exclusive mailing lists to be kept informed of progress in one's field. The pernicious problem of lost or stolen preprints experienced by some large institutions is as well definitively exorcised. Communication among colleagues at the same institution may even be enhanced, since they frequently cross-request one another's preprints from the remote server (for reasons I hesitate, in general, to contemplate). Many institutions have eliminated their paper distribution of preprints and thus already have seen significant savings in time and money. Others have begun to request specifically that paper copies no longer be sent to them, since electronic distribution has proven reliable and more efficient.

It is straightforward to implement charges for such a system if desired, via either flat access rates or monitored usage rates. Piggybacked on existing network resources, however, such systems cost so little to set up and maintain that they can be offered virtually free. Overburdened terminal resources at libraries are not an issue, since access is typically via the terminal or workstation on one's desk or in the nearest computer room.

These systems allow users to insert interdisciplinary pointers to their papers stored in related archives, thus fostering interdisciplinary distribution and retrieval of information through cross-linked databases. Electronic research archives will prove especially useful for new and emerging interdisciplinary areas of research for which there are no preexisting journals and for which information is consequently difficult to obtain. In many such cases, it is advantageous to avoid a proliferation of premature or ill-considered new journals. Cross-linking provides an immediate virtual meeting ground for researchers who wouldn't ordinarily communicate with one another. They can quickly establish their own dedicated electronic archive and ultimately disband if things do not progress as expected, all with infinitely greater ease and flexibility than is provided by current publication media.

In the long term, electronic access to scientific research will be a major boon to developing countries, since the expense of connecting to an existing network is infinitesimal compared with that of constructing, stocking, and maintaining libraries. Indeed, physicists in developing countries confirm how much better off they find themselves even in the short term with the advent of the current electronic distribution systems: no longer are they "out of the loop" for receipt of information. Others report feeling that their own research gets a more equitable reading, as it is no longer dismissed for superficial reasons of low-quality print or paper stock. The trend experienced over the past decade in the Western world, where data transmission lines have become as common as telephone service, and terminals and laser printers as common as typewriters and photocopy machines, could be repeated even more quickly as countries in eastern Europe and the third world develop electronic infrastructures. In the short term they certainly can continue to receive information via conventional means from the nearest redistribution point. Conformity to a uniform computer standard both in the United States and abroad to communicate results to the largest possible audience should pose no greater a burden than communication using a nonnative language—English—already imposes on the majority of the world. Similar comments apply equally to those less well-endowed institutions in the United States.

The trends experienced by physics and biology departments are soon to be repeated by the full range of conventional academic institutions, including teaching hospitals, law schools, humanities departments, public libraries, and ultimately elementary and secondary schools.

Publication companies, on the other hand, have been somewhat irresponsible over the past decade, increasing the number of journals and as well the subscription price per journal (some single journal subscriptions to libraries now run well over $10,000 per year) during a period when libraries have experienced continually decreasing amounts of resources and space. In the meantime, because these same publication companies have been slow to incorporate electronic communication into their production and distribution operations, e-print archives could ultimately result in dramatic savings in cost and efficiency for all involved. There remain numerous value-added enhancements (discussed below) that could vastly improve on what is possible in current automated archives. The resources necessary for production and distribution of conventional printed journals formerly allowed publishers to focus on only those mechanics, avoiding any pressure to rethink the intellectual content and quality of their operations. But the online electronic format will allow us to transcend the current inadequate system for validating research in a variety of ways. No longer will we be tied to a one-time all-or-nothing referee system that provides insufficient intellectual signal and to a static past database. We eagerly anticipate a vastly improved and more useful electronic literature, taking advantage of the flexibility afforded by the electronic medium and unhindered by artifacts of its evolution from paper.

Moreover, it is difficult to imagine how the current model of funding publishing companies through research libraries (in turn funded by overhead on research grants) can possibly persist in the long term. It is premised on a paper medium that was difficult to produce, difficult to distribute, and difficult to duplicate—a medium that required numerous local redistribution points in the form of research libraries. The electronic medium shares none of these features and thus naturally facilitates large-scale disintermediation, with attendant increases in efficiency benefitting both researchers and their sources of funding. Recent developments have exposed the extent to which current publishers have defined themselves in terms of production and distribution, roles that we now regard as trivially automated. But there remains a pressing need for organization of *intellectual* value added, which by definition cannot be automated even in principle, and that leaves significant opportunities for any agency willing to listen to what researchers want and need.

Concerns about interference from malevolent hackers have proved unfounded. Archives can be rendered highly resistant to corruption, and minimal precautions can assure users of remote database systems that their own system resources are not endangered. Anonymous ftp servers running on Internet have for years allowed the academic community an open exchange of executable software far more susceptible to malfeasance, and their safeguards have proven effective. At this writing, there has happily not been a single instance of attempted break in or deliberate malfeasance. Perhaps the recent rapid growth of the Internet has simply provided too many easy targets, and random electronic vandalism has lost any perceived attraction.

Some members of the community have voiced their concern that electronic distribution will somehow increase the number of preprints produced or encourage dissemination of preliminary or incorrect material, arguing that an electronic version is somehow more ephemeral than a printed version and therefore lowers the barrier to distribution. This concern first of all confuses the method of production with the method of distribution, and it is likely that most researchers are *already* producing at saturation. Second, the electronic form once posted to an archive is instantly publicized to thousands of people, so the embarrassment over incorrect results and consequent barriers to distributing is, if anything, *increased*. Such submissions cannot be removed but can be replaced only by a note that the work has been withdrawn as incorrect, leaving a more permanent blemish than a hard copy of limited distribution that is soon forgotten.

This is not to argue that refereed or moderated forums are obsolete or necessarily undesirable. In some disciplines, the refereeing process plays a useful role both in improving the quality of published work and in filtering out large amounts of irrelevant or incorrect material for the benefit of readers. The refereeing process plays the additional role of validating research for the purpose of job and grant allocation. It is useful to observe, however, that if citations alone are used as a criterion for influence of research, then these can be compiled in an unrefereed sector as usefully as they can be in a refereed sector: crackpot papers neither make nor receive enough systematic references in the mainstream literature to alter any "signal" in this methodology. A refereeing mechanism could be easily implemented for the e-print archives in the form of either a filter prior to electronic distribution or a review *ex post facto* by volunteer readers or selected reviewers. In either case, the archives could be partitioned into one or more levels of refereed as well as unrefereed sectors. Thus lifting the artificial constraints to dissemination of information and decoupling it from the traditional refereeing process will allow for more innovative methods of identifying and validating significant research.

Additional problems may arise as computer networking spreads outside the academic community. For example, hep-th would be somewhat less useful if it were to become inundated by submissions from crackpots promoting their perpetual motion machines or even by well-meaning high school students claiming to refute the special theory of relativity. Perhaps this will ultimately constitute no greater nuisance than is currently experienced by recognized journals, or become no more commonplace an annoyance than current unwanted physical or telephone intrusions into our offices and homes. It is clear, however, that the architecture of the information data highways of the future will somehow have to reimplement the protective physical and social isolation currently enjoyed by ivory towers and research laboratories.

Increased standardization of networking software and electronic storage formats during the 1990s encourages us to fantasize about other possible enhancements to scholarly research communication. USENET newsgroups, for reasons such as their lack of indexing and archiving and excessively open nature, are unlikely to prove adequate for serious purposes. On the other hand, it is now technically simple to implement, for example, a World Wide Web form-based submission system to build hyperlinked discussion threads, accessible linked for given points in individual papers and also started from a subject-based linked discussion page. All posted text could be WAIS-indexed for easy retrieval, and related threads could interleave and cross-link in a natural manner, with standard methods for moving forward and backtracking. A histogram-like interface would facilitate the finding of active threads, and the index could show the location of all postings by a given person (including the user) with date of latest followup to facilitate tracking of responses. This would provide a much more flexible format than USENET, specifically avoiding awkward protocols for group creation and removal, and as well avoiding potentially unscalable aspects of the network news transfer protocol (nntp). For the relatively circumscribed physics research community, a central database (with the usual mirrored nodes) would have no difficulty with storage or access bandwidth. To enable full-fledged research communication with in-line equations or other linkages, we require slightly higher-quality browsers than are currently available. But with hypertext transfer protocols (http) now relatively standardized, network links and links to other application software can be built into underlying TeX (and configured into standard macro packages) to be interpreted either by dedicated TeX previewers or passed by a suitable driver into more archival formats (such as Adobe Acrobat pdf) for greater portability across platforms. Multicomponent messages could also be assembled in a graphical MIME (multipurpose Internet mail extension) composing object to be piped to the server via the http POST protocol, thereby circumventing some of the inconvenient baggage of Internet sendmail or ftp protocols.

While the above is technically straightforward to implement, there remains the already mentioned issued of limiting access to emulate that effective insulation from unwanted incursions afforded by corridors and seminar rooms at universities and research laboratories. One method would be to employ a "seed" mechanism—to start from a given set of trusted users and let them authorize others (and effectively be responsible for those beneath them in the tree), with guidelines such as doctorate candidate, and so on. Permission to post or authorize would be revokable at any time and retroactive one level back in the tree. To allow global coverage, application to the top level for authorization could be allowed to start a new branch. The scheme entails some obvious compromises, and other schemes are easily envisioned; but the ultimate object remains to determine the optimal level of filtering for input access to maintain an auspicious signal-to-noise ratio for those research communities that prefer to be buffered from the outside world. This would constitute an incipient "virtual communication corridor," further facilitating useful research communication in what formerly constituted both pre- and postpublication phases and rendering ever more irrelevant the physical location of individual researchers.

Finally, we mention that the e-print archives in their current incarnation already serve as surprisingly effective inducements in the campaign for computer literacy and have succeeded in motivating some dramatic changes in computer usage. Researchers who previously disdained computers now confess an addiction to e-mail; many who for years had refused to switch to UNIX or to TeX are in the process of converting; others have suddenly discovered the power of browsing with World Wide Web. The effectiveness of the systems in motivating these changes justifies the philosophy of providing top-of-the-line search, retrieval, and input capabilities for cutting-edge power users, while maintaining "lowest common denominator" capabilities for the less network fortunate.

Conclusions and Open Questions

These systems are still primitive and are only tentative first steps in the optimal direction. Already, however, we have learned that the experiment has been widely accepted by researchers:

· The exponential increase in electronic networking over the past few years opens new possibilities for both formal and informal communication of research information.

· In some fields of science, electronic preprint archives have been online since mid-1991 and have become the primary means of communicating research information to many thousands of researchers within the fields they serve. People will voluntarily subscribe to receive information from these systems and will make aggressive use of them if they are set up properly. It is anticipated that such systems will grow and evolve rapidly in the next few years.

· From such experimental systems, we have learned that open (that is, unrefereed) distribution of research information can work well for some disciplines and has advantages for researchers both in developed and developing countries. We also have learned that technology and network connectivity are currently adequate for supporting such systems, and that performance should benefit from improvements expected in the near future.

Some unanswered questions amplify some of my earlier comments:

1. Who ultimately will be the prime beneficiaries of electronic research communication—researchers, publishers, libraries, or other providers of network resources?

2. What factors influence research communities in their rate and degree of acceptance of electronic technology, and what mechanisms are effective in facilitating such changes?

3. What role will be played by the conventional peer-refereeing process in the electronic media, and how will it differ from field to field?

4. What role will publishing companies play in electronic research communications, and how large will their profits be? If publication companies do adopt fully electronic distribution, will they pass along the reduced costs of increasingly efficient production and distribution to their subscribers? Can publishing companies provide more value added than an unmanned automated system whose primary virtue is instant retransmission?

5. What role will be played by library systems? Will information be channeled somehow through libraries or instead directly to researchers?

6. How will copyright law be applied to material that exists only in electronic form? Publishing companies have "looked the other way" as electronic preprint information has been disseminated as they did when the earlier paper preprints were distributed by mail—claiming that their philosophy supported free dissemination of information. Will they continue to be so magnanimous when libraries begin to cancel journal subscriptions?

7. What storage formats and network utilities are best suited for archiving and retrieving information? Currently we use a combination of e-mail, anonymous ftp, and window-oriented utilities such as Gopher and World Wide Web combined with WAIS indexing to retrieve TeX and PostScript documents. Will something even better—such as Acrobat or some other format currently under development—soon emerge as a standard?

8. How will the medium itself evolve? Conservatively, we can imagine interactive journals in which equations can be manipulated, solved, or graphed, in which citations can instantly open references to the relevant page, and in which comments and errata dated and keyed to the relevant text can be inserted as electronic flags in the margins, etc. Ultimately, we

may have some multiply interconnected network hypertext system with transparent pointers among distributed databases that transcends the limits of conventional journals in structure, content, and functionality— thereby transforming the very nature of *what* is communicated. This is the sort of value added for which we should be willing to pay. We do not wish to clone current journal formats (determined as they are by artificial constraints of the print medium) in the electronic medium: we are already capable of distinguishing information content from superficial appearance. Who will decide the standards required to implement any such progress?

The hep-th e-print archive began for me as a spare-time project to test the design and implementation of an electronic preprint distribution system for my own relatively small research community. Its feasibility had been the subject of contentious dispute, and its realization was thought even by its proponents to be several years in the future. Its success has led to an unexpectedly enormous growth in usage. It has expanded into other fields of research, and has in addition elicited interest from many others—I have received over a hundred inquiries about setting up archives for different disciplines. Each discipline will have slightly different hardware and software requirements, but the current system can be used as a provisionary platform that can be tailored to the specific needs of different communities. While it long remained a spare-time project with little financial or logistical support, as of 1 March 1995 it has been supported by the U.S. National Science Foundation under Agreement No. 9413208.

Further development will require coordination among interested re- searchers from various disciplines, computer and networking staff, and interested library personnel, and in particular it will require dedicated staffing. At the moment, hardware and software maintenance of existing automated archives remains a loosely coordinated volunteer operation, and little further progress can be made on the issues raised by current systems without some thoughtful direction. Perhaps the centralized da- tabases and further software development will ultimately be administered and systematized by established publishing institutions or professional societies, if they are prescient enough to reconfigure themselves for the inevitable. Since researchers have taken the lead so far, however, we should retain this unique opportunity to continue to lead the development of such systems in optimal directions and on terms maximally favorable to ourselves.

Acknowledgments

Many people have contributed (consciously or otherwise) to the development of these e-print archive systems. The original distribution list from which hep-th sprung in 1991 was assembled by Joanne Cohn, whose incipient efforts demonstrated that members of this community were anxious for electronic distribution (and Stephen Shenker recommended that the original archive name not include the string "string"). Continual improvements have been based on user feedback too voluminous to credit (although among the most vocal have been Tanmoy Bhattacharya, Jacques Distler, Marek Karliner, and Paul Mende). People who have administered some of the remote-based archives include Dave Morrison, Bob Edwards, Roberto Innocente, Erica Jen, and Bob Parks. Joe Carlson and David Thomas set up the original gopher interfaces late in 1992. The Network Operations Center at Los Alamos National Laboratory has reliably and uncomplainingly supplied the requisite network bandwidth @lanl.gov, and Joe Kleczka has been available for crisis control. Louis Addis and staff at the Stanford Linear Accelerator Center (SLAC) library moved quickly to incorporate e-print information into the SPIRES database, furthering their decades of tireless electronic service to the high-energy physics community. Dave Forslund and Richard Luce helped lobby for support from within the laboratory, and the Advanced Computing Laboratory has in addition provided some logistical and moral support. Finally, Geoffrey West repeatedly and against all obvious reason insisted that Los Alamos lab is appropriate to sponsor this activity, while simultaneously bearing the bad news both from within the laboratory and from certain government funding agencies.

5

Using Electronic Social Science Data in the Age of the Internet

Richard C. Rockwell

Only a few years ago most academic librarians did not customarily think of the primary data of social science as within their realms of responsibility. However, the ways in which academic libraries connect to learning, teaching, and research are changing, perhaps more rapidly and more fundamentally than ever before. This chapter on gateways to social science data is based on a paper presented at a Harvard College Library conference on "Gateways to Knowledge" and discusses fundamental changes in how researchers, teachers, and students will use electronic social science data in this age of the Internet.

Some basic changes in using electronic social science data are that artificial distinctions among kinds of information—graphical, textual, and numeric—are breaking down and that organizational lines that divided libraries, museums, research institutes, and computer centers are dissolving or being rethought. One such line of demarcation—that between academic libraries and the providers of the primary data of social science—had already broken down in many places. On some campuses the library simply absorbed a social science data service from some department, research institute, or computing center. On other campuses, the library recognized the inadequacy of existing arrangements for access to data and created an alternative system. On still others, the library began to take a proactive role in creating a set of services that the campuses had never before seen, including data services built around client-server facilities.

Like other data archives, the Inter-university Consortium for Political and Social Research (ICPSR) is now accustomed to working with libraries. When ICPSR was formed over thirty years ago, it usually dealt with departments of political science and young professors in those departments. Since its formation, a new profession—that of data librarian—has arisen, and increasingly these professionals find their homes in libraries rather than in departments or research institutes.

This new cooperation between data archives and academic libraries is occurring in the context of sweeping technological changes that have the potential for reshaping the academic library. These changes are fundamental and qualitative and are not merely incremental changes of the sort that libraries have forever experienced. As libraries engage in rethinking and reengineering over the next decade, that self-examination will transform libraries, hopefully under the guidance of professional librarians rather than just of those enamored of technical gadgetry.

In this chapter, I introduce the topic of access to social science data in this new environment by describing a remarkable ethic for sharing data that arose almost forty years ago in the U.S. social science research community. I then consider means for providing improved access for teachers, learners, and researchers to the electronic data sets resulting from surveys, censuses, administrative records, and other modes of social science data collection. Finally, I expand my perspective to a discussion of how access to the primary data of social science could be provided under the more general concept of the gateway library.

The Data of Social Science as a Shared Resource

The surveys, censuses, and other data collection methods used by social scientists generate most of the primary data for empirical research in fields such as economics, political science, social psychology, and sociology. Since at least the 1950s, the data have been stored in electronic data sets in forms appropriate for computerized statistical analysis. The "logical records" in the data sets pertain to individuals, families, households, groups, organizations, and governments, with each record usually providing dozens or hundreds of measurements. There are often thousands or even millions of individual data records. These data are, for the most part, raw data in that they contain measures for each unit of observation, whether the unit is a person or an organization. The nearest equivalents in most libraries might be parish or genealogical records. Where a promise of confidentiality has been given to the respondent, that promise is adhered to by eliminating all personal identification and by recoding information to prevent reidentification of respondents based on combinations of geographic, demographic, social, or economic characteristics. Confidentiality and privacy are assured, and a research resource of great power is made available.

The measures available in these data sets may include economic, political, social, demographic, attitudinal, or psychological information. Measures can be expressed in quantitative units such as dollars, in simple numerical codes for characteristics such as type of industry or sex, or in numerically coded summarizations of complex verbal information, such as responses to questions about occupation. All of these are commonly called *quantitative data* because numbers are used to record the information, but the data are often inherently qualitative and are only represented as quantitative.

Not all electronic data sets contain raw data. Some contain summarized data—percentages, counts, and other summary statistics or tabulations of several measures. Examples are tables of the percentage of families living below the poverty line in all census tracts in the United States and counts of persons in each ethnic group in each county. These summarized (or *aggregate*) data are familiar to libraries because their content derives from the concept of printed reports. Such printed reports have long been the staple products of federal data collection programs such as the decennial U.S. Census. Their release on the CD-ROM medium in recent years has not been problematic for most libraries, except for the uncertainty of acquiring needed equipment given libraries' limited resources. These electronic versions of printed reports are likely to characterize the products of the statistical programs of the federal government by the turn of the century as printed reports are phased out. Libraries should soon be prepared to receive many or most federal statistical volumes only in electronic form.

My emphasis here is on raw data rather than on these summarized data products, although data archives do maintain aggregate data as well as raw data. Historically, specialized data services on campus have uniquely provided access to raw data, while both libraries and data libraries have provided access to summarized data. The trend is strongly in the direction of libraries themselves providing access to raw data.

Why would a researcher make an investment in using raw data when experts have already prepared summary tabulations? The advantage of using raw data is primarily an issue of flexibility, one that is familiar to reference librarians who are asked questions such as: "This table tells me the relationship for the whole population between educational attainment and income. What is the relationship for people in Generation X?" Raw data permit a response other than, "There is no way to tell from this table."

From the perspective of the researcher, the power of raw data is much greater than the data that are provided by reports. Given access to raw data, analysts control the research they are conducting. They can ask questions about specific portions of the sampled population. They can introduce statistical controls not employed by the original designers of the tables.

New research can be undertaken with old data. Because original researchers rarely exhaust the analytical potential of a complex data set, researchers can apply new analytical methods to old problems, sometimes shedding new light on what we thought that we knew. Additional discoveries can be made about scientific and societal issues that arose after the original researchers moved on to other topics. Several data sets can be pooled to provide analytical potential that the original investigators never had.

In addition to these uses of raw data for new discoveries, researchers can perform analyses that test or extend the results published by other researchers. Those new results sometimes differ from published results, raising questions about the validity of prior findings and allowing researchers to implement the scientific method to replicate results before they are accepted as true.

This set of uses of raw data, commonly called *secondary analysis,* is thus an indispensable part of the process of discovery as well as of the process of replication and verification of reported results. The term *secondary* carries a connotation of inferior analysis, but in fact the process of looking again at data has yielded substantial primary research discoveries. Secondary analysis is annually the foundation of numerous journal articles, books, theses, and dissertations.

Secondary analysis in the social sciences has been made possible because original investigators have shared their data with other social scientists. In the 1950s, many leaders of social science around the world acknowledged that informal arrangements for sharing data resulting from major data collection projects were proving cumbersome and ineffective and recognized that it was necessary to develop institutional arrangements for sharing and archiving. Most libraries of that time were not talking about computer-readable data or even computers, so national electronic data archives—such as ICPSR—were created by the social science communities in several countries, well before their equivalents were created in the natural sciences.

Simultaneously, local campus data services were initiated, usually operating first out of an assistant professor's closet. Today, most of those campus data services are professionally operated by data librarians who combine library skills with computer and statistical skills. Data librarians have created standards for cataloging computer-readable data, software tools for finding data, sets of routines for archiving data, and a host of other accomplishments that may be germane to the problems now being faced by academic libraries. Data librarians are often an underutilized source of expertise and a resource for understanding the future direction of libraries in general; directors of libraries would do well to consult them.

The sharing of data has led to the social scientist's equivalent of the chemist's laboratory. This social science data-driven laboratory is the vehicle for replications and new discoveries, as well as for teaching. The social scientist at the workstation, personal computer, or terminal has access today to data from much of the world, and this access lays a foundation for both research and training.

Campus administrators have often been slow to recognize that, just as chemists need laboratories, social scientists need data services and adequate access to computing power to do their work. An administrator who would not flinch at an expenditure of $90,000 for one piece of equipment for a single natural scientist questions an expenditure of that size to benefit an entire campus community of social scientists. Social scientists need to better articulate their needs and demonstrate that both computing and access to data are integral to social science research. Moreover, teachers are bringing the computer into the classroom, replacing lectures with laboratories in which students work with real data and discover for themselves some of the principles of social science. Students so trained are likely to understand social science's need for data if they take administrative or political positions.

Some data sets collected with public funding have been designated by the National Science Foundation as "national resources" that are available to shared access. In many other cases, original investigators share their data with others after a brief period of exclusive access. Public opinion polling firms, university-based research institutes, private organizations, as well as governmental agencies have typically made some provision for public access to data they collect. This was not the mode in many of the natural sciences until recently, and it seems still not often to be the mode in the humanities where the original collectors of the data are viewed as the owners of the data and share their data with others at their option.

The predominant ethic in much of social science has been that data collected with public resources should be publicly shared through public archives, and this ethic is reinforced by rules of some granting agencies. For example, award letters for data collection projects funded by the National Science Foundation contain this paragraph: "All data sets produced with the assistance of this award shall be archived at a data library approved by the cognizant Program Officer, no later than one year after the expiration date of the grant. In cases that involve issues of confidentiality or privacy, precautions consonant with human subjects guidelines shall be observed." In addition, there is a strong community expectation that researchers will provide copies of data on the request of those attempting to replicate published results. This data-sharing culture has led to the creation and expansion of vast archives such as ICPSR.

These archives have enabled social scientists to exploit the enormous data resources generated by a diverse assortment of data collectors: the surveys and censuses of the federal government, the significant national studies conducted in universities and research institutes (usually funded by the federal government or private funders), national and regional polls, and many other local and regional studies. These data sets constitute a multibillion dollar resource for society. Social scientists are often the side beneficiaries of these major data collection programs, with the major client being an administrative agency or the Congress. Without access to these data sets, empirically driven social science as we know it would not exist. In addition, archived data are increasingly of interest to historians, whose work has been enriched by the appearance of a new form of evidence in recent decades. Even humanists may begin to view quantitative social science data as within their purview, perhaps as cultural artifacts.

From the Desktop Back to the Desktop

Secondary analysis became possible when social scientists gained computational power. Social science computing began with primitive desktop hands-on analysis, moved to batch and time-shared remote computing, and has reached the sophisticated desktop computing of today. For several decades prior to the 1960s, hands-on social science computing involved punched cards, card sorting machines, and desktop rotary calculators. Cumbersome as these devices were, they provided for direct interactions of the researcher with the data, often with the aid of a small army of graduate students. The calculator-equipped desktop was a workbench for many social scientists, providing independence from central machines and the ability to process fairly large amounts of data.

In the 1960s the migration began to magnetic tape and central mainframes in either batch or time-sharing modes. During this period the researcher was separated from data analysis by time and space—and analyses and the computer operations preliminary to analyses consumed increasingly larger proportions of research budgets. Researchers were separated from their analyses by a new priesthood of programmers, who muttered arcane incantations to large machines and asked the researcher to place blind faith in their results.

By the mid-1980s a reverse migration stream (which has now turned into a flood) began, leading to today's powerful desktop computing environments. Mainframes are disappearing from many campuses or are being assigned peripheral roles in distributed computing environments. Hands-on computing has returned to social science.

Today's computing environment is sharply different from what it was even five years ago. We have seen the evolution of client-server architectures; widespread access to and familiarity with the Internet; the advent of effective standards-based software tools such as Mosaic for using Internet services; the declining cost, expanding capacity, and increasing speed of magnetic disks; the installation of CD-ROM drives in a substantial percentage of personal computers; and the proliferation and declining prices of powerful desktop computers that are the equivalent in processing power of the mainframes of only a few years ago. The effect has been a revolution in computing in the social sciences and in everything associated with computing, such as access to data. As in many revolutions, there has been no clear leader and no consensus on how things are changing. There are at least as many visions of the future as there are players in the game.

These revolutionary developments have led to a new set of expectations among social scientists. They wonder why we, the campus data services and national archives, are not already

· Delivering data, documentation, and analytical power directly to their desktops;
· Employing modern client-server architectures and a friendly desktop interface in client software;
· Providing a single interface to all the resources and services of the world's social science data archives, thereby lifting from them the burden of learning peculiar protocols for each data archive;
· Responding to their requests more quickly, more cheaply, more intuitively, more powerfully; and
· Pushing rather than trailing the state of the art.

These expectations are far-reaching, and the resources available to meet them are small. Nevertheless, it is clear that data archives and campus data services must work to provide the kinds of services that researchers demand. It would be highly desirable for them to do so in cooperation with academic libraries. They can learn from each other. The concept of the gateway library provides a way to think about how cooperation among national archives, academic libraries, and campus data services might blossom.

A Concept of the Gateway Library as a Provider of Remote Social Science Data

I view the gateway library as an electronic means by which a researcher or student can access resources and services collected at many different locations. The gateway library provides a simple integrated electronic interface between the inquirer and the resource—and the interface is the same no matter which resource the inquirer is seeking. The print collections (books, journals, data sets) locally held by the gateway library may be among its less important assets. The gateway library might, in fact, have no print collection at all, and it might not even have a physical location. Users of the Internet are undoubtedly familiar with the directory service known as Yahoo. This service maintains no resources; it is purely a searchable directory of more than 32,000 Internet sites. In a sense, Yahoo is a primitive form of the gateway library in its least physical form: it provides access to information on a large scale but maintains nothing itself.

This observation about the nonphysical nature of some gateway libraries should not be read as a declaration that print collections are unimportant or that libraries will go out of the business of building and maintaining collections. Some institution somewhere must have responsibility for maintaining a collection, just as the Internet sites to which Yahoo points must remain functional for Yahoo to have any value. I do claim that libraries must provide access to far more resources than they can possibly collect locally.

The range of resources to which the gateway library provides access and the effectiveness with which it provides that access will be the hallmarks of a successful gateway library. Those resources may be present on campus, be held by an academic library, a publisher, or a data archive, or be half a world away. Popular resources will be widely duplicated for ease and speed of access, but resources with very small numbers of users will be held by only a few specialized libraries. Some resources may exist at only one place in the network. If an effective form of access is provided, it will be immaterial to the researcher and to the student where the resource has been collected—as long as an electronic form of access is satisfactory and as long as the integrity of both the collection and access to it is ensured.

It is clearly *not* the case that the only way to provide access to a resource is to acquire that resource for a local collection. Libraries have provided access without ownership for many years. The gateway library is simply an extension of the concept of the library itself as a shared resource. I do not have to acquire for my personal collection everything that I might ever want to read; as a member of the academic community, I have access to the resources of the university's library. The academic library did not need to be housed in the building where I am officed because I could access materials from its collection without physically going to the library. In fact, I would have been equally well served whether the library collection had actually been housed a block away or a continent away had service been equally quick. Departmental and satellite libraries exist all over campus without anyone expecting them to replicate the collection of the main library; the fact that the resource is available, and not precisely where it is, is what matters. The gateway library is a means of access to distributed resources and therefore is an extension by electronic means of the access that I already have to library materials.

Similarly, every social scientist at every member institution has access to the data collections of ICPSR without the relevant part of those collections necessarily being housed on campus. ICPSR headquarters has responsibility for acquiring, processing, documenting, and archiving the data sets, and it provides access to those data sets in a variety of forms. Individual campus data libraries need not assume responsibility for acquiring the data sets for their own collections, although many do so; their primary function is to provide access to those data sets for faculty, staff, and students.

The gateway library will be, I suspect, the significant library trend of the future, connecting directly to and supporting the concept of the digital library. This will be because simultaneously the demand for access to resources is growing, the costs of collecting and processing materials are skyrocketing, and the technology for electronically sharing a resource around the world is becoming economically feasible. It remains unclear whether this technology will save money compared to present access methods or even whether electronic access will be fully acceptable to most library clients. However, it is likely that electronic access will become a major thrust because it offers one of the few cost-containment strategies available today, because it is faster than physical relocation of materials, and because it can open access to a world of resources that it would be unthinkable for most libraries to acquire.

A Scenario for Access to Social Science Data[1]

Under this model of the gateway library, one of its services would be to provide access to data and documentation housed in social science data services all over the world. The following scenario of how that access could function assumes that the user is using a desktop machine of the Intel 486 class or better, a high-resolution large-screen display device on which images of documents are easily readable, a pointing device such as a mouse, a networked laser printer, and an Ethernet-speed direct connection to the Internet. This is a common configuration and can be purchased for less than $2,500. (It will also rapidly become an obsolete configuration, although still functional.) Many scholars and students do not yet have access to such machines, but any college or university that wishes to maintain its academic standing will have to make appropriate hardware and software investments, including infrastructural investments in Internet access. An institution that fails to provide suitable equipment and infrastructure will soon be seen as being in the same class as an institution that neglects to provide a library.

In this scenario, the user—an undergraduate student enrolled in a political science course—is preparing to do an analysis of one of the "national resource" data sets, the General Social Survey (GSS). The GSS is taken as the example because the National Science Foundation is funding a project to provide exactly the services described below. What is said about the GSS will generalize to most of the primary data sets of social science.

The GSS covers the last twenty-two years (1972 through 1994) with twenty probability samples of adults living in households in the United

States. The cumulative data set covering 1972 through 1993 contains 29,388 respondents and 2,173 variables (over 800 variables tracked over time), and the 1972 through 1994 cumulative file has about 2,400 variables, including over 900 trend variables. Most major topics in the social sciences are covered: intergroup relations, gender roles, social control, social stratification and mobility, social inequality, poverty, civil liberties, national priorities, social supports and networks, AIDS and sexual behavior, and so on. It also has an extensive battery of demographic information that not only covers the basic current background variables for respondents but also includes considerable information on family of origin, spouse (such as labor force participation, occupation and industry, education, and religion), and current household (such as the age, gender, martial status, and relations of all family members).

The user's first task is to discover whether the GSS, in all its richness and complexity, includes data on ethnicity and political participation in the form that she needs. Using free text search capabilities, the ability to form Boolean expressions, and a system of indexes and key words, the user specifies the kinds of data in which she is interested. Successful usage of a survey data set requires that this information be accurate, complete, and readily available. Users need full question text, full listings of response categories, sampling information, skip instructions, field notes, working papers, methodological reports, and so on. In this scenario, the full documentation of the GSS is available to the user in an integrated, organized way.

Hypertext documentation addresses these needs. A hypertext document is composed of one or more other hypertext documents. These documents have links in them to other documents, which appear in NCSA Mosaic or Netscape as highlighted words or phrases. A user positions the cursor over a link (usually underlined, in reverse video, or in a different color) and then either presses the return key or clicks with a mouse. This action causes the software to retrieve the linked document. Sometimes this link is within the same document and repositions the user within the document, but the link also can extend to other documents in layers below the source document. Those linked documents can be provided by remote servers; they need not exist on the server on which the user began her search.

Using documentation thus becomes far less linear than it was in the days when scrolling through screens of electronic documentation was the only option available to users. In the place of screen after screen of scrolling text (sometimes aided by search capabilities), hypertext services return the user to the days in which one could jump through the pages of a book, marking some pages for easy return or even tearing out a page from time to time. This is functionally equivalent to having dozens of books and articles laid out on the table, all indexed and all with context-sensitive pointers to each other. The implementation of hypertext documentation for the GSS will permit the external user to obtain and correlate information that even the GSS staff itself cannot now obtain. If this is true for a research project in which the documentation is already well organized, it will be even more true for other data sets, including many federal data sets.

The user obtains information about the GSS through a layered set of documentation, supported by online help and a tutorial. The experienced user will have access to all these services but will also have shortcuts that can go directly to such services as extract and statistical analysis. The documentation will begin with the GSS Guide:

The GSS Guide
This brief overall document is designed to explain the survey and the services available and to direct users to various services marked up for hypertext access. Users may access all GSS services from the Guide page. The Guide leads the user to the following five sources of documentation, which are themselves linked by index systems, including by the familiar GSS mnemonics:

· GSS *Electronic Codebook:* The Electronic Codebook provides full question and response wordings. It includes frequencies and percentages for each year. The user has the ability to view a formatted version of the codebook either by scanning through it or by jumping through the document by hypertext links and searches. It is possible to search for questions using key words, mnemonics, and topic headings or to do a free-text search with a WAIS index. The capacity to print from the codebook is provided by the network browser. The user sees not simple ASCII text but formatted text, which is much more readable on the screen and in print.

- *GSS Electronic Codebook Appendices:* The GSS Electronic Codebook Appendices provide documentation on sample, interviewing, and other essential study information. From the viewpoint of the user, these are no longer appendices but instead are directly accessible from the Guide and the Codebook.
- *GSS Trend Tables:* The Trend Tables provide 1972 through 1994 trends for all items with proper weights and special adjustments. They are searchable by using the same tools that are provided for searching the Codebook.
- *GSS Bibliography:* The 1994 edition of the GSS Bibliography has over 3,100 listings, and all are indexed by and searchable by mnemonic as well as by standard keyword searches and WAIS free-text searches. The Bibliography is continuously updated by the GSS staff—a service impossible to offer through print.
- *GSS Reports:* The GSS Reports include over 150 project reports in their complete text, indexed by mnemonics and WAIS and fully searchable. New reports will be added to the system as they are produced.

Option for Core Research Articles

In addition to the five forms of documentation available through the GSS Guide, it would be possible to electronically capture many of the core research articles, permitting the user to read the full text of the article by clicking on the highlighted articles in the Bibliography. The articles would appear as formatted text and include graphics. This would permit users to "come up to speed" rapidly on the GSS, learn about research done by others, and avoid unknowingly replicating the work of others. Eventually, all new journal articles will surely become available electronically. Implementing this capability today depends more on whether a suitable licensing agreement can be struck with publishers than on technical or financial considerations.

GSS Cumulative Data File   The GSS Cumulative Data File is the core data file and is updated after each survey. It provides case-level data for all cases and all variables for all years. File transfer protocol (ftp) service for the full cumulative data file is available, enabling the user to obtain the entire GSS data file over the networks, but the Extract service (described below) may prove to be so attractive that users may repeatedly come back to the service for new extracts rather than obtaining the full file and then doing their extracts on local machines.

Extract   A researcher rarely requires a full data set; far more commonly a researcher requires only a subset that contains observations on some variables for a selected group of subjects. Subsetted data sets are usually much smaller than the source data sets and more amenable to usage in statistical packages. Indeed, drawing an extract is a routine step in preparations to do analyses. Efficient use of both network bandwidth and local storage capacity could be attained if researchers have the capacity to obtain the subsets of data sets that they need. What is needed is a generalized, highly efficient extracting program directly accessible from the user's desktop. The Extract facility enables the user to prepare flat files or transport files representing a sample of items, cases, or years drawn from the cumulative data file in formats suitable for use within SPSS, SAS, or other statistical or spreadsheet systems. It automatically prepares data definition statements for either SAS or SPSS. Customized codebooks are also prepared on request.

Users can select a list of variables, a filter for the selection of cases, and a range of years. No programming experience is required; users simply type the specifications for the desired extract or click the mouse on icons. For example, one could click on or type SEX, RACE, AGE, and POLPART and get a file with the three demographics (gender, person's race, and person's age) and the political participation variable, or one could click on or type GSS1993 and get all 1993 variables. Many users recode variables or compute new variables as they create customized extracts.

Statistical Analysis   In some cases the user's research question requires exploration of the data before an extract can be drawn. In other cases the analysis requirements are limited and suitable for execution at the remote server and do not need even the importation of extracts to the local machine. All of these options are offered through analysis services provided to the client by the server. This makes the user's analysis very simple to perform and will not require that the user have any statistical analysis software at the desktop. It requires only that the user have a machine capable of running Mosaic or some other WWW browser.

The level of analysis services provided is limited because it is expected that the user will do heavy-duty computations at the local desktop. Analyses to be made available include the computation of frequencies (with means, modes, and medians); basic descriptive statistics (mean, standard deviations, confidence intervals, measures of skewness and kurtosis, and range); graphics including bar and pie charts, frequency polygons, and Lorenz curves; bivariate and multivariate contingency tables or cross-tabs, with row, column, and total percentages, expected frequencies, and measures of association; and correlations with scatterplots.

Ask GSS   The user can send queries to the GSS staff at Ask GSS and receive answers quickly.

GSS Roundtable   Users can join the GSS Roundtable, an electronic conference moderated by GSS staff, and engage in conversations with one another. This consolidates the community of users of the GSS and has already led to collaborative research.

Benefits for Both Expert and Novice Users

Novice users of electronic research technologies—as well as persons who are trained to be social scientists, including journalists, students, and public servants—are able to locate questions of interest and view the distributions and trends where applicable because access is easy and the downloadable products (question wordings, distributions, trends) are presented in simple, clear, and self-contained formats.

The educational applications for these services could be significant. Faculty will be able to assign exercises involving studies of trends, comparisons of ethnic and racial groups, or other research questions that can be answered with the GSS. High-school students will be able to undertake data analyses. These services will move us further toward the goal set by a founder of the GSS, James A. Davis: that social science at the undergraduate level should be a laboratory science.

At this point social scientists and other expert data analysts are making far heavier demands on electronic services than are novices. Because data and documentation will be integrated, they will be able to do this work more easily and effectively than ever before. An example of use may convey the power of this system of services.

An expert enters the system with an interest in a particular subject matter, such as characteristics of nonfeminist women. First, the user locates appropriate questions by either searching the topical headings covering all questions, making a keyword search, or using other built-in retrieval techniques. Users already aware of appropriate GSS mnemonics (such as FEPOL or FEHELP) can ask for those variables and also have the system locate related questions and wordings (such as FEPRES or FEBEAR). Once the user identifies the items, the analyst examines wordings and response categories, including frequencies, and studies trends. A question about sample design (such as, Does the sample include older women living in institutions?) might lead to a query about sampling information. The analyst searches technical notes for any observations about response bias, question order effects, and other technical details of measures and searches the literature for other studies on this phenomenon (a substantial number of articles would appear in this case).

The analyst might perform exploratory research before committing to reading an extract or even to using the GSS. Once the decision is made, the analyst obtains raw data for incorporation into analyses employing the most widely utilized statistical programs (SPSS and SAS) and even can draw custom extracts for immediate use with the statistical programs on desktop machines. Through NCSA Collage, which is compatible with NCSA Mosaic, the analyst can engage in synchronous (real-time) collaborative research with colleagues at distant locations, fully sharing access to the services and retrieval of information. The analyst can join GSS Roundtable or query Ask GSS when questions arise.

There is currently no way for an analyst to perform all of these information retrieval operations. Doing so is even beyond the present capacity of the GSS staff. The integration of data and documentation afforded by this system thus does far more than make work easier and faster: it strengthens survey analysis by opening the way to better, more thorough work.

The old tape- and print-dependent system clearly has worked in many ways, although it was not easy or fast. A generation of social scientists has produced volumes of high-quality research using the existing technologies of tape and print. Perhaps we should question whether anyone really needs to have data available at the desktop within a few minutes of the request, accompanied by a customized codebook. I, however, see no scholarly virtue in waiting for mail deliveries or in depending on computer experts to draw an extract or perform a statistical analysis.

Desktop services return to the analyst the ability to directly interact with data and documentation that was once afforded by the card sorter but with an efficiency that far exceeds those sorters.

When users encounter problems, they can address them to a local campus data librarian, who has the capacity (over the campus network) to join users on screen in a collaboratory mode of work. The user also can choose to participate in a conference about this and related data sets, address questions to the staff of the data archive, or send messages to the study's designers.

Fundamental Changes in How Libraries and Data Libraries Operate

When the user is finished using the GSS data and documentation, she probably will discard everything that is archived elsewhere, knowing that she can easily obtain the information whenever she needs it again. This conserves local disk space, relieves the user of archival responsibilities, and ensures that she will receive the current edition of the data set when she next queries it.

More generally, network access to archived data will radically change the role played by the campus data service. For every campus, access to data will be markedly improved, even as thousands of reels of computer tape of social science data that once cluttered computer centers around the world vanish, and few are found in the campus's data collections. Now even the smallest college can provide access to the entire ICPSR data collection for its faculty and staff, at the cost of providing access to half a dozen print studies. By shifting from seeking to acquire local collections to seeking to provide local access, campus data librarians have found their jobs strongly shifted in the direction of being expert consultants and away from being archivists. The archivist role is performed by organizations like ICPSR.

This scenario is already partially realized. Some of the search functions for ICPSR data are now provided by a gopher server at ICPSR that is accessible from anywhere and by anyone in the Internet. An X-windows-based and more sophisticated documentation search facility is provided by the Swedish Social Data Service for the data in its collection. Data examination and extract services are provided at the University of California–San Diego and by the California State Federation of ICPSR members. The U.S. Global Change Research Program and its components are making strides toward unified directory services. Albert H. and Paul Anderson of the Population Studies Center, University of Michigan, have functioning extract and exploratory data analysis programs that have cut to seconds the turnaround time required for exploratory analyses of the large Public Use MicroSample data sets resulting from the 1990 U.S. Census.

Considerable momentum is building in the direction of providing such services. The technology is ready. Development projects are being mounted on many campuses, often under the rubric of the digital library. The challenge will be to provide these services in an integrated way worldwide, so that the user does not need to learn one procedure for accessing San Diego data resources and another for accessing Swedish data resources. We need one common gateway to all social science data archives that is accessible from a single client—either Mosaic or its sibling, Netscape. That client ought also to serve the other needs of the gateway library. This is, again, the core concept of the gateway library as a simple common interface between the user and the resource (Rockwell, Hardin, and Loots 1995).

What Kinds of Data Will Be Provided by Gateway Libraries?

The above scenario concentrated on just one of the major data resources of the social sciences. Several other data sets are similarly major resources, plus there is an enormous outflow of data from the statistical agencies of the federal government and the polls conducted by survey organizations worldwide. Added to these are literally hundreds of data sets, often with smaller samples and narrower foci, that are generated by individual research projects. Many of the latter are also archived by ICPSR. What might librarians of the future expect to see among the mix of data sets for which they have responsibility?

No overview of the requirements of the social science community for the data resources of the future could be complete or even reasonably trustworthy. Social science evolves, and among the principal ways that it advances is by changing its conception of the kinds of data required for research. Nevertheless, a brief list of possible data priorities might be helpful in conceptualizing usage of social science data through the gateway library.

· For a couple of decades, longitudinal data sets have been recognized to be the most powerful way of studying change over time, and this approach is likely to persist. Either these data sets follow the same respondents—individuals, groups, organizations—over time in what is called a *panel design,* or the study is replicated with different samples across time in what is called a *repeated cross-sections design.*

· An increased emphasis on comparative research is drawing on a long tradition of conducting studies designed to be comparable across several countries. Because cross-country studies do not exist for most topics and for most of the world, we are now attempting to pool data sets that were not originally collected with an explicit eye toward comparability. There is also an interest in comparative analyses for units other than the nation-state.

· Certain subject areas are rising in importance because of public or scientific priorities. Prominent among these areas are studies of global environmental changes and of the environment more generally. This is the fastest-growing part of social science in terms of increased funding, and it is inherently interdisciplinary. The volume of data associated with this research can be stunning.

· Similarly, health services are an increasingly important area of research. Among underexploited data resources are the enormous data sets collected in the administration of insurance and Medicare programs. As with most social science data, problems of ensuring confidentiality and privacy in these analyses are serious but surmountable.

· Throughout the social sciences, there seems to be a renewed attempt to combine quantitative and qualitative data in analyses. As pointed out above, we previously used numbers for two purposes in the social sciences: as a measure of some quantitative attribute such as income or number of children and as a placeholder for qualitative or categorical data such as race or an attitude. The latter use of numbers was introduced when the card sorter entered our technology; the machine could not analyze text punched into the card. Computers have removed that restriction and allow us to analyze text and even images without prior numerical coding. However, constructing suitable methodologies for qualitative data is conceptually an extraordinarily difficult task. It is conceivable that social science can import pertinent methodologies from the humanities as well as from remote sensing and image-enhancement technologies.

· New approaches to analysis are also rising in importance and will affect the kinds of demands made on gateway libraries. Among these new approaches are Geographic Information Systems, a way of organizing data of various kinds into many layers that are built on an underlying geographic core. Historical time series can be organized in this form. These systems permit the analysis of data collected under considerably different geographic coding schemes. Their widespread use might serve to reintroduce the concept of space into social science analysis—beyond its present home in geography. There is reason to expect some federal data products to be released in this form within a decade or so. The implication for gateway libraries is that users will need machines with very fast CPUs and high-resolution display devices.

· Visualization tools are rising in importance for training, for exploratory research, and for understanding complex nonlinear systems. At one time we acted as if regression coefficients summarized what we could know about relationships among variables, but today we understand that a picture is indeed better than a thousand words—and probably better than ten-thousand numbers.

· Many statisticians feel that resampling analytical methods ("bootstrap" and "jackknife") will become the dominant form of statistical analysis in the future. These computation-intensive algorithms eliminate the need to make strong parametric assumptions about data structures. They demand high-performance computing (ideally, storage of large samples in RAM), meaning that linkages to campus facilities that provide such performance may be important to gateway libraries.

· Modeling of complex systems, including chaotic systems, is similarly receiving renewed attention. Formerly, social science modeling was primarily stochastic or probabilistic; today, deterministic modeling is of rising importance. These models are simpler in many respects but more mathematically demanding. Models often involve data from both the natural and the social sciences in such fields as global environmental change and health.

These are only a sample of the kinds of social science data that gateway libraries are likely to be expected to provide in the future. Developing the necessary expertise to manage the new technologies will be a formidable challenge. My guess is that libraries will need to develop new forms of collaboration with campus research institutes and even with individuals. It is probably unrealistic to expect libraries to cultivate substantive expertise on this range of topics. What will be provided instead is access—in this case, to people rather than to data. That need for access to people will, in fact, probably be as true in the future as it has been in the past: the most valuable resource of a great library is not its books, its reference system, or its electronic card catalog: it is the library's people. The greatest challenge to directors of today's academic libraries is to train and retrain their staffs so that they will be able to function well in the bright new age of the Internet.

Note

1. Most of this section is adapted from a successful proposal to the National Science Foundation jointly submitted by the National Opinion Research Center (NORC) of the University of Chicago (Tom W. Smith, principal investigator) and by the ICPSR (Richard C. Rockwell, principal investigator). The author expresses appreciation to NORC for permission to adapt these materials for this purpose.

Reference

Rockwell, Richard C., Joseph Hardin, and Melanie Loots. 1995. "Surviving the Three Revolutions in Social Science Computing." *Social Science Computer Review* 13, no. 2 (Summer): 149–162.

6

Some Effects of Advanced Technology on Research in the Humanities

John Unsworth

I recently read in the *Boston Globe* that QVC (a company held by Liberty Media) was preparing to bid on Paramount, giving up merger talks with Home Shopping Network, and that Bell South was discussing buying a 22 percent stake in QVC in order to provide cash for the Paramount bid. Liberty, which had pledged $500 million toward the $9.5 billion Paramount bid and held a controlling stake in the Home Shopping Network, was itself the subject of a merger proposal from TCI (Tele-Communications Inc.), which with Bell Atlantic had just completed one of the largest mergers in history. QVC was bidding against Viacom for Paramount (Viacom and TCI are old corporate enemies: Viacom owns MTV). Paramount owns Fox (heads of Paramount and QVC used to work together on the Fox network), the Knicks, and, incidentally, Simon & Schuster, the largest book publisher in the United States.

I mention this tangled tale from the business section because the largest book publisher in the United States appears in it as a footnote. If we're not fairly aggressive and organized about our role in the emerging national information infrastructure, humanities scholarship will be a footnote as well. A great deal of hype has been focused on the national information infrastructure and the information superhighway, and behind that hype a great deal of money is riding on the idea that the Internet of the future will be amenable to the models and practices and values of broadcast or (at best) cable television. As telephone and cable companies slug it out for ownership of the road, they are both head-hunting the executives of broadcast television to program and run their new networked services. Frankly, we probably don't have a chance here: our best hope is that the new market will behave differently from the old one and that new materials may find new audiences in it. But whatever we think our chances are, we are bound to participate. As Stuart Moulthrop (1991) argues in an essay called "You Say You Want a Revolution? Hypertext and the Laws of Media," humanists must engage the technology: if we don't do that, we can't complain when it turns out to be hostile to our needs and ambitions. The University of Virginia's Institute for Advanced Technology in the Humanities is one effort to effect this engagement, to generate these new materials, and to find these new audiences.

The Institute for Advanced Technology in the Humanities

The Institute for Advanced Technology in the Humanities was established in 1992 to advance computer-mediated research in the humanities. It does this by bringing in faculty fellows in residence—most from the University of Virginia but some from outside—and by supporting a number of associate fellows, on grounds and off, each year. Fellows are selected in a competitive application process adjudicated by a committee of faculty from the humanities and computer science, and fellows receive equipment, technical support, project-design consultation, and access to shared Institute resources. Fellowship at the Institute allows humanists to work with technologists as partners, to participate in the design of software that will meet general needs in humanities scholarship, and to discover tools and resources that already exist. The Institute encourages cross-fertilization not only between fellows and technologists but also among humanists from divergent disciplines—indeed, catholicity and collegiality are its distinguishing features.

The Institute was made possible by a major grant from IBM and by matching commitments from the University of Virginia. Our technology base, at the moment, consists of about 20 Rs6000 workstations, 270 gigabyte tape archive, about 40 gig of disk, a dozen X-Stations, a few Suns, Decs, IBM PCs, and Macs. Our work is UNIX-oriented, working with X-Windows, Motif, and the Web, and most of our development efforts are based on the RS/6000 platform, but we have rigorously observed open-systems standards for tagging, image formatting, and data collection in general. Our work, from both a technical and a humanities

point of view, is aimed at the research and telecommunications environment of two to three years in the future: the technology we are working
with is already available but is a couple of years from being on everyone's
desk.

Current Research Projects

Current research projects underway at the Institute include the following:

· Ed Ayers's documentary history of two towns (Staunton, Virginia, and
Chambersburg, Pennsylvania) during the Civil War. This project collects
thirty years of newspapers from each town that have been digitized from
microfilm, many different kinds of census information, period and contemporary maps and photographs, diaries, military rosters, and a host
of other materials. Overlaid on this rich archive of primary materials is
Professor Ayers's historical narrative examining the effect of the war on
the daily lives of ordinary people.

· John Dobbins's Pompeii Forum project, a CAD-based reconstruction
of the Forum. This project began with a meticulous survey of the site
using laser measuring devices and then, based on the results, created new
two-dimensional digital plans and three-dimensional models of the Forum. Extensive photographic evidence is also included in this project, as
are animated tours of the models.

· Hoyt Duggan's edition of the medieval manuscript poem *Piers Plow-
man*. This "diplomatic critical edition" seeks to represent all fifty-four
extant versions of the poem, using the computer to collate and explore
the variant forms and to preserve and present the manuscript pages
themselves.

· Ken Schwartz's study of several low-income neighborhoods in Char-
lottesville, Virginia, aimed at designing affordable housing based on the
architectural history of those neighborhoods. Maps, GIS (Geographical
Information Systems) data, photographs, text, architectural plans, and
many other sources of information make up this rich planning resource.

· Gary Anderson's study of medieval narratives concerning the life of
Adam and Eve after Eden. This project collects texts in Hebrew, Greek,
Latin, Cyrillic, and Arabic character-sets, using SGML (Standard Gener-
alized Markup Language) tagging and unicode character representation.

· Elisabeth Crocker's study of immigration and assimilation in the United
States at the turn of the century, focusing on the representation of identity
in popular texts such as the cartoon strip Krazy Kat.

· David Gants's digital catalog of watermarks and type ornaments used
by William Stansby in the printing of *The Works of Benjamin Jonson*.

· Jerome McGann's hypermedia archive of the complete works, visual and textual, of Dante Gabriel Rossetti. This archive includes a vast number of manuscript images, galleys, editions, SGML-tagged transcriptions, drawings, paintings, and translations.

Upcoming Projects

Upcoming projects at the Institute include the following:

· Joe Viscomi's, Morris Eaves's, and Bob Essick's Getty-funded electronic edition of all the illuminated works of William Blake, in multiple editions, and many of Blake's commercial illustrations,
· Elizabeth Meyer's interpretive study of the evolution of slavery in Hellenistic and Roman Greece,
· Richard Guy Wilson's study of the architecture of Thomas Jefferson,
· Frank Grizzard's documentary history of the building of the University of Virginia,
· Constanze Witt's project on the origins of Celtic art, and
· Rob Leventhal's "Responses to the Holocaust: A Hypermedia Sourcebook."

In addition to these projects, the Institute sponsors associate-fellows projects in history, religion, linguistics, landscape architecture, music, film, and literature. My own work at the Institute is focused on *Postmodern Culture,* the oldest peer-reviewed electronic journal in the humanities, now publishing networked hypermedia.

This is the body of work, then, that I would like to use as my example of advanced technology in the humanities for the purposes of discussing the impact of technology on research and on teaching in the humanities. In particular, I'd like to focus on the research of Jerry McGann and his Rossetti archive.

The Rossetti Archive

Like all of the Institute's research, the Rossetti archive is available through the World Wide Web. Our home page is at http://jefferson.village.virginia.edu/home.html, where readers will find research reports in annual series, plus related publications, course materials, technical reports, software demonstrations and distribution, and a collection of humanities-related Internet resources.

In the Rossetti archive, Jerome McGann has begun to bring together all the material that make up Dante Gabriel Rossetti's work and a healthy slice of the other books and images that informed that work. It is worth noting that a work such as *The House of Life*—Rossetti's sonnet cycle— may exist in many versions, editions, and revisions. The same is true of what may be more familiar works—Whitman's *Leaves of Grass,* Wordsworth's *Prelude,* and others. What makes Rossetti an ideal subject for hypermedia research, though, is not only that he worked in many media but also that he was interested in the connections between poems and paintings and between texts and other texts. Conceptually, Dante Gabriel Rossetti was an early hypertext—or hyper*media*—author, generations ahead of his time. And as McGann (1994) has pointed out, the book is not a particularly well-adapted tool for studying or presenting the work of this type of writer:

When we use books to study books, or hard copy texts to analyze other hard copy texts, the scale of the tools seriously limits the possible results. In studying the physical world, for example, it makes a great difference if the level of the analysis is experiential (direct) or mathematical (abstract). In a similar way, electronic tools in literary studies don't simply provide a new point of view on the materials, they lift one's general level of attention to a higher order.

To uncover the intricate connections that criss-cross the oeuvre of Rossetti, and to analyze the many layers of his compositions, electronic tools are a practical necessity.

What we have in the Rossetti archive, then, represents a shift in paradigm and a significant change in the critical medium, but not a radical break with established scholarly practice. It takes the notion of the book—an idea whose form has seemed to be fixed for only a couple of hundred years—and subsumes its metaphors and operations under a companion metaphor, that of the archive. If, in a critical edition, every text potentially refers to every other text and to nontext objects in an archive, then in the electronic version all states of the manuscript and all connections with other texts and images are potentially available.

Copyright

Of the great quantity of text and images already collected in the Rossetti archive, a small percentage is not publicly available because of copyright or contractual restrictions. For example, a user who comes on a transcription of one of Rossetti's manuscript poems might ask for the page image itself but find that the server refuses to provide it if the user is not within the Institute. At a later date, when permission to publish that page image has been granted, we will simply unlock that particular link, and the information will become publicly accessible. In all likelihood, though, these pieces will never be made available through the Institute's publication but only through the University of Michigan Press, which has undertaken to publish the finished version of the project as an integrated combination of CD-ROM and networked database, probably licensed on an annual basis to university systems.

Depending on one's point of view, copyright is either one of the major impediments to, or one of the principal enablers of, networked research in the humanities—*especially* in the humanities. It is an impediment mostly from the point of view of users, who want to be able to get at information regardless of copyright status; it is an enabler from the point of view of publishers and some authors because copyright at least promises some protection for intellectual property in an apparently lawless information frontier. In the long run, though, the media of the computer and the network—where copying and redistributing are the basic character of the technology itself—are bound to force the establishment of new copyright practices, either through new legislation or by case law (Barlow 1994). Of course, those changes will not necessarily be for the better: some of the most vocal and well-represented lobbying forces in the battle over copyright are conservative or even reactionary ones: approaches to the problem of electronic copyright that emphasize maintaining the status quo (or revoking basic information rights in order to cope with new problems) will, if they are successful, result in the electronic environment becoming more restrictive and inflexible than ever before.[1]

If we can think only in old ways about new problems, we will overlook critical new economic opportunities and practices. If a library or museum sets prices for rights based on the book model—twenty or so plates, a few thousand copies, a high per-image price—it won't work for projects like networked databases with thousands of images. On the other hand, as automated and secure mechanisms for collecting revenues over the network come into existence, it may be possible for rightsholders to collect pennies from each of hundreds or thousands of users, effectively competing with photocopying machines. There are also opportunities for new kinds of site-licensing arrangements, such as the those being investigated by the Getty-sponsored Museum Educational Site Licensing project (in which the Institute participates).

Computers and Humanism

The Rossetti archive and indeed the work of the Institute as a whole raise the issue of the compatibility of computers as tools with the aims of humanism as a cultural movement. In the popular press and in the imagination of some humanists, there seems to be a *de facto* opposition between print literacy and computer literacy. This opposition, and the dire predictions of what we will lose by moving from one to another, are based for the most part on uninformed and unexamined assumptions (Amiran, Chaski, and Unsworth 1992). Nonetheless, the electronification of scholarly communication is effecting a gradual but apparently inevitable change in the way we go about our business. This change is affecting scholars and students in many different disciplines of the humanities and the sciences, as well as academic and commercial publishers, tenure committees, university administrators, MLA policymakers, private and government funding agencies, and librarians.

The community of humanists has responded to this change and its implications with everything from despair to rejoicing, but for the most part we have focused on the local effects of the situation rather than on understanding our circumstances as a limited and special case of a much more general shift in the culture as a whole. With few exceptions, academics have not successfully addressed the public on the more global effects of computers, networks, and electronic communication, except in the form of an elegy for vanishing values in an electronic age. In the Arnoldian lament for culture in the age of the chip, the defenders of traditional academic practices find themselves in strange collusion with both the traditional and the emergent enemies of intellectualism: this particular resistance to change within the academy serves the interests of those who would like to see these new technologies integrated into current markets with the least possible alteration of the property system or the role of the consumer.[2]

From my point of view, one of the most important and revolutionary implications of networked humanistic research of the kind represented by the Rossetti archive and the other projects at the Institute is the potential for scholarship to become the occasion for collaboration and, through that collaboration, to grow and develop over time. In addition, when the original scholar or scholars are finished with the archive—if ever—what will be published is not only the result of research (the book, as it were) but also the research material itself. It is as though all notes, records, and findings were published with the book—and remained there, to be expanded and used for different purposes. In principle, those who use such an archive could also propose the addition of new material to the editor of the archive, and related archives could be linked to one another.

For students, this means not only greatly expanded access to primary documents but also a more meaningful opportunity to apprentice in the disciplines. In addition, networked hypermedia archives are easy to assemble. I taught my graduate assistant, a first-year master's student in English with little computer training, to do basic HTML markup in about an hour; she has since gone on to become the managing editor for *Postmodern Culture* and the project manager for both the Blake project and the Rossetti archive. In a real sense, then, the tools of networked publishing are now sufficiently accessible that students can easily master them, moving from traditional roles as research assistants into new roles as partners in the research and publishing enterprise.

I'm neither a techno-optimist nor technodeterminist, but to some extent technologies do have a character. The telephone is a one-to-one communications technology; TV and radio are one-to-many technologies. Computer networks are inherently many-to-many communications medium. This in itself will change research and teaching more than anything else. One immediately available consequence of that many-to-many capability is real-time conferencing facilities such as IATH-MOO, the Institute's real-time, text-based virtual conferencing facility. While we browse the Rossetti archive in one window, we can be in the Rossetti room of the IATH-MOO in another window, talking to others who are looking at the same materials. This might be compared to the opportunity one has of meeting another reader in the library stacks, and it demonstrates that the edited online hypertext archive can, if we wish, have a common room.

Conclusions

In this period of great creative ferment we are experiencing the freedom and the peril that accompanies the rise of any major new technology. I expect that we will spend the next generation sorting out our respective roles, identifying our needs and our goals, and generally finding our bearings in this new terrain. I think it very likely that the basic missions represented by the library, the publisher, and the researcher (scholar or student) will survive, though these activities may in some cases look very different when we've translated them to this new medium. But the medium itself might, by analogy, offer us some guidance: on the Net, layers and layers of protocols—TCP, IP, Winsock, perhaps Z39.50—are running to enable what we do, each handling a different aspect of getting information from where it is to where we are. We need, in planning academic use of the nets, to think in similar terms about the distribution of tasks. I'd argue that campus computing needs to take care of communications standards and protocols; librarians need to take care of information formatting (tagging, file formatting, access methods), cataloging (how to find things), collection development (what to highlight for users), and archiving (as opposed to backing up); and scholars need to attend to quality, peer review, and presentation (how data tagging gets used). Finally, there needs to be a handful of experimental centers like the Institute, where concerted effort is applied to developing the tools that researchers—in our case, scholars in the humanities—will need.

The roles of author and reader are likely to undergo some reorganization, too. In "What Is an Author?" Michel Foucault (1977, pp. 124, 138) writes,

In our culture—undoubtedly in others as well—discourse was not originally a thing, a product, or a possession, but an action situated in a bipolar field of sacred and profane, lawful and unlawful, religious and blasphemous. It was a gesture charged with risks long before it became a possession caught in a circuit

of property values. . . . The author—or what I have called the "author-func-
tion"—is undoubtedly only one of the possible specifications of the subject and,
considering past historical transformations, it appears that the form, the complexity, and even the existence of this function are far from immutable. We can
easily imagine a culture where discourse would circulate without any need for
an author. Discourses, whatever their status, form, or value, and regardless of
our manner of handling them, would unfold in a pervasive anonymity.

Although we can see, at the moment, some rear-guard actions intended
to protect the perceived interests of rights holders against the perceived
threat of an open information environment, I think that the next generation will live in a world where the concepts of authorship and intellectual
property have substantially changed and where writing is once again
considered "an action" more than "a thing, a product, or a possession."
Collective authorship, sampling, distributed hypertext, human-computer
interaction: all these are already eating away at the idea of writing as a
product of a unique and identifiable author—the foundation of copyright—and it seems unlikely that this part of the property system will
survive the decade intact. This is not to say that we will, in the year 2000,
step into a utopia of free information: on the contrary, we may find that
the conditions under which information can be exchanged are much more
restrictive than now.

The same forces that are working to reshape our understanding of
authorship and of intellectual property are, necessarily, going to revise
our understanding of the scholar's enterprise, sometimes in surprisingly
conservative ways. In the near term, I expect we will see textual and
bibliographic criticism come back into vogue: computers offer us a
chance to create new, comprehensive editions of major and minor writers
alike, including—as in the Rossetti archive—every phase of every composition in every medium. Literary theory, on the other hand, may find
that computers render older methods and practices obsolete: the stand-
alone philosopher-critic may not translate well into a world where networked collective performances are the rule. As for the student, we
already can see that networked computers may level the field in interesting ways, bringing the practice of scholarship into reach sooner and, in
some cases, obfuscating distinctions of rank and age.

In closing, I'd like to pull back to the frame and remember that QVC
and Home Shopping are also in here somewhere. The great threat is that

while we argue with one another about the degenerative effect of computers on reasoning or the relative merits of print and pixels, billions of dollars are concentrated on laying down a national information infrastructure with no better idea of what to do with this fabulous, historically unprecedented medium for cultural growth than to bring you the Domino's Pizza Channel. I do not think this technology spells the end of humanism, the end of rationality, the end of libraries, the end of publishing, or the end of learned inquiry—though the marketing of it might. If we take advantage of the opportunities that open up before us in this moment of massive rearrangement and reapportionment, it is possible that scholarship in the humanities will emerge with a new mission, a new method, and a new audience. If Rosenzweig and Brier's *Who Built America* or McGann's Rossetti archive or Ed Ayers's Civil War project were available on our souped-up, interactive television, who can predict what audience might choose them?

Notes

1. If you doubt this prediction, look at the Clinton administration's July 1994 Green Paper on intellectual property (Lehman 1994) (the product of a working group on intellectual property rights chaired by Bruce Lehman, Assistant Secretary of Commerce and Commissioner of Patents and Trademarks) and see Pamela Samuelson's (1994) rebuttal of this green paper, where she argues that Lehman's recommendations "would, in fact, bring about a radical realignment in the historical balance between publisher interests and the public interest in access to information products, pushing the law in a direction that would favor publisher interests to the detriment of the public interest. [The Lehman report] would abolish longstanding rights that the public has enjoyed to make use of copyrighted works, rights that have been consistently upheld in courts and in the copyright statute."

2. This paragraph and the one that precedes it are excerpted from a longer discussion of humanists' reactions to computer technology in Unsworth (1996).

References

Amiran, Eyal, Carole Chaski, and John Unsworth. 1992. "Networked Academic Publishing and the Rhetorics of Its Reception." *Centennial Review* 36, no. 1 (Winter): 43–58.

Barlow, John Perry. 1994. "The Economy of Ideas: A Framework for Rethinking Patents and Copyrights in the Digital Age (Everything You Know about

Intellectual Property Is Wrong)." *Wired* 2, no. 3: 84–90, 126–129. Also available on the World Wide Web at http://sunsite.unc.edu/wxyc/economy.ideas.html.

Foucault, Michel. 1977. "What Is an Author?" *Language, Counter-Memory, Practice: Selected Essays and Interviews*. Ithaca, NY: Cornell University Press.

Lehman, Bruce, chair. 1994. "Intellectual Property and the National Information Infrastructure." Green Paper produced for the White House. Available at the Electronic Frontier Foundation's World Wide Web site at http://www.eff.org/papers/ipwg.html.

McGann, Jerome. (In press). "The Rationale of Hypertext." In *The Electronic Text*, edited by Marilyn Deegan and Kathryn Sutherland. Oxford: Oxford University Press. Also available on the World Wide Web at http://jefferson.village.virginia.edu/public/jjm2f/rationale.html.

Moulthrop, Stuart. 1991. "You Say You Want a Revolution? Hypertext and the Laws of Media." *Postmodern Culture* 1, no. 3: paras. 1–53.

Samuelson, Pamela. 1994. "Legally Speaking: The NII Intellectual Property Report." *Communications of the ACM* 37, no. 12 (December): 21–27.

Unsworth, John. 1996. "Electronic Scholarship, or Scholarly Publishing and the Public." In *The Literary Text in the Digital Age*, edited by Richard Finneran. Ann Arbor: University of Michigan Press.

IV
Concepts of the Gateway: Libraries and Technology

The idea of the gateway library is still emerging, and at this stage, as Peter Lyman observes, it is "defined by the problems it is attempting to solve more than the solutions it has achieved." The underlying tension between the theoretical and the practical—the need to solve immediate problems even as the gateway library responds to the influence of information technology on scholarship—is apparent in the following four chapters. The essays in this part differ not so much in the direction they take as in the time they think the journey will take.

The Harvard College Library, responding to the need to refurbish its undergraduate library program as well as its building, confronted the need to devise a way to provide library reference and instructional services in a radically decentralized library system. In chapter 7 I explain that Harvard's problem was also how to introduce technology to a faculty who have not achieved consensus on its usefulness and to find a middle ground between opponents and proponents of electronic information. The response was a gateway that explored the potential benefits of technology without abandoning the historic print collections. The aim was to begin a conversation at Harvard about the role of technology in learning and about how the library might best support teaching and learning in the new environment.

Richard Rockwell begins his analysis by working back from a model shaped by his vision of the future. He rejects past agendas and assumptions and takes a more theoretical tack. The virtual library is the ideal that he believes librarians should aspire to create. For Rockwell, the gateway is a process and not a place, and any attempt to accommodate old assumptions misses the point and the potential of a gateway library.

Rockwell's vision is shaped by the reality of the ICPSR (Inter-university Consortium for Political and Social Research), which is already moving toward a model of networked information in which local clients access, rather than own, resources. From this vantage point, it is but a step to the virtual library he and many others predict will be the library of the future.

Jan Olsen's vision or, rather, her implementation of the gateway is tempered by the day-to-day reality of a library director. Her chapter also reflects the transitional character of the gateway. Although she clearly sees the gateway as evolving toward a fully electronic library in which services and uses will be delivered at a distance, she is obliged to address the immediate increase in onsite use of the library and its collections experienced in the Mann Gateway Library at Cornell University. Even her emphasis on genres—that is, different categories of information, such as text, numeric data, multimedia, images, and sound—represents an interim response to the volatile nature of the emerging technologies and the complexity of these sources. Although she does not suggest that the need for genre specialists will one day disappear behind a seamless web of user-friendly electronic information, she does think that the role of librarians will evolve toward providing services online to remote users.

Peter Lyman, like all of the authors, emphasizes the teaching role of the gateway. But Lyman, more than the others, sees a fundamental polarity between the traditional culture of scholarship and the market-place. Both he and Rockwell are acutely conscious of the costs of delivering information in the electronic age and the need to factor this into library plans for delivering information and services. For Lyman, however, there is a real concern about whether or not libraries can survive in a world in which information is increasingly viewed as a commodity. The gateway, he believes, is a strategy for balancing "the free access of the traditional library with more efficient and cost-effective collections."

7

Gateways to Knowledge: A New Direction for the Harvard College Library

Lawrence Dowler

Dramatic developments in electronic information and telecommunications are beginning to alter the way students learn and scholars do research. For Harvard University, the question raised by these changes is, How should the Harvard College Library support teaching and research in a highly decentralized institution during a period of dramatic technological, intellectual, and economic change?

One major goal to emerge from the university's strategic planning process is to improve the quality of undergraduate education, and enhancing library support for instruction and student learning is essential to this effort. In the past, the library provided access to users according to their presumed level of competence and their position in the academic community. Having access to collections and services depended on whether a reader was an undergraduate, a graduate student, or a member of the faculty. With a core collection of basic works in the humanities and social sciences and ample study space, the Lamont Library was designed as the undergraduate library. Students who needed to use the research collection in Widener Library were required to obtain a letter from a sponsoring faculty member. Then in the late 1960s the Widener stacks were opened to undergraduates, signaling a fundamental shift in undergraduate instruction and their use of libraries. Freed from the regimen of textbooks by the paperback revolution, faculty began to introduce new courses that altered the undergraduate curriculum and reflected significant changes in academic research. An increase in interdisciplinary and cross-cultural research resulted in a proliferation of new courses and areas of intellectual inquiry. In a sense, the adoption of the core curriculum, like the opening of the stacks to undergraduates, was a recognition of this new academic reality and an attempt to introduce a measure of order and discipline to undergraduate instruction.

These changing patterns of scholarship and their subsequent influence on curriculum and instruction have increased undergraduate use of the research libraries and blurred traditional distinctions among libraries based on the status of readers. Experience suggests that the nature of inquiry and familiarity with research tools and resources, especially electronic information, determine the level and kind of library support that is needed. Certainly, there are obvious differences between a freshman writing an expository writing paper and a graduate student working on a dissertation. But like all parts of the educational process, the transition between these two extremes must be constantly attended to. During those transitions, a student's status does not always define the level of assistance needed and therefore defies easy categorization.

Not surprisingly, undergraduate use of research collections in Widener has continually increased so that it now nearly equals use by graduate students and faculty. Over the past ten years there also has been a pronounced growth in the use of government documents and microforms—traditionally viewed as a research collection—by undergraduates in a variety of academic disciplines. At the same time, because of the visibility of Lamont's records in HOLLIS, faculty and graduate student use of the undergraduate libraries also has increased. Other libraries that are at least partially dedicated to undergraduate use have experienced increased use by faculty. Faculty use of the Cabot Science Library, for example, comprises 40 percent of its total circulation. Clearly, then, the historical distinction between undergraduate and graduate and faculty use no longer reflects reality.

Emerging information technologies are affecting both undergraduate instruction and academic research in ways that further alter the usefulness of separate and distinct library facilities. Faculty, under the twin pressures to publish and participate in the governance of the institution, require convenient access to the sources they need for research. For the humanist, especially—whose method of research is associative and hence requires browsing—proximity, as well as the richness of research sources, will likely affect the direction and perhaps even the quality of research. Improvements in the efficiency and effectiveness of research will increasingly depend on information technology for locating needed sources or retrieving books from storage as well as for examining texts and images, the very sources used by scholars in research.

An increasing proportion of information is becoming available electronically. For the next five years we can expect that most information in electronic form will be of a bibliographic nature (such as indexes, catalogs, and abstracting services), but we already have several full-text sources. *Thesaurus Linguae Graecae*, for example, is a growing database of more than 8,000 works of Classical Greek literature, and the *Medieval and Early Modern Data Bank* contains a master data set of tabular works concerning medieval and early modern history. Indeed, the National Center for Machine-Readable Text in the Humanities estimates the number of converted texts to be approximately 8,000. These texts will begin to be accessible over telecommunication networks.

For Harvard faculty, who have access to an exceptional collection of printed material, immediate access to local and national networks may not seem vital. But as bibliographies and texts become available solely in electronic form, networked access will become increasingly important. To foster access to materials in electronic form, the library must develop appropriate instructional and reference services. Since it is not economically feasible or cost-effective to provide staffing and expertise at every library within the College Library, we must develop a program that can provide an effective level of support concentrated in one or two locations. This approach will permit more specialized subject expertise at the research collections and libraries, including Widener. For the researcher, what is most needed is convenient access to research sources—print, manuscripts, images, artifacts, sound, and electronic texts, indexes, and data—and library support for locating and using these sources. Thus, the gateway is the point of entry into the rich and varied elements that comprise the system of research resources at Harvard and the world beyond.

What Is the Gateway?

The gateway is a metaphor for access to knowledge and evokes the image of crossing a threshold and entering a dramatically expanding world of information and learning. The library, as gateway, is the means by which students and faculty will locate and use this information. The gateway we envision is the constellation of services, the organization required for providing these services, and the spaces dedicated to student learning.

The very ambiguity of the term *gateway* has the advantage of inviting support for what many will wish it to be and the disadvantage of seeming to discard some things it never intended to reject. The gateway's emphasis on electronic information, for example, may be perceived by some as inimical to the traditional role of the library as a repository of scholarly publications and cultural artifacts, although we have consciously avoided making distinctions among research sources based on format. Blurring traditional distinctions between undergraduate, graduate, and faculty in Lamont may appear to some as the loss of a useful library dedicated exclusively to undergraduate needs, although one objective of the gateway is to enhance opportunities for student learning. The notion of a gateway also raises the specter of centralizing some functions and services and coordinating others in ways that cut across existing institutional boundaries, contrary to Harvard's decentralized system of libraries. Moreover, viewed from the perspective of networked information, in which computers are ubiquitous and information is accessible from virtually any location, some may wonder why library space is needed for a gateway. These apparent contradictions derive from the theoretical notion of the gateway as a portal to an expanding universe of information, on the one hand, and the library's operational use of the term as a way of organizing services in a highly decentralized environment, on the other.

There are four defining elements in our definition of the gateway. First, the gateway suggests an electronic means of access to expanding sources in all formats that are needed for research. Second, the gateway includes the various services that will support access to these sources and make study and research more effective and efficient. Third, the gateway is a flexible physical space that supports student learning through individual study space, small group and class study, and demonstration facilities, which can be altered in response to future changes in technology and the needs of readers. Fourth, the gateway may be seen as the organization within the Harvard College Library that will coordinate gateway functions and services throughout its individual libraries.

Electronic Information and Historical Research Collections

The gateway is the electronic means of access to information and sources that are needed for research regardless of format, genre, or location.

The use of the term *gateway* suggests information in electronic form. Computer and telecommunication technologies are an increasingly visible part of the academic environment, and managing these resources *and* helping students and scholars to use them will command a significant share of a university's resources. The technically oriented associate the gateway with Internet-based e-mail, which they use to communicate with colleagues, electronic bulletin boards, computer conferences, and listservs that promise to transform scholarly communication. Library users can browse electronically for materials from hundreds of libraries, search and retrieve the texts of journal articles, and, increasingly, find libraries of reference sources.

But the growing importance of information technology masks an equally dramatic growth in the quantity and variety of artifactual evidence that has increasingly been used in research over the past four decades. Research libraries are obliged to acquire not just scholarly publications but also the evidence on which scholarship is based. These artifacts—texts, images, sound, ephemera, even the objects of everyday life—are part of the documentary evidence increasingly used by students and scholars in many disciplines.

Traditionally, libraries have separated resources according to their formats—microtext from print, primary from secondary, visual from audio. There is a danger that emerging information technologies will, for reasons of format and means of delivery, spin off from the library and operate in isolation from related research sources. Librarians, who have expertise in the categorization and content of information, will need to provide the bridge between information and users, whatever the format. Separating electronic sources from other forms of information will create a kind of technological ghetto and undermine the promise of information technology to bring together all media—audio, textual, visual—in a form that is both interactive and highly manipulable. The strength of Harvard's historic book collection and the decentralized nature of the university and its libraries provide compelling reasons for linking electronic research with the book collection and providing an integrated approach to library services. Thus, a conscious aim for the gateway is to provide the space and services that will help students and scholars to integrate the use of research sources in all formats.

Picture this:

A graduate student in American urban history struggles to collect information for a seminar paper. His topic is the ethnic evolution of a small neighborhood in Boston that is now part of the South End. While he has no trouble finding secondary sources on Boston urbanization using HOLLIS and some periodical indexes online, he has trouble identifying primary sources. On a friend's recommendation, he sets up an appointment with a gateway reference librarian.

On his arrival, he finds that this librarian has already contacted a subject specialist in Widener who has given the gateway librarian an extensive list of potentially useful primary sources. The student is referred to several other Harvard locations: Schlesinger Library for some original settlement house papers, Houghton for the papers of Robert Wood (a major leader in the Boston settlement house movement), and the Government Documents and Microforms section for help with finding demographic information from census sources. In addition, the reference librarian recommends that the student contact the libraries of the Massachusetts Historical Society and the State House.

The student is also given more detailed HOLLIS instruction on how to locate turn-of-the-century learned society papers in the Widener collection as well as manuscript collections throughout the university. On the reference librarian's recommendation, he signs up for a special gateway seminar on primary source material in American history at Harvard that is being taught jointly by a Houghton librarian and a subject specialist from Widener.

The Gateway as Service Center:

The gateway provides services that enable researchers to locate and use the resources they need and make study and research more effective and efficient.

The aim of the gateway is to increase library support for teaching and instruction and help readers to become self-sufficient in locating and using the resources they need. To this end, the gateway will coordinate dispersed library functions and services and make library policies and procedures more consistent and predictable. The goal is to make use of the library more efficient and research more effective.

Historically, the eleven units of the Harvard College Library have provided a level of service consistent with the needs and requirements of their individual clienteles. But as physical barriers to access become less significant, physical location must not determine the quality of service.

For the reader, good service means availability, predictability, and reliability. Improving access services for using research materials in Harvard's decentralized environment involves coordinating functional areas such as circulation, interlibrary loan, document delivery, photocopying, library privileges, orderly maintenance of books on shelves, aggressive enforcement of policies that aim to have books promptly returned for other readers, and security to ensure that the books are still there for future readers. Library services need to be available at times and places that are convenient for readers, who should be able to predict the type and level of services the library will provide. Finally, services must reliably connect the reader with the resources they need. These are fundamental aims of the gateway.

Imagine this:

A professor in fine arts is collecting a set of readings for a seminar she is giving in three weeks. She selects the bibliographic files she is interested in searching and enters her search. As she goes through the ranked list, she identifies items that she is interested in by using a GET command. This command works regardless of the database from which the citation was drawn.

After selecting GET, she is provided with various options for delivery, along with an estimate of the cost and the time for delivery. During her work session, the professor identifies, locates, and requests the following items:

· From the CD-ROM version of the Avery Index provided by the Design School Library, an article is located on another CD-ROM database licensed by the Design School Library. The GET command has the article sent to her local print station. Depending on the print queue, she may have to wait up to five minutes. She will not be charged for this transaction.

· From the Legal Resources Index maintained as a HOLLIS mainframe file, she locates an article from a journal available in NEXIS. She asks her workstation to open a window to NEXIS, scans the article in ASCII format, and requests the SGML file to print a copy identical to the printed page. The copy arrives at the department laser printer. There is no extra charge for the article.

· From the Expanded Academic Index maintained as a HOLLIS mainframe file, the professor locates an article from a journal received by the Widener Library. Her GET command sends a message to the Harvard College Library's Interlibrary Loan Department. A copy of the article will be sent to the Ariel workstation in the Fine Arts Library within forty-eight hours. She sends an e-mail message to the library to have the image transferred to her course file on the library's Image Server when it arrives. She will not be charged for this transaction.

· From HOLLIS, she discovers a book owned by Widener Library. She can see that it is not currently on loan. Her GET command means the book will be retrieved from the stacks and held for the professor at the circulation desk. Unless she is sent a message to the contrary, she may pick up the book after noon tomorrow. No charge will apply.

In 1991, Widener Library established a new unit, Research and Bibliographic Services (RBS), as an experiment to assess demand for consultative reference and for instructional services to graduate and undergraduate classes and seminars. We also wanted to know what kinds of instruction, if any, were of value to faculty and students. Although RBS has not been widely advertised, the response has been overwhelming. Services range from instruction in using HOLLIS to exploring the Internet, from individual research consultations to discussions of sources and reference materials needed for a particular class or project. Research workshops introduce students and faculty to new resources in the humanities and social sciences, including resources available through the Internet in selected fields (for example, psychology, economics, religion), periodical indexes on CD-ROM (for example, the *MLA, Historical Abstracts*), full-text CD-ROMs (for example, English poetry—600–1900, the second edition *Oxford English Dictionary,* the *Patrologia Latina,* recent acquisitions by the Documents and Microforms Division (LegiSlate, an online database bringing up-to-date information on the activities of the federal government, the National Trade Databank, and various other electronic products covering census information), and, CD-ROMs available in the Harvard Map Collection. Research and Bibliographic Services is a precursor of the kind of services we envision for the gateway.

Picture this:

A junior faculty member in the history department brings his tutorial into the gateway for an hour's session on basic sources in American history. The research librarian introduces the class to several print sources and shows them how to use HOLLIS and *America: History and Life* on network-accessible CDs.

The faculty member's own work in nineteenth-century urban development requires that he use several government population data sources. He returns therefore the following afternoon, to attend a class given in the library by a staff member from the gateway's Economics and Government Information Service on accessing and analyzing population data. As the year passes, he finds himself frustrated in his attempts to set up a simple bibliographic database to store secondary citations. A reference librarian in Widener suggests that he talk with OIT (Office of Information Technology) about the advantage of a modem purchase versus network access and that he sign up for a gateway class in downloading data into PBS (Personal Bibliographic Software) packages.

The Gateway as Learning Center

The gateway is a place for individual and group study by undergraduates and houses a center for interactive learning using technology, faculty course reserves, and a collection of the basic literature in the humanities, sciences, and social sciences.

The gateway continues the College Library's commitment to supporting and enhancing undergraduate education through appropriate library support. The goal is to create a highly flexible physical environment that supports study and learning by individual students as well as by small groups. Since electronic information will be a pervasive feature of life— one that students will use throughout their lives—preparing them to do so will be an essential element in their education.

Perhaps the most compelling argument for conceiving the gateway as a dedicated space within the College Library is related to the traditional notion of the library as a center for learning. Students still need places to study, and Lamont, in particular, however else it may change, must continue to provide study space for undergraduates. In addition, recent studies show that students learn best in small groups. One goal of the gateway library, therefore, is to provide spaces—for group study, for small classes needing access to electronic information, for a limited number of workstations that support interactive, multimedia applications, and for librarians who can answer questions and guide students to materials and sources related to their particular interest. In addition, a collection of approximately 150,000 volumes covering the basic literature in the humanities, sciences, and social sciences and faculty course reserves will be part of the gateway. Eventually, course reserves will include scanned images that can be distributed to any location on campus.

Interest is growing among universities in improving the quality of teaching and instruction. The Bok Center at Harvard is just one indication of the university's commitment to improving quality of instruction.

Developing skills in evaluating and using information from a variety of sources, including electronic ones, will continue to be an important aspect of student learning. Working with the Office of Information Technology, the Science Center, the Bok Center, and faculty research projects for improving student learning, the library should develop programs and provide space to support these initiatives.

The gateway's equipment and facilities would support a growing number of interactive multimedia databases. Hypermedia, for example, for interactive learning that involves all of a student's senses may provide avenues of learning that adapt to individual aptitudes and learning styles. There are already software programs that enable one to view a filmed play by Shakespeare and simultaneously view the text, stage-blocking materials, dictionaries, historical notes, and still photographs. Other applications focus on computer simulations of historical events and offer powerful tools for understanding the past. As students, faculty, and librarians gain access to multimedia programs, they will be able to integrate programs into particular courses or subject areas. The center would be configured for maximum flexibility so that new electronic products and applications can be made accessible as they become available. The intent here is to bring together students, faculty, librarians, and research sources, to provide support for programs and experiments for improving access to research sources, and thereby to enhance opportunities for creative learning.

The Gateway as Organization

The gateway is the organization within the College and Faculty of Arts and Sciences libraries responsible for coordinating services and programs identified with the gateway.

The Harvard libraries and the university itself have often been compared to a federation of autonomous states. A better analogy for the Harvard College Library or, at least, the College Library as we envision it through the gateway, is what some social historians have described as "a social web." Picture the blue and white checkered homespun cloth of eighteenth-century New England, and imagine that the white threads represent the unique functions of each library and the blue represent functions and services that are increasing in demand but that cannot adequately be supported or duplicated by each individual library. Where the white and blue threads cross, creating a third square of lighter hue, reside those coordinated functions and support services—described here as the gateway—that serve all the libraries. The gateway helps preserve individual distinctions by creating a new organization that supports and enhances the delivery of services throughout the College Library.

Convenience and efficiency are important goals of the gateway. By concentrating some services in the gateway libraries and reducing duplication, the subject-based research libraries and Widener can devote more resources to offering specialized reference materials and research support. Improved coordination of services among the research collections and libraries will not only reduce costly duplication but will also clarify for readers where they can get assistance in locating the resources needed for particular research projects. Providing a central place—the gateway—where all readers may receive general assistance and instruction will permit greater subject specialization in the research collections and libraries.

The gateway will be a locus or place where one can be introduced to resources scattered throughout the university's libraries and receive instruction in how to locate them. This is the role Lamont Library can play for the humanities and social sciences and Cabot Library can play for the sciences.

Picture this:

A senior physics student is taking a history of science course and must write a thirty-page term paper. At the Cabot gateway she is given some general bibliographic guides on the history of science coproduced by a Widener reference librarian and a gateway research librarian. Then she is referred to the Lamont gateway and spends an hour with the Lamont gateway librarian discussing how she should organize her time and research and which library to use for source material (Widener). She also has an ISIS search on her topic done for her on Citadel and receives recommendations for other indexes to search on CD-ROM. After the librarian encourages her to return for more help if she needs it, the student leaves with her search results, a referral to a particular reference librarian in Widener who will help her there, and printed materials on how to use Widener.

Coordinating library services for locating and using the resources needed for study and research is the heart of the gateway. Because the library does not reside in one building or location (the College Library consists of eleven separate libraries plus many important faculty libraries, especially in the sciences), when scholars outside the primary constituency use the collection they encounter a bewildering array of locations, regulations, and services. Because there is no central library, Widener Library notwithstanding, readers must navigate this system without a chart or a clearly established place to begin. What the gateway will try to do is balance the services and functions that ought to remain distributed with those specialized functions that ought to be concentrated in a few locations to provide the services our users increasingly indicate they want and need.

One model for the coordinated services we envision for the gateway is the Economics and Government Information Service (EGIS). Currently, government publications are scattered across the campus, and bibliographic access to these sources is idiosyncratic. Documents sometimes are cataloged in the general collection, but usually they are not. There is no standard policy among university libraries for cataloging or accessing these materials: in effect, each library has developed its own procedures for handling government documents. Moreover, responsibility for government publications within the College Library is divided among Widener, Littauer, and Lamont's Documents and Microforms. Important government data is also located in the Government Department's Data Center, which is not part of the College Library.

The recent renovation of space in Lamont for Government Documents and Microforms was the first step toward creating the gateway and may serve as a model for future gateway developments. EGIS brings together data and published government information in a variety of formats and provides access to some information via electronic network. At several locations, EGIS also offers instruction in locating information and help in using it effectively. The same information often resides in electronic, print, and microtext formats, and the form to use may well depend on the nature of the inquiry. An undergraduate student writing a paper may need only printed reports, but a faculty member or graduate student in government or economics may need help in using a statistical package to analyze complex data. Still another user may want to display certain statistics, such as voting behavior, geographically by country, state, or region. At whatever level, patrons ought to be able to enter the system, locate the information they need, and be directed to the persons or places that can help them use the information they need in the form in which they need it. This is the purpose of EGIS and also the gateway.

Picture this:

An undergraduate enters the Lamont Library with her laptop computer in hand. Her paper on the effects of acid rain on the environment is already several days overdue. She sits at one of a selected group of study carrels and plugs her personal computer into the open data jack. Through this data jack, the student has the option of browsing the Internet, checking her e-mail, or connecting to various library resources throughout the world. With a little guidance from the reference librarian the student can use the College Library's resources to (1) download bibliographical information concerning acid rain, (2) capture photographic images of specific landscapes in North America where acid rain has been particularly devastating, (3) read the postings of a discussion group on the Internet dedicated to acid rain research, and (4) retrieve research results from a CD-ROM entitled *Canadian Acid Rain Research*.

The student loads a diskette found in the back of a book she retrieved from the shelves. The disk contains data tracking changes in the acidity of rain in New England over a twenty-year period. She uploads the data covering Massachusetts for the period 1980 to 1990 and incorporates it into her Lotus 1–2–3 spreadsheet.

Via the bibliographic citations she has downloaded the student discovers that the United States Department of Energy (DOE) has spent a significant amount of money on acid rain research. She then heads down to the first level of Lamont where government documents reside and retrieves several microforms containing DOE research on acid rain. She plugs her PC into the data jack in the Government Documents section and makes notes in her word processor while reading off the microform reader. Meanwhile, the librarian has downloaded data from the *Boston Globe* database onto a floppy disk. The student copies the data to her PC and heads home to write her paper.

Conclusion

The gateway is the College Library's response to the changing informational needs of students and faculty. Harvard's version of the gateway is neither a radical departure from library tradition nor a detailed blueprint for the future. Instead, the gateway sets in motion a process that aims for organizational flexibility, premium services to readers, and maintenance of a system of libraries devoted to the excellence of its collections. In the end, the gateway offers a way for the Harvard College Library, as an institution, to be more responsive to the evolving needs of readers at all levels and to continually reinvent itself in the future.

8

The Concept of the Gateway Library: A View from the Periphery

Richard C. Rockwell

The gateway library of the twenty-first century will be an integral part of a computing and network environment that is far more complex than the one universities knew in the 1980s and early 1990s. If users are kept fully in mind as this environment is created, the gateway library will represent a qualitative improvement in how people obtain and use information. Identifying and linking information will be done in ways that are simply impossible today, even in the richest library with the best cataloging and reference personnel. It will be possible because a larger change has already occurred, a change sufficiently dramatic to call "the information revolution."

Planning for the gateway library must begin with a rethinking of what libraries can accomplish and what librarians ought to do. Because fewer distinctions can be drawn today between information and the tools for managing it or between libraries and campus information infrastructures, assumptions based on past levels of computing and network performance, on the persistence of user-hostile software, and on excessive labor and hardware costs will be invalid and dangerous guides for the librarians who are charged with designing the future. If we do it right, all users will find the new library services more powerful, more friendly, more flexible, and more adaptable to their personal needs.

Outside the province of the traditional library, qualitative changes are already occurring. These improvements illustrate the power of the new computing environment. Data analysis no longer requires the major investment of time and money that was required in the mainframe environment. It was once common for most of the effort (and 90 percent of the computing budget) on a research project to go into drawing an extract from a large data set. Today researchers can today explore data sets from their desktops and pursue clues that before they could not afford to explore. Computing is delivering new teaching capabilities to the classroom, as well, enabling professors to display everything from the attachment of muscle to bone to the expansion of habitation in China over millennia. Just as chemistry professors now do experiments in class, professors in the social science classroom will engage in live exploratory research. As students increasingly approach the social sciences (and perhaps some humanities) as laboratory subjects, the transmission of knowledge will occur by discovery rather than by lecture. Subjects once learned by memorizing glossaries and parroting received wisdom can thus become intellectually alive expeditions of discovery.

How the gateway library organizes information will be a critical element in the success of these innovations. The gateway library will electronically connect users into a worldwide information resource that is organized for effective and easy access. Even at the most financially deprived institution, students and faculty can have access to the resources of the world's finest libraries. Libraries can deliver interlibrary loan services directly to the dormitory or office desktop computers, including provisions both for ordering materials and for delivering electronic copies to the researcher. People will construct and maintain these loan services, but they will not be directly involved in any particular transaction, sharply reducing the per-unit cost of providing interlibrary loan services. Further, these libraries will integrate dispersed campus information sources—libraries, museums, departments, area studies centers, field stations, research institutes, and even private investigators—over which no bibliographic control usually exists today.

Distributed Computing and Its Benefits and Hazards

Both globally and locally, the gateway library will manage information with *distributed computing.* Because it is no longer necessary to concentrate a campus's major computing resources under one roof, there is no monopoly in computing on campus—no single brand of hardware employed, no single form of computing service, no monopolistic provider of most services, and no authoritarian control of computing. Providers of computing services will distribute throughout the campus hardware, support staff, databases, directories, and catalogs.

The distributed computing environment will be hospitable to innovation. When demand increases, it can be scaled up without discarding the existing system and starting over. No solution will ever be locked permanently into place. The specialized computing services that are offered by each campus unit will yield the usual rewards of high performance. Librarians will feel themselves to be in control of the services they offer and not dependent on the caprices of a central authority.

Distributed computing will make possible all of the benefits sketched above but at a high price. One cost will be an increase in the amount of institutional funding directed toward computing. Although some administrators believe that distributed computing will decrease overall computing costs, actually costs will shift from central administrations to departments and institutes. These units will recognize, perhaps for the first time, the actual cost of the computing services that they consume. The institution as a whole will pay more, perhaps much more, for computing and the infrastructure supporting it, but most purchasing units will find the costs of these greatly increased services to be justified.

Purchasers of computing will have strong incentives to tailor their purchases to fit their own needs. This could erode the idea of a computing community that can communicate, share software and data, offer mutual support, and benefit from economies of scale. On some campuses the computing community will fall apart unless institutions find effective ways to coordinate computing and to provide leadership without the authority of hierarchy. Islands of varying computing abilities could develop within the campus community, and units without the funds to invest in computing will have to depend on the central administration, make cuts in other areas (such as in graduate student support), or bow out of the information revolution.

Expertise also will be distributed unequally across campus. Some users will have direct access to needed expertise, while others will have less support. There will be sharply differing levels of demand for services, with some users not knowing to ask for services that they need, and services needed by the novice user will differ dramatically from those needed by the most sophisticated. Libraries may play a major role in providing expertise to users of all skill levels because they have a long history of providing effective help to users of all levels of sophistication. In fact, it is conceivable that libraries will become a focal point for the coordination of computing across campus.

Even after this electronic revolution has progressed for a decade, no one will be entirely confident about the future of rapidly evolving technology: if a computer is now on your desk, it is not the current model. Funding this computing environment will be increasingly problematic in a period of declining federal support. Coordination among campus units might be elusive, and the learning curve may leave some people behind. We may be embarking on a difficult period on many campuses.

The Gateway Library as a Process and Not a Place

I define the gateway library as *an integrated and organized means of electronic access to dispersed information resources.* The gateway library is therefore a *process* that delivers services to the user. Stating clearly what that definition does not entail might be useful. First, under this model the gateway library is not itself a collection of resources. It may physically hold few resources but will provide access to books, journals, films, CD-ROMs, and many other media from all over the world. Second, the gateway library is not a place; indeed, it would defeat much of what the gateway library could do for a campus if users had to travel somewhere to use its services. Those services ought to be available from the faculty office, the dormitory room, the classroom lectern, and the home. The gateway library is thus as distributed and decentralized as campus computing has become.

Any design for a gateway library that requires people to journey somewhere to use it has simply missed both the point and the potential. Architects will not build the gateway library; sophisticated librarians will build it. Libraries must free themselves of any vestiges of the edifice complex and its associated centralized thinking. Funds spent on monumental new buildings would better be spent on training and retraining the people who will construct the gateway library. Investments in people will be critical to success. Librarians know a great deal that is necessary for the building of the gateway library; if they do not know some of the computing technology, they should be taught it.

Even before the technological revolution, the library was never its building. The loss in Alexandria was not of a marble edifice; for centuries we have regretted the burning of the manuscripts inside that structure and would gladly have sacrificed the building for their preservation. The loss of the books and documents of Sarajevo's library, and not the loss of a magnificent building, is today's cultural atrocity. When faculty members claim to a prospective colleague "We have a great library!" they don't mean the building.

The library was always the people inside the building, the information-retrieval systems they had created, and the collections they had built. The gateway library simply carries this fact to its logical conclusion: the grammar of the gateway library will be that students work "through" or "with" the gateway library and not "at" it. University presidents who point to "the new library site" are only pointing to the location of the facility that would house the library, although the prospective donor may envision only a grand new building bearing his name. Perhaps someday a donor will posthumously endow the Harvard College Gateway Library, which is not to be seen anywhere but instead is to be experienced everywhere, a virtual monument to a vanished benefactor.

Two terms—*digital library* and *gateway library*—contend today for the status of high jargon in the library community. The digital library indeed is an important idea, but it is only a step along the road to creating the gateway library as I have defined it. It will certainly be necessary to digitize all texts and images that will be used through the gateway library. However, digitization itself provides no service to those seeking information: the digital library is only a collection in another form. Until the data in the digital library are organized into information, we will have what we now see often on the Internet: an unedited, unevaluated, unusable mélange of documents.

We require something more than a collection. We require the creation of effective gateways to knowledge, and that means organizing the collections. That is not a task for technologists; the likelihood of computer scientists providing the organizing structure for the world's knowledge is small. Instead, this has been and is still a task for librarians—albeit librarians who have shed the limiting assumptions from the past and can run with the technological wolves.

Issues Facing the Gateway Library

At least six issues—cost, indexing, integration, data imperialism and piracy, economic disadvantage, and print media—face the designers of gateway libraries, and each involves research and development as well as good management. The solutions will never be final because the information environment will continually evolve as users discover new needs, as new technologies become available, and as the structure of the university itself changes. Once the profession of librarian was a relatively well-defined job with clear boundaries—the acquisition and management of a books and journals collection and its circulation. It has become one of the most exciting and demanding jobs on campus as the boundaries of the library and of the profession have become more permeable.

The Pricing of Access

Some new services that libraries will offer will carry a more obvious price tag than before. It always cost money to acquire, catalog, shelve, and circulate a book. Because there was a real per-user cost, nothing was ever free, although some services were fully subsidized by the university. Moreover, that cost was rarely quantified in the individual transaction itself, so the user never knew the cost. Few libraries arranged for recovering costs directly from users.

As resources increasingly are shared rather than owned, new costs will accrue to libraries. The rich collections that provide access to deprived institutions must recover some of their costs from those institutions. Providing access to such services as interlibrary loan, bibliographic information services, and databases usually will be associated with either a site license or a per-user fee. The organization of information itself will be an expensive proposition, one for which someone—users or an institution—must pay.

Most librarians will seek to deliver services at no charge, fearing that economic inequities could lead to people not seeking information that they need and to the creation of a class that is economically poor as well as information poor. However, the costs are real, and someone must pay them. Moreover, if an institution provides a service at no direct cost to us, we often undervalue and occasionally exploit that service. The "tragedy of the commons" could become the problem for libraries that it has for the environment and health services. By imposing no fee for service libraries will continually expand their personnel and equipment resources to meet unconstrained demand and to pay higher site license and per-user fees. This, in turn, might cause libraries to budget some of their services beyond the capacity of universities to support or to withdraw services in times of budget stringency.

Is there a way to provide open and equitable access to services while restraining the growth of budgets and usage? One method for controlling growth might be the allocation of subscriptions for services to all members of the university community. A subscription would buy a package of services designed by the user. Libraries could offer subscriptions at many levels for different parts of the community, depending on expected use of resources, with the university fully subsidizing first-level subscriptions for everyone. Exceeding the services offered by the subscription would lead to billing, which would require an accounting system that ensured that collecting payments would not cost more than the fees that are raised in collecting them.

If this suggestion distresses librarians, they should recognize that a hidden constraint on use is already in place. Budgetary limits *already* impose an overall cap on services that libraries can provide to the university community, but such a global limit on services has no mechanism that fairly apportions services among members of the community. In particular, those seeking new services from libraries frequently find that the budget has no room for anything other than what has always been done. Equity might increase under the proposed subscription model because those seeking new services would be permitted to fund those services.

Another factor that can ensure equitable access to services is to constrain costs. Two complementary strategies for cost containment merit consideration. First, client-server architectures should be implemented wherever possible. Unlike terminal-host architectures, which require further investment in hardware as the number of users grows, computing in a client-server environment is done at desktop terminals and by servers that can be reached through networks. As libraries decentralize their computing and as commercial suppliers of library software learn to do more than just adapt their software to the UNIX operating system, client-server architectures will lead to cost savings.

Second, libraries must avoid the "roll-your-own" syndrome. Despite the attraction of developing something that "meets the needs of Harvard" or of another particular institution, developing something only marginally different from an on-the-shelf product is a wasteful strategy. It wastes finances on expensive software development, and it wastes time on starting a service when something else almost as good is already available elsewhere. It also is wasteful of the talent, creativity, and skill that already have been exercised elsewhere. Talent that is available locally should go to solve problems that no one else has solved. At a minimum, library management must insist that commercial software developers adopt and abide by international standards for software and documentation, beginning with the capacity to use Standard Generalized Markup Language (SGML) documents. In sum, library management must ruthlessly weed out the "not invented here" syndrome: no accolades should accrue to the manager who reinvents the wheel.

Guides to the Information Superhighway

As the resources accessible through the gateway library multiply and diversify, finding useful information reliably and simply will become increasingly problematic. Full-text search is often touted as the solution, but requiring the user to know a battery of alternative terms for the same idea is unrealistic and undesirable in a learning or exploratory situation. What we need, instead, is indexing.

Indexing has always been a major conceptual challenge facing librarians because indexing schemes can constrain searches rather than ease them. Because librarians have the capacity to structure rigidly the way that people can know their world through the indexing schemes that they employ, they could block off entire areas of discovery if serendipity is made impossible. Serendipitous discovery through browsing would particularly suffer in an environment where access is entirely electronic and is offered only through rigidly constraining indexes.

I favor quirkiness in indexing schemes. I would like to see index entries that make no sense to me but do make sense to another inquiring mind. Further, the indexing of a document should be the cumulative result of team efforts rather than the work of a single individual. The way to achieve this is not by training people to be professional indexers according to some standard method or by adopting anything remotely like a standard indexing scheme. Ideally, a team of indexers, each with training in a different discipline but with common core training in librarianship, would be free to structure index entries however their minds lead them.

This could, of course, result in confusion on a large scale, with our searches progressively degraded by a ballooning index system that takes forever to explore and has many false trails in it. Perhaps one way to avoid this outcome would be to embed the index search system in an artificial intelligence environment that permits the system to learn how people use index entries in order to set priorities among entries and build linkages. Such a facility could even "age" some index entries into the archives if they never lead anyone to a resource.

The Wal-Marts of Information

The virtual library will come to encompass diverse sources of information not commonly thought of as within the purview of university libraries, including the resources of museums and research institutes. This raises the possibility that libraries might seek to become the Wal-Marts of information, housing all campus information services in one system managed and operated by one team of librarians, metaphorically placing information under one enormous roof. This is not likely to be a viable outcome. The holders of information are also its builders and are usually protective of their rights as developers and experts. Furthermore, libraries could never have sufficient financial or personnel resources to offer all information services in great depth. An imperialist strategy will not work for libraries.

The campus information system of the future may more resemble a mall of upscale boutiques and department stores than it does a Wal-Mart.

Under this model, librarians will more often play the role of the developer of the mall than the role of the manager of a department store. Librarians also will provide the maintenance services, including opening the doors and sweeping the floors. Successful execution of this development model will require an extraordinary degree of coordination among the suppliers of information resources on campus. Because there will be no single management of the virtual library, except in the person of the university president, integration through cooperation will become essential.

The gateway library is the key to providing integrated access to information without creating a locus of control and consolidation. Because it is a process and not an organization, the gateway library allows people and their units to work within it without sacrificing their autonomy and without foregoing the development of services to meet their specialized needs.

Imperialism, Piracy, and the Virtual Resource
Data-hungry organizations like my own, the Inter-university Consortium for Political and Social Research, have been accused of data imperialism. The charge is that we acquisition data for our use from all over the world without making it equitably available to the people who produced it. Latin Americans, for example, wonder why data on Latin America have been available to U.S. scholars but not to Latin Americans. In the natural sciences, data imperialists employ scientists in developing countries as data collectors, export the data they collect to the developed world, and then never find a way for the data collectors to become data analysts. Libraries have acquired rare resources for their own collections, physically removing them from their original owners. Museums have similarly acquired artifacts by employing both political dominance and financial persuasion. Such practices create inequities in access to information.

We can avoid many of these long-standing problems in the new information environment. It is no longer necessary to export data and other information resources from their points of collection because information can be archived at local sites but made broadly available through electronic networks. This enables local analysis of data, retains local control, and puts the task of updating and correcting the information in the hands of those most knowledgeable about it. Data collectors can thus participate in a worldwide matrix for storage of and access to information as information is archived at its home but is available worldwide.

The most difficult issue arising from this move away from data imperialism is how the security of materials archived all over the world can be assured when resources and skills vary widely internationally. An additional issue is how international archival standards can be adopted so that all users can search the matrix of information effectively.

Economic Disadvantage and Power

Information is power, and in a modern society access to information often determines wealth and political voice. If access to information depends on economic standing, then economically advantaged individuals and countries will further concentrate power, and long-standing economic differentials are likely to be exacerbated. Equitable schemes for the pricing of access to information are a concern, but a greater concern is the inability of many people even to get on the information superhighway.

As long as college professors in poor countries earn less in a year than the cost of a personal computer of the 1990s, there is ample reason to doubt that the age of the Internet will dawn everywhere at once. Equitable pricing schemes have little meaning in a country with no information infrastructure; any price would be too high. Nevertheless, some developing countries may be able to leapfrog the developed countries by skipping our stages of mainframe computation and communication over copper wires. Sunk costs in infrastructure may hinder the United States from replacing its system quite as rapidly as Mexico could install an entirely new system. Despite the possibility of leapfrogging, some societies are unlikely to have full access to information, and every society will have its information-disadvantaged people. This is a political issue that demands a political solution and is not something that libraries have the capacity to solve.

The Future of Books

Throughout the land libraries are filled with wonderful things called books. Many are beautiful, some are unlikely ever to be reproduced electronically, and all are convenient ways of storing and accessing information. Investments in books are emotional and financial. People who love libraries love books and feel chilled by the thought of the printing of the last book. Industries have been built around the production and distribution of books, buildings devoted to them, and a profession dedicated to their acquisition, care, storage, and circulation. Most of the world's significant memories are preserved on paper. In fact, electronic bytes still preserve mostly the transient and the insignificant and will continue to do so until the objectives of the digital library are accomplished. Even then, organization will be required before the digital library matches a book collection in its accessibility.

What happens to our books matters to the future of our cultures. When thinking about the gateway library, we must view books and their future as objectively as possible. Sometimes mulling over an alternative history is a way of gaining that objective viewpoint.

Consider, then, a world in which Arabs sustain and enrich the scientific heritage of the Greeks in a unified and peaceful Arab-dominated Asia and Africa. After about a millennium of sustained theoretical and engineering momentum, Arab scientists invent the transistor, which soon leads to the development of "text and image processors." These devices prove particularly useful for dealing with Arab languages because of their graphics orientation and also for doing arithmetic computations (so some call them "computers"). In a short time most citizens of the Arab world have access to vast information resources stored on plug-in solid-state memory, and this leads to further dominance by Arabs of science and technology. News, scientific journals, magazines, poetry, art, and novels—once the privilege of the elite—are now widely and cheaply accessible to most citizens. Sales to China and Japan are brisk.

Meanwhile, Europe continues its decline into religious obscurantism. Science is suspect, and those who formulate scientific theories can be burned at the stake for heresy. Aspiring European scientists recall with horror the fate of Galileo Galilei. Religious authorities ban contact with Arabs and other foreigners and view Eastern technology as the work of the devil.

In what we know as the twentieth century there emerges a global consensus that the developed countries have a responsibility for lifting Europe out of its dark ages. They take literacy, at least among the small European middle class, to be a prime goal. However, Europe has none of the infrastructure required to sustain the information technology of the Arabs and their partners—no electrical service, no way to maintain the equipment, and little capital with which to make these adaptations. An alternative to the text and image processor has to be found.

The peoples of the Middle East for millennia used stamps to cut impressions into wax and clay. The Chinese carried that idea further by developing wooden blocks that could be moved around to impress an image on an entire page of paper. In one of the great R&D laboratories in the mountains of the western continents, the Cherokees develop an efficient means for using the paper-making technology acquired by the Arabs in their battle with the Chinese in Samarkand in 751. This technology employs movable metal type and can produce multiple copies of documents that require no electronic infrastructure to read. They soon print newspapers and magazines, and some of these documents are bound for preservation, leading to books that can be distributed throughout Europe at much lower costs than electronic media. A teaching program is mounted around these new printed documents.

The Arabs adopt this new document—the book. Are books good for anything other than helping the Europeans to lift themselves out of the dark ages? A new habit arises: that of reading in bed, but the possibilities seem richer than that. Luddites oppose the introduction of this new technology of printing, but most people are willing to explore whether books and other printed forms of information have certain advantages over electronic forms. They ask, "For what purposes are books particularly suitable or even preferable?"

That is, I think, the question that librarians and many others ought to ask today. Until we give sharp answers to that question, some university administrators will tend to consider books obsolete and their defenders Luddites. Some proponents of information technology for libraries may be entranced by the technology without deeply considering what they seek to replace and why and without knowing much about how people use information. If their technocratic thinking guides decisions, we shall willy-nilly replace books and other printed media with electronic media on the assumption that electronic forms are always cheaper, more accessible, and "more modern."

Before the book becomes a relic of the technology of the past millennium, it deserves a spirited defense. That defense must start with a positive argument and not just arguments about sunk costs and personal preferences. If you had the technology of printing given to you for the first time today, what would you choose to print and why?

Conclusion

This chapter began with a statement that gateway libraries are processes and not places and ended with a fantasy about the Cherokees' opening of a new world of possibilities with the invention of the book. Because the new technology of information has the capacity to challenge our deepest assumptions, I see libraries as inextricably involved in development and application of this new technology rather than as relegated to the sidelines while technological elites reshape the world.

Libraries can still make themselves irrelevant to the new information age, however, by repelling all invaders from information technology, by allowing job-protection strategies to dominate decision making, or by failing to provide librarians with opportunities for appropriate training and retraining. Libraries can avoid these mistakes, however, by becoming the prophets of the information revolution.

9

The Gateway: Point of Entry to the Electronic Library

Jan Olsen

The Traditional Paradigm of the Research Library

The research library connects scholars to society's recorded knowledge. In the paradigm for achieving this—the library based in the printed record—librarians have developed theories, practices, and standards to evaluate, organize, and provide access to the printed record of knowledge.

But the computer revolution has introduced an anomaly into the traditional paradigm: scholarly information is now electronic in form. It is widely dispersed and not carefully organized and classified by librarians and publishers. The scholar can sit at home and access electronic information through a low-cost personal computer and national networks. The theories and practices of handling information in printed form within the traditional paradigm of the research library are being challenged by the emerging electronic library.

Toward the New Paradigm of the Research Library: The Electronic Library

The vision of the electronic library centers on a user at a workstation—that is, a microcomputer connected to a local network, which is in turn connected to state, regional, national, and international networks. The user enters the electronic library through a single gateway and window. The locus for the user's access to information is now outside the four walls of the library; it has become the home, the office, or the laboratory.

The electronic library consists of categories or genres of information. Each genre requires particular expertise to select items for the collection, to add them to the collection, and to provide service to users. Genres include applications, software, bibliographic files, full-text documents, numeric files, and multimedia.

Some of the electronic library's resources are held at the local level and loaded on computers on the user's campus. Databases such as ABI Inform or BIOSIS can be loaded on a library computer under a license agreement and accessed by the campus community. But the electronic library also encompasses resources that are available via the Internet. The mode of access to any of these resources should be equally transparent for the user.

The scenario then is that of scholars sitting at individual workstations accessing data and the full text of literature regardless of the location of the resource. In this ideal scenario, information resources are varied, easily accessible, and usable, workstations perform their search functions well, and telecommunications systems have sufficient bandwidth to support the transmission of information. Until scholars can rely predominantly on the electronic library to excel at these tasks, printed documents will continue to be a significant medium for publishing and storing information.

The Gateway

Having a great variety of resources in the electronic library is not practical unless users understand what is available and can connect easily to any resource. A single point of entry is the key—a front door to the electronic library. It should present the user with a catalog of resources available, assist the user in making a choice, and then connect the user to selected databases on either local or national networks.

At Cornell University's Mann Library we have built such a front door and earned the first ALA/Meckler Library of the Future Award for our accomplishments. It is called the Mann Gateway, and since January 1991, it has been used at workstations within Mann Library, elsewhere on campus, at home, or anywhere in the world with network access. The faculty, students, and staff at Cornell maintain that the gateway has changed the way they conduct their work. For example, members of the Cornell debate team have used the Mann Gateway to prepare for their meets as they travel across the country, and a student studying abroad for a semester used the gateway from France.

The gateway provides a single, convenient, uncomplicated entry point to a carefully selected library of bibliographic, full-text, and numeric information. Users simply need to find and log in to the system to search a wide range of databases located on various computers in diverse locations. Once at the gateway, users see a menu of choices with explanations and helpful prompts. When a user chooses one of the more than 500 available databases, gateway software handles the log-in process and connects the user to the selected database, which may be maintained on a Mann Library computer, on a computer elsewhere at Cornell, or on an off-campus computer. Location of databases is tracked by the gateway.

The first gateway, developed as a joint effort of Mann's technical staff and librarians and coordinated by a librarian, was sophisticated in its capabilities, easy to use, but quite primitive technologically. The more technically advanced present gateway is based on Mosaic client-server architecture and can deliver graphic images, better access to full-text resources, subject access, and an alphabetical menu to its 500 databases. The gateway is open to international use, but access to some databases is restricted to Cornell users only. The Uniform Resource Locator (URL) is http://www.mannlib.cornell.edu.

The gateway has been very well received: usage has grown from an average of fewer than 100 logins per day to often more than 900 sessions per day.

Information Genres
The five electronic information genres are essentially a broad taxonomy of electronic publications selected by specialists in each genre of information, such as numeric file specialists and multimedia specialists.

By defining the characteristics of the information resources and how these resources are used, specialists in each genre take into account similarities among categories of electronic information resources in terms of systems of access. These access requirements include search and retrieval software, operating systems software, and hardware. The Mann Gateway currently supports the following five information genres.

Applications Software   This genre is made up of productivity tools that are used to accomplish a set of tasks or to manipulate information. It includes tools such as word processors, spreadsheet programs, and database management programs as well as subject-specific programs such as diet-analysis packages for nutritionists and plant-selection programs for landscape architects. Some of these are available primarily on floppy disks and run directly on the user's microcomputer, but most are accessed from a file server.

Bibliographic Files   This genre includes abstracting and indexing programs, electronic dictionary and online catalogs, and bibliographies, which all can help users identify publications on a particular subject. Bibliographic files provide citations and possibly abstracts but do not include the full text of the publication cited. They require special search and retrieval software that retrieves by field or free text and conducts author, title, subject, and other defined searches. Bibliographic files are widely available in print, on CD-ROM, and on magnetic media.

Full-Text Documents   Traditionally, this is the largest genre collected by libraries. It includes the text of publications—everything from pamphlets and encyclopedias to annual reports and daily newspapers—meant to be read or consulted for their content and often includes graphics in the form of charts, tables, photographs, and drawings. Full-text documents are available in various electronic formats, ranging from CD-ROM and other optical media to various magnetic media. They require specialized search and retrieval software, advanced display requirements, and large amounts of computer storage space.

Numeric Files   This genre is comprised of publications presenting numerical or statistical data such as census materials, financial data, crop production reports, and meteorological data. Also included in this genre are genetic sequence databases and spatial data, including geographic information systems. Numeric files usually involve long time series and frequent updating and often are used by researchers who are studying relationships among a number of variables. The sophisticated statistical search and retrieval software required for extracting subsets of a file and manipulating data is very different from that required for a bibliographic database or a full-text database. Numeric files are available in print, on floppy disk, on CD-ROM, on magnetic tape, and through remote network searching.

Multimedia   Multimedia is a combination of sound, graphics, animation, and video. Whereas other genres are categorized to a large degree by the type of information they convey, regardless of the form of presentation or access mechanism, multimedia is categorized entirely by form of presentation. For example, a multimedia presentation of spatial data on meteorological phenomena may be available on a CD-ROM in a graphical modeling mode, along with relevant full-text and bibliographic files. Although multimedia currently is treated as a separate genre while the library explores the many technical issues involved in making multimedia available through the library, over time, as the many interesting collection policy questions raised by multimedia are resolved, its distinction as a separate genre may be eliminated. Other components of multimedia publications that we have not begun to mainstream include sound and image data.

Genre Specialists
Just as libraries currently employ specialists in audiovisual services, music, government documents, and various subject and area studies, they soon will develop specialists in various genres of electronic information. The genre specialist is an expert on the publications in all formats in a given genre. This person identifies and evaluates new information resources, selects those that fall within the collection subject scope and meet quality standards, determines the most appropriate mechanism of access, and recommends selection to the Electronic Resources Council (see next section).

A genre specialist may be either a full-time bibliographer in the collection development division or a part-time selector in public services or technical services. Whatever the primary administrative appointment, the genre specialist works, through the Electronic Resources Council, with other librarians to coordinate the library's policies and procedures on new formats. A genre specialist must be analytical, imaginative, dogged in the pursuit of format integration, comfortable with technology, and a real librarian's librarian. The successful genre specialist must be able to (1) analyze a new publishing medium against the backdrop of traditional and evolving professional practice for the genre, (2) discover the extent of conformance and assess the anomalies it presents, (3) make the resource fit existing operations where it can, and (4) work with colleagues throughout the library to adapt policies and procedures as necessary to the idiosyncrasies of the resource.

In the Mann Library's organizational model, genre specialists evaluate and select resources, identify the major issues attendant to their selection, and present their selections to the head of collection development. Then the selection is reviewed with the library's central forum for coordinating the mainstreaming of electronic resources across functional units, the Electronic Resources Council.

Electronic Resources Council
Acquiring electronic information affects every part of the library, from budgeting and selection, through acquisitions and cataloging, to reference and instruction. To ensure that adequate resources are available to handle a new format, an organizational audit or impact study is conducted by establishing a standing committee called the Electronic Resources Council (ERC). The ERC reviews electronic publications recommended by genre specialists for purchase or lease. Its dual role is (1) to assess the effect of new electronic resources on the total organization *before* they are selected and determine whether the library can handle a particular resource and (2) coordinate activities among the functional units of the library in acquiring, organizing, and providing services for the new format. The goal of the ERC is to mainstream the selection and handling of new publishing formats so that ERC review of such selections eventually will be unnecessary.

Genres and Technical Services

Mann Library's conscious decision to divide the information universe into genres has certainly affected collection development very strongly. However, it has probably had an equal impact on the conduct of technical services as the following case studies illustrate.

Bibliographic Information Case Study   The technical services department at Mann Library had extensive experience in creating bibliographies representing the resources of the library's collection. Drawing on this expertise, the library director created a joint committee of public services, technical services, and information technology staff to develop a searchable catalog of electronic resources for the library's gateway. As the number of electronic resources grew, it became increasingly evident that both staff and users required better tools for identifying and using electronic resources. Although most of the over 500 electronic resources available through Mann Library have bibliographic records in the online catalog, the MARC records cannot be retrieved easily from the OPAC and used within the gateway. In addition, the records often lack detailed access information. The goal of the committee was to create a subject guide to the library's electronic resources and have this database serve as a major finding tool in the library's gateway.

The records in the subject guide are created jointly by the cataloging staff (who have been involved in determining the record structure, organizational model, and guidelines for creating records) and the genre specialists (who often provide details on subject coverage or specific access instructions). The perspective provided by the public services staff has influenced the content of the MARC record as cataloging staff uncover complications related to access and the need for additional subject information. The core of the record is a selection of fields from the MARC record with enhanced information on access instructions, subject coverage, and Internet instructions, which are embedded in the 856 field, a newly defined MARC field that records network access information.

This database of records is an essential finding guide that allows users to look at different views—by subject, title, and genre—of the library's holdings of electronic resources. With WAIS indexing, users also can perform a keyword search of titles and descriptions.

Full-Text Information Case Study　Although Mann Library has long been interested in the research questions related to delivering full-text information, only recently has delivering this electronic information become a service priority. The library began exploring the questions related to the selection, delivery, and archiving of electronic journals two years ago. The library's goals were (1) to provide a network environment that would facilitate browsing and full-text retrieval of electronic journals and (2) to create a system that could process the journal issues. Because of his background in cataloging and computing, the electronic resources and monographs cataloger, a staff member whose responsibilities included programming, systems analysis, and cataloging, was asked to develop such a system. Additional insights were provided by a project team consisting of the library's interface designer, a collection development librarian, the technical project manager (who was a specialist in full-text resources), and the head of technical services.

Initially, the team examined BRS/Search software, a commercially available search and retrieval software, which the library was licensed to use within the gateway environment. BRS/Search provided field-based searching, and since many of the library's bibliographic databases were mounted under BRS/Search software, it was an environment familiar to both staff and users. These development plans changed, however, as the library began exploring the second-generation gateway to the electronic library and based the second generation on National Center for Supercomputing Applications (NCSA) Mosaic. The move to Mosaic provided several distinct advantages for electronic journals. Mosaic provides flexibility in handling a range of document types: ASCII text, graphic images, and multimedia documents. Mosaic also has a built-in markup language, hypertext markup language (HTML), which facilitates processing and supports an effective display using hypertext as an organizing principle. It supports the three most common platforms—i.e., Macintosh, X-Windows, and Windows—and its key navigational tools can be used within documents and among networked resources.

Numeric Information Case Study   Mann Library acquired 140 data files from the U.S. Department of Agriculture's Economic Research Service (ERS). The majority of the files from the ERS were in Lotus 1–2–3 format, and titles ranged from agricultural statistics on individual crops (such as Wheat Yearbook and Feed Grain Yearbook) to comprehensive surveys of farm-sector economics. Mann Library determined that the model for delivery would be a gopher server, which would facilitate navigation and downloading of specific files. The library also decided that the processing of these files would be mainstreamed—that is, we would use the current organizational structure and build on newly developed skills to process and service the ERS files rather than have a specialist handle them in a parallel process. For technical services, the process of acquiring, organizing, and cataloging included the following steps:

1. Acquire the physical disks,
2. Determine the organizational structure of the gopher,
3. Create the directories and subdirectories,
4. Upload the files,
5. Perform quality control checks,
6. Provide bibliographic access through the online catalog, and
7. Create online check-in records to track the ongoing receipt of files.

Although steps 1, 6, and 7 were traditional technical services responsibilities, steps 2 and 5 were new areas of concern. Technical services staff needed to broaden their understanding of processing to include the establishment and organization of a gopher for ERS data. The library needed to consider the concerns of both the producer (in this case the Economic Research Service) and the library user. Working closely with the numeric files librarian, the cataloging librarian analyzed the README files and the publication patterns of the ERS, created specific directories and subdirectories for each file, and directed the acquisitions staff to upload the files into individual directories. The processing of new titles and the regular updating of the file are handled in the acquisitions unit.

Impact of the Gateway

The Cornell community has enthusiastically embraced the Mann Gateway. Usage continues to increase as electronic resources are integrated into the daily academic work of faculty and students. The utility of the gateway is well described by the following users:

I just wanted to give you some positive feedback about your efforts. I used BIOSIS extensively in preparing my lectures for Bioscience 687 this fall. You saved me a tremendous amount of time and improved the quality of my lectures greatly. I was able to provide the students with the latest data and a list of references to boot.[1]

One of the things that I missed the most about Cornell during my sabbatical in France were the support and collection of Mann Library. . . . I was shocked and disappointed at the limited collection and accessibility to bibliographic databases that my French colleagues have to accept. This experience made me realize even more how valuable the Mann resources are for the development of strong and visionary research programs.[2]

Despite the ever increasing use of the gateway, its availability has not lessened users' needs to consult the printed literature (with the exception of some indexing and abstracting tools), nor has it made obsolete print-based information and document delivery services. In fact, the printed collection has seen more use as the electronic library has grown. Although the size of Mann's user population has not grown over the past decade, the volume of in-building use and external circulation has almost doubled. The print collection has grown, and the OPAC and the widespread availability of computerized bibliographic indexes and other reference tools have made the collection more available than ever before. The electronic library seems to stimulate use of the print collection.

The gateway has affected almost every area of the Mann Library. Staff members have responded by learning new skills, offering new services, and developing new documentation and instruction sessions. The reference staff handles questions undreamed of a quarter of a century ago. Support staff now participate in information services in new ways and have incorporated digitization into daily document delivery processing. The instruction program has been completely redesigned and focuses almost entirely on hands-on classes to teach skills on finding and using information in electronic form.

The number of questions brought to reference desk staff by users has increased, and staff believe that this traffic increase is due largely to the growth of the electronic library. The availability of many databases in a variety of formats has apparently contributed to a higher volume of reference and information questions. More databases for users seem to bring more questions from users—questions about database content, database selection, and system use; equipment and operation problems; about finding printed material identified through electronic resources.

Some questions about the electronic library come from users who are in the library building, but an increasing number come from remote users, who are accessing the Mann Gateway from locations outside the building. Remote users of the gateway contact the reference desk with questions about choosing the right database and using search software. Search software questions often are about how to use Boolean logic, search for author names, or limit search results by date or language. Regular system users are interested in using database update codes to limit searches to the most recent records added to the file. With training and practice, all reference desk staff have learned a number of new command languages and are able to answer most questions of this kind. Staff who were used to working with users in person have learned how to respond to search questions over the phone or via e-mail. Reference staff have expanded their technical knowledge in order to handle effectively other types of questions from electronic library users. For example, the reference desk staff are often the first to learn about technical problems because they are contacted by concerned gateway users. Although the system is reliable, there is occasional downtime when the gateway system itself is down or when individual resources are unavailable due to network or equipment problems. Staff at the reference desk are now able to determine, in many cases, whether a problem is local to Mann Library's hardware or software so that referrals to the appropriate technical staff can be made.

Another set of common questions received by staff at the reference desk involves the use of telecommunications software: prospective gateway users need guidance in choosing software that is the best for system access; new users sometimes have difficulties connecting to the system; many gateway users want to save data in electronic form. Some of these questions cannot be resolved by Mann staff because the answers may involve actions that must be taken by users' local network or computing coordinators. However, many are *best* answered by Mann staff who know the gateway system's configuration and have used several major communications packages available for gateway access.

Recent articles on staff training and competencies have discussed the importance of ongoing staff training and development in an evolving technological environment and the level of technical knowledge that should be expected of library staff. Although Mann has computer professionals to install and maintain computer systems, all staff in public services are now expected to be knowledgeable about basic electronic library functions.

The life for Mann librarians will be somewhat different in the future than it is today. The Mann Gateway and its electronic library are here to stay, and the reference and information questions from walk-in users will begin to decrease as the number of remote out-of-library users of the gateway increases. An effective support model will have to be developed for these remote users that includes a question-answering process that retains a human presence with users. As long as users recognize that the service they are getting is from the library, they will automatically turn to librarians with their questions. Support at the users' workstations will be a significant aspect of users' expectations, and if librarians do not meet these expectations someone else will.

Acknowledgments

Thanks to Susan Barnes, Sam Demas, and Janet McCue, whose writing is included in this article and whose commitment to Mann Library has made possible so many of its achievements.

Notes

1. Kenneth Kemphues, associate professor, genetics and development, Biological Sciences Department.

2. Larry P. Walker, associate professor, agricultural and biological engineering, Agricultural Engineering Department.

10
The Gateway Library: Teaching and Research in the Global Reference Room

Peter Lyman

Research libraries are homes for scholarly communities. As places, the library's buildings contain specialized collections that reflect the literature of the university's scholarly disciplines and professions, which together reflect its identity as an institution. Yet collections are necessarily only a sample of all literature; a library also must develop and provide tools that act as a gateway to the totality of published literature. In turn, published literatures are only a gateway to the research activities of the various disciplines, professions, and scholarly communities—activities that by definition extend across generations and around the globe. Thus, although libraries are always gateways, it is not a contradiction to say that they are also the physical and symbolic center of the university because their collections constitute an intellectual organization of highly specialized activities that otherwise might seem quite fragmented. It is through the library that members of an institution are best able to experience themselves as members of an academic community.

Since the turn of the twentieth century, research libraries have provided a sense of order for scholarly research—a center for teaching and research that is local and yet extends across time and even national boundaries. In partnership with scholarly publishers and disciplinary societies, the research library has been the cornerstone of an organized system of scholarly communication. Yet clearly this system can no longer absorb rising information costs, new modes of technology-based research, and an information explosion. The research library, and indeed the entire system of scholarly communication, has begun an irreversible process of change.

The idea of a gateway library is still emerging and at this stage is more defined by the questions it asks than the answers it provides:

· What kind of *place* will the library become when collections include information that is available in many technical formats and media (reflecting the new technologies used to create information) and that is accessed through a network gateway as well as collected locally? Specifically, can the network be designed as a place where scholarly communication is possible?

· How will the relationship between scholarly communication and scholarly publishing change, as information becomes the intellectual capital of an information economy and the price of information as a commodity dominates its use in scholarship and learning? How will the role of library collections change as scholars communicate directly with each other and exchange documents by "publishing" them on the network?

· How will the epistemology of scholarship and learning change as technology becomes a necessary part of reading and writing and as new rhetorical structures (like hypertext and databases) create new relationships between reader and text?

· How will the work of librarians change? What is the new role of the librarian in the gateway library as a catalyst for the transformation of information into knowledge?

These questions will shape teaching and learning in the gateway library as it adapts to changes in the nature of information and the economy, in publishing, and scholars' information needs. The gateway library cannot possibly contain all scholarly publications but instead contains tools that enable the reader to identify, access, and adapt particular information from the universe of all possible information. Creating the gateway library will require a partnership between scholars and librarians to preserve the essential values of a scholarly community even as economics and technology require us to reinvent the organization of the research library itself.

The Gateway to Collections

The research library has always been a gateway to scholarly communication in the sense that collections are built on the quality filter provided by scholarly publishers that began as disciplinary societies and have become increasingly commercial. Other gateway mechanisms, such as papers presented to professional meetings for public discussion, more directly reflect current research but are not authenticated by the editorial process and therefore have not become part of the library collection. (This authentication, even more vital to professors' promotion and tenure than to library collection policy, is directly supported by the price of scholarly publications and is thus indirectly subsidized by library budgets.)

Technology is changing scholarly communication much faster than scholarly publishing, but changes in scholarly publishing alone are sufficient to change the library. The price increase in scholarly publications has caused a fiscal crisis in collections budgets, but even more important than upward cost spirals are the fundamental changes in the sociology of knowledge that have caused this price inflation. As scholarship has become increasingly specialized, the number of scholarly journals has increased to over 200,000. As advanced economies have become increasingly technological, the economic value of scientific, technological, and medical information has increased, which in turn increases the price and decreases the availability of information that is patented rather than copyrighted. International commercial publishing companies have established near monopolies in the publication of journals in these fields, where research is strategic in the economy and international trade. These changes raise fundamental issues for library collections: even if a library could afford to collect everything published, given disciplinary specialization it is not clear that the totality of published information is a coherent whole or that what is published represents all of what scholars have to find in a library.

No physical library collection can be more than a microcosm of the totality of knowledge in any field. In an age of expanding information and increasing specialization of knowledge, both the researcher and the learner face the same challenges—to find the right information or knowledge, to determine the quality of information, to understand the most efficient and cost-effective methodology for access to published knowledge, and to choose the technical format most appropriate to the content and use of a given kind of information.

Since the turn of the century the system of scholarly communication has attempted to balance the customs of academic gift cultures with the legal structure of the marketplace. Within academic gift cultures, research is subsidized by the economic structure of tenure and promotion and by the nonmaterial rewards of prestige, and scholars build a sense of community by exchanging information and ideas freely. Research libraries preserve the idea of knowledge as a gift between scholars through the subsidized use of information in libraries, and the law recognizes it through the doctrine of fair use, which allows limited copying of copyright material for educational purposes.

The boundary between gift exchanges and market exchanges has been defined by the transfer of intellectual property rights to scholarly publications. After a century of use, this system is changing as an economy based on intellectual property emerges, as technology changes how scholars exchange and use information, and as the price of printed published scholarly information increases. Some research has such commercial value it is patented and never enters the system of scholarly communication.

In a world in which research often increases in economic value, scholars must join with research libraries to define a strategy for preserving the traditional infrastructure of scholarly culture from destruction by the information marketplace. As collections are increasingly constrained by the growing price of printed published information, and the amount of printed information grows beyond the capability of any library's budget to acquire, the library user must change research strategies. An alternate scenario—and this is a strong possibility—is that the research library will disappear and the reader will buy access to knowledge in the marketplace directly from the publisher. Between the two poles of the traditional library system and the marketplace, the gateway library is emerging to balance the free access of the traditional library with more efficient and cost-effective collections.

The Gateway to the Global Reference Room

The Internet is a new mode of scholarly communication that is becoming a global reference room as it overcomes the geographic limits that have defined traditional scholarly communities. Today's Internet offers only a suggestion of the global reference room that research libraries eventually could build. Two-thirds of the activity on today's NSFnet is dedicated to communication (electronic mail), document exchange (file transfer protocol or ftp), and name look-up; only one-third is computation. Over 500 library catalogs are now accessible on the Internet, and when the Z39.50 standard is completed and implemented, users will be able to explore information and transfer data from those catalogs on other library systems to the desktop. Early studies by the Faxon Institute of scholars in science and technology indicate that the network is the preferred method for finding information at every step of the research process up to publication. Thus far, the Internet has not been widely used by publishers for document delivery systems because it lacks mechanisms for auditing, charging, marketing, and enforcing copyrights.

Yet these are only technical problems. The Internet removes many (but not all) of the constraints of distance and potentially reduces the cost of inventory and shipping to perhaps half the cost of many scholarly publications. Scholarly publications can be distributed globally by the network and printed locally. In response to this ready access to information around the globe, worldwide scholarly communities are beginning to grow.

This network will be entered through a gateway—to the library. The new mission of the library is to transform a medium built by engineers for engineers as a technology for shared computation into a medium for scholarly communication. This transformation will require librarians to design network software and interfaces, to understand the relationship between the content of information and the format in which it is stored, accessed, and to perform the library's traditional roles of controlling quality, organizing knowledge, and teaching the art of navigation. Every researcher or learner will have to navigate the global digital network to participate in international disciplinary and professional communities and their information resources.

The information resources of the Internet are being built by library consortia (such as the RLIN—the database of the Research Libraries Group) and by important experiments sponsored by disciplinary societies and scholar editors of electronic journals. The most important example is the Online Mendelian Inheritance in Man (OMIM), a comprehensive database that suggests an alternative to the system of scholarly publishing.

Yet libraries have yet to take the most important steps in building a global reference room: developing cooperative collections, finding aids for digital exchange of archival documents and images, and delivering documents. The gateway library cannot exist on one campus until research libraries begin to think of themselves as part of an international research community.

The Teaching Mission of the Gateway Library

What research skills will faculty and students need to conduct research in the global electronic reference room? Although the network is the only global reference room for scholars, television and radio also are global media for global communication, and cable and cellular communications are likely to be. At this point in designing the national information infrastructure, it is not even clear that the Internet will survive as a noncommercial network.

In the emerging world of information, critical thinking cannot focus only on printed scholarly publishing but must enable students to analyze the way everyday life is saturated with information from television, information technology, entertainment, advertising, government, and business.

Information Literacy

Because of the cultural prestige of technology, the word *information* connotes objectivity. However, *information* has its origin in scholastic training: *to inform* meant "to give form to the mind," "to discipline," "to instruct," "to teach," "to train." Critical thinking about information requires that each of the senses be taught to make a critical reading of each of the media that present information. Just as psychoanalysis trains the ear to listen and the mind to understand the meaning of emotional speech and as ethnography trains the eye to see and understand nonverbal communication and the meaning of space, so liberal education must train researchers to understand the rhetorical and lexical structures of writing in every format:

· To understand how the format of knowledge shapes its content and use;
· To understand the appropriate use and limits of each medium's form and the origins and purposes of the rhetorical structures that it uses;
· To understand enough of how information is created in each medium to make judgments about its quality, use, and potential misuse;
· To understand how deception and truth differ in each format and how deception is used for the purposes of both entertainment and exploitation.

The Future of Information

All readers must continuously evaluate and apply new information as it changes the organization of work, the value of knowledge in the economy, and cultural values. Up to this point, the information explosion (which refers to growth in both the amount of information and the number of formats for accessing information) has not led to fundamental change in the organization of higher education or the research library. This is largely true in the corporate world as well, where investment in information technology has often led to improvements in the quality of information, but growth in productivity has required the reorganization of work itself. After the business office, the research library is the first unit within an academic organization to feel the transformative effects of the information economy. The faculty's sensitivity to changes in the research library reflects a concern that every other aspect of the organization of academic work may be forced to change as well.

And yet almost every faculty member recognizes that the traditional research problem, finding scarce information, has changed; today the researcher often encounters too much information, and the problem is not scarcity but abundance. New skills are required—selectivity, quality control, and management of data. Learning to organize knowledge requires managing personal information resources, selecting and customizing digital knowledge, participating in collective forms of knowledge, publishing on the Internet, reorganizing work, and developing conceptual tools and scholarly environments that take advantage of new technology and information resources.

As the cost of information continues to rise, and indeed as commercial publishing continues to replace nonprofit scholarly publishing, the library will be unable to subsidize access for all users to all information. Subsidized information, which appears to be free to the reader, has been the foundation of the academic gift culture. Certainly subsidized access to information will be impossible without new discipline and skill on the part of the readers, who must use knowledge efficiently to minimize the cost of information as knowledge becomes a new form of capital. But even with new discipline in the use of information, it seems inevitable that some costs will be passed along to the reader. Inevitably, the research library of the future will include a gateway to the information marketplace.

The Future of the Reader

Reading and libraries have been so closely linked that historically scholars and students were called *readers,* not the contemporary *user.* But digital texts are not only read; they are searched, customized, copied, and combined into new kinds of texts. It is fundamental to the gateway library that the reader be thought of as an author, and perhaps as a publisher as well. (This approach is not entirely new: nearly every library researcher is both a reader and an author.)

The gateway library may well serve some of the functions of the bookstore, especially as a distribution point for customized texts. By using McGraw-Hill's Primus database, instructors can create custom versions of a textbook, which are then printed on demand. McGraw-Hill reports that twenty years ago 97 percent of students assigned a textbook would buy it but that today only 53 percent will buy assigned texts. In a digital environment, instruction will increasingly resemble research in that the student will be asked to select texts from a vast array of networked resources.

Instruction will resemble research in a deeper sense as well. Digital texts are created through interaction with technology and with content; they are not static like printed texts. Ultimately there must be a link between creating a text, doing research, and reading a text. Pedagogically, the gateway library resembles a craft workshop in which students apprentice themselves to masters to learn how to use the new technical arts of scholarship in a manner appropriate to their content and use.

Readers may become publishers in two new senses as well. First, digital texts have a communal character: they may be shared across the global network and written by groups of writers who are located around the world. Second, the act of reading the digital text may change it by adding recorded remarks or gloss. The character of digital texts is clearly different from printed texts, and their use and abuse are only beginning to be explored.

Designing the Gateway Library

The gateway library is emerging from experiments being conducted by many libraries and technology companies across the world: the OMIM genetics database from the Welch Medical Library at Johns Hopkins University, the British Library's document delivery service, and online bibliographic databases and catalogs such as HOLLIS. These experiments do not replace traditional libraries but seek to take advantage of technology to control the costs of information and to provide scholars and students with the information resources and skills they need in the emerging information age.

The Gateway Collections

Every library collection reflects the history of the community that created and uses it; it is a microcosm of the array of possible collections. The gateway library collection must define a strategy: In what format should information be collected? What piece should be part of the physical collection, and to what items should the library provide access?

The concept of access is problematic on at least two grounds. First, the library could either subsidize all the information needs of its community or could pass along the cost of new collections. Second, electronic access signals fundamental changes in scholarly habits—an end to browsing the shelves, a willingness to select information based on an abstract alone, a time delay in delivery of information, and the use of computer databases and networks.

The principles guiding collection development also are changing. A gateway library's collections will provide three things:

· *Access to information and knowledge will be provided in the format appropriate to its content.* The question is no longer whether to purchase information but how to select the format in which the information is most useful. Census data was historically printed but is virtually useless in print format today; researchers need to use it collected in a form that can be subjected to computerized statistical analysis. Other examples are more ambiguous and require a decision about how information is going to be used: Should art history images be collected as color prints, as slides, or as digital images that can be distributed on the network and analyzed by computer?

· *Users will learn how to select the information they need to conduct research.* Digital information resources require technical skill to access and to use. The gateway library must acquire appropriate technologies and be prepared to teach scholars and students how to use them.

· *Information will be provided in a form customized to meet the reader's needs.* Scholars and students will need to make copies of digital information in the format in which it will be most useful. This will require selecting the right information, having the right to include it in one's own works (although copyright policy will regulate this in new ways on the network), and printing, e-mailing it, or copying it by diskette.

Gateway to the Global Reference Room

The gateway library is founded on the recognition that no library collection can be complete and that scholars must have access to information on a global scale. Every library is simply an access point to the information resources of the global Internet.

The gateway library must train students to make their own information judgments to select, evaluate, and use information and knowledge in every format. Today's Internet is defined by four applications—electronic mail, file transfer protocol, Telnet, and Gopher—which suggest uses for the global reference room and yet are still primitive applications.

Electronic mail is the prototype of a new medium for dialog among widely geographically dispersed speakers. Thus far, electronic mail combines the immediacy of the telephone with the limited expressiveness of plain text to produce a convenient message system. Electronic mail, however, is only a prototype for the more sophisticated networked multimedia communication (including video and voice) that is being developed. Partnerships between the faculty and research library will be needed to explore the scholarly potential of these new formats.

In the network medium, reading implies writing and publishing, and those in reference services are finding that there is no longer a viable distinction between a content problem, a software problem, and a hardware problem. Some collections, mainly print but also microform, come in fixed formats; others are do-it-yourself collections (network, authoring).

The *file transfer protocol* (ftp), enables document sharing around the world. This program allows collections to be shared and yet lacks the bibliographic structures and quality control of print collections. It suggests a future where authors and researchers distribute their writings without mediation—without quality control or authentication. Clearly, publishing (and all of its related legal controls in copyright) must be reinvented for the network medium.

Telnet means that in principle any computer has access to any other computer's software and hardware capabilities. In practice, this access is often restricted, but it suggests a future in which even a library terminal will provide access to the means to conduct serious research. In such a library there is little distinction between reading and research, which again redefines our assumptions about the activities of library users.

Gopher is the first client-server application to join the top ten software applications on the network and is a prototype (with WAIS, MOSAIC, and Netscape) of the global reference room. Gopher suggests that information literacy must include network navigation—the ability to follow (fairly complex) information trails around the globe.

The Teaching Mission of the Gateway Library

The gateway library has as its premise an ideal of literacy that includes the ability to use information resources in printed or digital formats. Today's students are often computer literate in a technical sense and yet often are unskilled in using either traditional print libraries or new digital information resources. Students have learned about digital technologies and multimedia in the commercial world of entertainment, in which images and information are to be enjoyed but not analyzed in any scholarly sense. Yet they will graduate into a world in which information technologies are changing the structure of organizations and the shape of knowledge. Similarly, faculty members often face the challenge of adapting new technologies to their research and instructional activities without institutional support. The gateway library may well be responsible for supporting innovative teaching technologies and the faculty's introduction of new kinds of information resources into the curriculum.

The gateway library will be a place for the solitary reader but also for students who collaborate in learning. Libraries should be designed specifically to support group work.

As information technologies redefine the idea of literature and the relationship between author and reader, they are making the discovery and creation of knowledge part of the activity of reading. When this happens, the library is a place for student writing and publishing, as well as reading.

The Gateway Librarian

If the structure of knowledge and the organization of the library are changing, then inevitably the profession of the librarian is changing as well. The closing of library schools at research universities suggests a downgrading of the profession, and yet librarians are among the few professionals who have skills and experiences in the structure, organization, and management of information. Clearly, the gateway library requires an interdisciplinary staff that combines traditional librarian skills with technical skills and very likely advanced training in the disciplines. Gateway librarians will play at least three roles in information management:

· Gateway librarians will be practitioners of "clinical informatics" and experts at diagnosing information problems in the learning process. As the field of theoretical informatics evolves, it certainly will include librarianship, computer science, the sociology of knowledge, and a grounding in the research traditions of the various disciplines.

· Gateway librarians will be organizers of information communities and will experiment with ways to foster learning through relationships between people and between people and information.

· As information access is commercialized, gateway librarians will be agents for consumers in the information marketplace.

This incomplete definition stresses the new dimensions of librarianship rather than the continuities in the profession, yet it suggests the new kinds of curricular elements that must be part of the training of the librarian and the new kinds of professions that will staff the library. Most fundamentally, the faculty must accept the librarian (and other information professionals) as partners in the vital enterprise of recreating the library.

V

Technology and Education: The Role of Libraries in Teaching and Learning

The themes of teaching and learning wind through many of the essays in this book, but the following three chapters all conceive of the gateway as an opportunity to create a new environment for teaching and learning. All three examine new technology primarily with regard to its impact on learning—that is, on how students learn and what they learn. For Richard A. Lanham, technology changes the conceptual world created by print and challenges the traditional tenets and organization of higher education. The basic structures of the university—course, class, major, department, academic discipline, textbook—are reexamined from the perspective of a world no longer defined exclusively by the culture of print. The defining issue for Lanham and, indeed, the underlying motif for all these authors, is the role of the library in a curriculum being transformed by the emerging digital culture.

Karen Price also examines the ways that digital technology changes how we learn and use information and even how people express themselves. The issue is not technology but its uses. The challenge for the academy is to define its goals for education and learning and turn technology to these purposes. As Price points out, information is not knowledge, and the success of the gateway will depend as much on the goals as on the tools selected. By embracing many pedagogical values from the past—helping learners develop the skills to find information so they can be self-directed learners and linking information and knowledge to people's needs—she believes the gateway can create a new environment for learning.

James Wilkinson, while acknowledging the role played by technology in changing the way we learn, focuses on its convergence with changing concepts about teaching and learning. New methods of teaching, for example, are closer to research than traditional lecture methods of instruction. But technology has taken little note of these changes in teaching, and much of the current instructional software has limited value for learning. For Wilkinson, the role of the library is not simply to provide access to information but to connect learners with the information they need. Like Lanham and Price, Wilkinson believes one of the problems we face is too much information. Librarians, he believes, can provide the missing link between information and technology by understanding both.

The gateway provides an opportunity to address the fundamental issues of education—teaching and learning—and to redefine the mission of the library in this basic enterprise. As Lanham observes, in an information society the scarce commodity is not information but human attention. The critical role for the gateway library is to allocate scarce student attention in an optimal way by integrating the library with the process of instruction.

11

A Computer-Based *Harvard Red Book:* General Education in the Digital Age

Richard A. Lanham

To: The Select Committee on the Undergraduate Curriculum
From: The University President
Re: A curriculum for the digital age

Dear Colleagues:

I thank you for undertaking the most difficult task a university faculty can confront—the periodic rethinking of its curriculum in the face of changing circumstances. To judge from past experience, your deliberations are likely to be long and, if not acrimonious, at least galvanized by profound conviction. To armor you against these perils, I have scheduled your meetings in the Regental Caucus Room, which has the most comfortable chairs on campus.

Background

In 1943, in the middle of World War II, President Conant of Harvard University appointed a faculty committee to ponder "the objectives of a general education in a free society." The committee's deliberations lasted nearly three years (a salutary warning, this) and bore lasting fruit: their report, *General Education in a Free Society* (Harvard University, 1945), known more familiarly as the *Harvard Red Book,* is a landmark document in American higher education.

The committee saw itself as inheriting an educational revolution already begun in the public schools. In moving from an agricultural to an industrial economy, America had increased its high school population ninetyfold. Mass public education had really begun. In 1945, when the committee issued its report, American higher education was about to institute a similar revolution—to welcome students of different kinds and in much greater numbers than it had ever before, to extend its curriculum into uncharted ground, and to expand its research task and its financing in ways that would transform the university.

President Conant sensed the coming revolution when he charged the committee: "The primary concern of American education today is not the development of the appreciation of the 'good life' in young gentlemen born to the purple. It is the infusion of the liberal and humane tradition into our entire educational system. Our purpose is to cultivate in the largest possible number of our future citizens an appreciation of both the responsibilities and the benefits which come to them because they are Americans and are free" (Harvard University, pp. xiv–xv).

The *Harvard Red Book* makes interesting reading now, immersed as we are in culture wars between the "politically correct books" left and the "great books" right. The Harvard committee was perhaps more polite and judicious than we have been, but it wrestled with the same issues—an increasingly diverse student population, a proliferating and increasingly specialized curriculum, and the desire to teach both skeptical and inquiring habits of mind a commonly accepted body of information. All this was to be accomplished without redeploying the rigid classical curriculum that Harvard had repudiated in the nineteenth century. The recommendations that the Committee made endured for half a century: they differ hardly at all from the "distribution requirements" now in force on our campus.

Now it is time to rethink the problem again as we face the third stage in the democratization of American education. We are expanding the educational franchise still further to a yet more diverse student population and must teach our students how to meet the higher and different demands for symbolic thought imposed by an information-based society. A new force has now been added to the mix of social, political, and educational forces that animated the first two revolutions—digital technology. The digital revolution and the information society it animates alter all the terms in the carefully balanced educational equations the Harvard committee worked out. I am asking you to develop a new *Red Book* for our university.

Some Fundamental Questions to Be Addressed

As we heard at a recent faculty conference, it's time to address the art of teaching, changes in the tools of instruction, societal changes, such as the increasing diversity in background and experience of those being taught, and questions concerning what must be taught and how to teach it. I especially want you to consider how the most unprecedented of the changes we face—the digitization of information—affects all these topics. To help focus your deliberations, consider our undergraduate curriculum as a small "information society." How can we reconceptualize it, just as the larger society for which we educate our students is reinventing itself?

Looking at the problem in this way, you may find that the university library will loom large in your deliberations. As you know, like most major universities these days, we are closing our library school and putting a draconian spending cap on our library budget. Even considering how short we are of money, have we done the wise thing here?

Now on to some of the particular questions that I hope you will consider.

What Kind of Literacy Will Our Students Need in the Future?

Students are growing up in a world that increasingly offers them information on an electronic screen rather than in a printed book. As the late O. B. Hardison, Jr. (1989, p. 264) wrote in his last book: "We are coming to the end of the culture of the book. Books are still produced and read in prodigious numbers, and they will continue to be as far into the future as one can imagine. However, they do not command the center of the cultural stage. Modern culture is taking shapes that are more various and more complicated than the book-centered culture it is succeeding."

What effects will this change bring? The goal of the printed text was *fixity.* That is what those great Renaissance scholars I used to study before I went into administration were after—fixity and the authority that comes from it. The volatile electronic text would seem to undermine that fixed authority. The electronic reader can now change the text being read, reformat it, reorder it, revise it, and reprint it in another typeface in another place. Our students will be growing up with this freedom as their native way of reading. Doesn't this freedom undermine the whole idea of textual authority? Isn't this digital subversion really a much graver threat to cultural authority and continuity than heated discussions about replacing the canonical great books with modern revolutionary ones?

What effect will these habits of electronic reading have on the reading of traditional codex books? After all, our library has several million of those, and not all of them are printed on self-destructing acidic paper. What will students brought up to read a volatile electronic text think about reading a fixed printed one? Will it seem recalcitrant and rebarbitive? Will they prefer what they can read, and thus manipulate, on screen? Will they be accustomed to accessing "books" from a network rather than going to the library? If so, what do we do with all those books? Digitize them? Spend more money? Who will decide which ones to do first—the library or the faculty?

I'm far from an expert on multimedia, but it seems that the basic operating system for information will be a richer sensory signal than black-and-white print provides, one that includes image and sound as well as print. Books have always had illustrations, of course, but now the whole world of imagistic expression is much more available, much easier and cheaper to reproduce, and as volatile and user-manipulatable as text. Sound too now forms a regular part of the expressive mixture: we can talk to our computers and have them read to us, play music, and listen to as well as read an author. I'm only a university bureaucrat, but aren't we creating a whole new semiology of expression?

The classic reading experience we cherish is built on a black-and-white printed surface that is deliberately made as unnoticeable and unselfconscious as possible and that allows us to concentrate on the conceptual world created by the words rather than on the words themselves or their printed manifestation. This has been true, as the great Harvard Hellenist Eric Havelock pointed out, ever since the Greeks adapted the Phoenician alphabet. Doesn't this transparency, and the silence and isolation that accompanied it, radically change when the expressive surface mixes words, images, and sounds, and does so in *color*? Look at one of the new media magazines, like *Wired* or *Mondo 2000,* that mimic computer design practices in print, and you'll see what I mean. If information will be available in this new way, how are libraries going to store it and disseminate it? And how will they translate their books—as to some degree they will have to—into this new and richer mixed-media signal?

This all seems very much like an electronic game room, but we already are beginning to use the same kind of media mixture here on campus. We've just gotten a National Science Foundation grant for our scientific visualization group. Aren't those folks really doing the same thing—exploring a new interface between alphanumeric expression and iconic expression? I've also just been asked by a faculty group for seed money to start a data *sonification* group, to add sound to help conceptualize various kinds of scientific data and asked by another group to supply funds for a Center for the Digital Arts. We also just funded an interactive fiction conference for the creative writing people, and for two decades we have supported the pioneering Center for Electronic Music. You all know how resolutely I have defended and funded our freshman composition program. But what will it look like in this universe? Will we continue to use the essay as the basic expressive training unit, and if not, what will replace it? What kind of faculty will we recruit to teach this new literacy? The library staff is developing skills in designing informational packages. Could we think of a digitally-based library as the locus of this new kind of instruction, and if so, will the library perform a new kind of instructional role?

As I add up all these mixed modalities, I seem to see a fundamental change not only in *how* we learn but in *what* we learn. If so, will this change affect everything we teach and how we teach it, and will we need to build a different conception altogether of what human "literacy" is? If so, how would we instruct our students? Or should we, as our English Department wants to do, *defend against* it as the end of the world? Won't that leave our students as the last clerks of a forgotten mode of apprehension?

What Happens to the Course or Class in an Environment of Electronic Information?

One of the central issues discussed by previous curriculum committees has been the fatal disconnection of one course from another. The student carries over little wisdom from one course to another, even within a single major, and some connections between courses are discouraged by the finality of the final grade. Does this mean that we should stop teaching Shakespeare, for example? Or cross another great author off our lists? The course even varies widely depending on who teaches and who takes it.

Suppose that an enterprising instructor assembled an electronic sublibrary for a particular course and included the texts studied in the class, those most closely associated with it, some secondary research materials, and perhaps some primary sources? Wouldn't this improve the quality of the student writing in the course? At our university many students live off campus and often commute long distances to be on campus only two or three days a week. These students have great difficulty using secondary sources, even if they are placed on library reserve in plentiful numbers. Suppose they could access the best articles on an assigned topic from home through their modem, and suppose further that their papers and exams were published on a class network. Might this kind of publication improve student writing in yet another way, by giving them a less artificial audience than a single instructor? I remember, when I was teaching, forever photocopying good papers and exams as examples. Published electronically, examples of student excellence would be more naturally visible. If the network would allow it, the student essay might well become some kind of multimedia product.

Occasionally, when someone asks me to speak at a dinner, I puzzle about the kind of work that is going on at our institution. If I could call up the syllabus, the assignments given and executed, and a student computer bulletin board about the course, I could understand better how instruction is shaping itself—and so could students who are considering taking the course at a future time. If we project such a process as occurring year after year, the course would possess something that now it so markedly does not—a *history.* Would your colleagues find this an intolerable intrusion on their teaching privacy, or might they learn from what their colleagues across the university are doing?

If one imagines a series of these courses connected hypertextually, we might have a new kind of answer to the central question of your committee—the search for some kind of common ground for general education. Such a series of connections at first might be planned but would soon become a series of stochastic encounters, using the initial connections to devise new ones based on interest and the kind of chance that favors the prepared mind.

A digital sublibrary would be available as a resource for high school students who aspired to advanced placement, or just to independent study. The next step beyond that, which already is being done, is to prepare a course for use in distance learning of various kinds. Such a digital course library would open our courses to all kinds of groups now excluded from them.

I can see three problems, at least, in such a reinvented course. First, it would cost a good deal of time and money to set up. But could not those costs be offset by reduced textbook costs, by fees paid by those who access it from the outside, and by the savings in duplicating and disseminating the basic and secondary course materials? Another possible economy in this regard is student *productivity*. Many of you may recoil from the word, but our university is under great pressure to maximize student learning and to keep the baccalaureate degree down to four years. Students themselves are under pressure to maximize their very expensive undergraduate educational time (according to our new survey of student employment, our undergraduates work an average of twenty-five hours a week at an outside job). We have scarcely begun to ponder this question of student productivity, yet increased costs of all kinds, especially tuition, force us to. At present, waste is built into how students enter courses, often stay only half a term, drop, resume, buy books they don't need, can't get ones they do need, and so on. Can we improve this segment of the curricular information society?

The second problem I can see looming in creating a digital course library is that clearly it stands outside the capacity of an individual faculty member. Who would create such a system, and how might it be done? To some extent, as the Intermedia program at Brown has shown, the department could do it. But building such a sublibrary generally will have to lie outside professors' regular scholarly and teaching obligations, or it will simply swamp them. Would such a task be a function of the library, and if so, how should the library be equipped to perform it? This kind of course design would be performing a central evaluative and judgmental one—a primary teaching task. It would be a new task and require a new kind of training.

Third, it seems likely that a digitized course system would gravely aggravate a problem that already vexes us—plagiarism. I need not spell out the fresh problems such a system would create. But might we not turn this to our advantage? The nature of authorship and originality is one of the issues that changes most radically as we move from print to screen. The absolute originality that the Romantic tradition of authorship bequeathed to us and that current intellectual property litigation is doing so much to set in concrete directly contradicts a central characteristic of digital information—its iterability and ability to replicate itself. That is why copyright issues loom so large on our campus. In a world of electronic text, which collapses the reader–writer distinction, the very idea of individual creation is now up for renegotiation. Why not use this new kind of course to discuss it? When I talk to business groups, I'm often asked why we do not train our students for the kind of *collaborative* creative work they will be doing later in groups. Might we not begin such work here with a discussion of original creation and intellectual property in a digital environment?

What Happens to the Idea of a Classroom in a Computer-Based Environment?

At the first level of changes that occur in a computer-based environment, professors barrage the administration with requests for money to install multimedia apparatus in class and to set up networked computer class-rooms. One proposal I reviewed included a description of a fascinating new program that supports complete interchange of information among students about particular assignments. Does this make the classroom a series of smaller work groups? If so, how should the room be arranged, and how do you teach in such a room?

Beyond these first-level problems, I hope you will consider issues that are both more futuristic and more immediately rooted in the present. The logic of current work in what is called virtual reality suggests that perhaps digital magic may blend a single classroom out of many different distant locations. Much of the "ubiquitous computing" work done at, for example, Xerox PARC seems to point in this direction. Will the naturally disembodied nature of electronic information mean that we don't need classrooms at all? I would guess and hope that the need for human society will prevail. Such issues may sound a little far-fetched but I have on my desk the legislature's proposal to axe two of our projected classroom buildings. How hard should I fight back? And who will plan these new instructional spaces, however virtual—the administration, the individual departments, or, again, the library that plans the information system of which they will be a part? If the library designs and administers an instructional network for a course, will it also administer a virtual classroom? Again, please consider issues of faculty and student productivity and costs. Surely here the labor intensivity of individual classroom instruction can be addressed; we must get some electronic leverage on it somehow.

What Will a "Textbook" Look Like in the New Digital Environment?
Who will publish these new textbooks, and who will pay for them? Committees like yours generally do not consider textbooks to be part of curricular planning, but the issue may become a central one. If we are concerned with improving student productivity (the ratio of student learning to student costs), we have to consider how much student texts cost and how much benefit students obtain from them. We also might consider whether the university should provide them in a form customized to our instruction, rather than depend on outside publishers. The print publishers, which have been slow to adapt to digital textuality, are now making their texts available in customizable form and licensing end-users to take parts from various texts, and many of you use the custom anthologies that campus copy shops prepare. Perhaps the university should buy in bulk and then customize for our students.

The technology seems clearly headed to some kind of genuinely portable digital reading and writing device and to a storage medium of extraordinary capacity. In a real sense, individual students will carry around their own miniaturized libraries. Your committee might explore whether our library people are thinking about this miniaturization of their function. Is this part of their thinking about *gateways*, for example? Such a distribution system inevitably makes the library into a publisher, but would that be a bad thing? The entertainment business is converging with the publishing business, which is converging with the computer business; and the university probably is not exempt from these kinds of technological pressures.

The class network I've described is another way to publish customized texts. I would like your committee to inquire into the net-cost-to-students of the present system of bookstore ordering, reordering, returning, and so on versus network course costs. You might consider doing a trial run in one department or a big class that fulfills one of our general education requirements. Judging from recent sales in our campus computer store, the kind of computer both our students and our faculty now buy includes a CD-ROM player. Should we think of publishing custom textbook CD-ROM disks for our students? This technology is now much cheaper and easier to operate than it was even a couple of years ago.

I don't think we can depend on print publishers to solve these textbook problems, as we have in the past. In the first place, they are thinking about profit maximization, and we are thinking of student productivity and cost containment. Beyond that, outside publishers cannot be expected to consider our curriculum as a single integrated information system, and that surely is the direction in which we want to go. The whole logic and direction of publishing changes in such a system.

We need to consider the place of our University Press in all of this. It has lost money for years, and we are going to eliminate its subsidy soon. Last year, when I fired the director, I threatened to shut it down entirely but backtracked and appointed a faculty committee that has not succeeded in improving the financial picture. Could the Press create a campus digital publishing service? CD-ROM technology offers the Press and the library an extraordinary opportunity for (to use perhaps too commercial a term) re-packaging—reconfiguring information. Is there some way to combine the Press's publication functions with the lending functions of the library? Despite clashes of institutional cultures, such mergers are occurring all across the American spectrum, wherever digital technology has transformed it.

In our current system of academic publishing, our faculty produces information and gives it to publishers (usually for a song), publishers publish expensive books in ever-smaller lots, libraries can no longer afford to buy these books because they are spending their money buying journals, journals obtain their material for free from our professors, and professors urge me to give the library and the Press more money to continue this self-bankrupting process. It will have to stop soon. Textbooks, the library, the Press, and the campus bookstore are all parts of a campus information system: doesn't digital technology suggest that there may be a better way to orchestrate these parts?

In a digital world, textbooks (the word itself is an anachronism) are a fundamental part of the curriculum problem. They always were: think of the changes brought about by the paperback. But why did the university wait for somebody else to invent the paperback, if it was to mean so much to how we taught? All those custom anthologies are being driven by internal pressures for curricular change; the custom anthology itself models an emergent curriculum struggling against a recalcitrant medium. In this current revolution in expressive technology, can the university lead rather than follow?

How Will Digitized Information Affect the Basic Organizational Unit of Our Undergraduate Curriculum—the Major?
In a digital universe, the arts that use words, those that use sounds, and those that use images now share a common notational base. The union is tighter even than that because it is data driven. I can create a song from your picture, and a directly data-driven visual image from your poem. The separation of the arts does not inhere in nature; they have always drawn as close together as they could. The expressive media have kept them apart. In a digital world, that barrier no longer obtains, and they surely will, as John Cage said in one of his stimulating lectures here on campus, all return to some kind of operatic center. We see this already in the popular arts, and the learned ones—always in the vanguard—will surely follow suit. MTV is the most notorious such new mix, but the multimedia programming now emerging offers countless instances. If you want to see a brilliant example, look at my friend Professor Robert Winter's new "program" of the Dvorak *New World* symphony. In the world of the sciences, about which I am not really qualified to speak, are the same things happening in the visualization and sonification spheres?

What will this convergence do to the undergraduate major and to the relationships among majors, at least in the arts and letters? The major, seen in this new light, seems to be based on a particular technological medium—print—which is now metamorphosing into something else. The major, of course, reflects the larger organization of the department and the discipline it embodies. Surely these will change—or pickle themselves in nonstrategic resistance. Suppose digital technology forces the department—the basic building block of the university—to change? Departments, disciplines, and majors are not eternal. In fact, the whole modern cluster of specializations isn't much more than a century old. When—not if—they dissolve, what will take their place as a central organizational principle? Who or what will supply new principles of order?

These questions run deep into the charge of your committee—general education. At present, all campus voices are disciplinary. The cross-disciplinary ones really only transpose the melody an octave upward into a hybrid that is itself disciplinary. Nondisciplinary jobs—mine for example—are immediately dismissed as bureaucratic. Yet everything in the digital revolution and everything in my charge to you moves in the other direction toward some transdisciplinary voice. Where will it come from?

Could it be that in a digital world the lower division of the undergraduate curriculum will change places with the upper? Or will they change at least relative significance and reverse their present figure–ground relationship? The innate logic of the common digital base, at least for the arts and letters, seems to be *relational* rather than *specialized,* which indicates that a very profound reversal will take place. The general education problem was created by disciplinary specialization and the disciplinary major that followed it. Once you define a real university education as a concentration in a specialized subject, preparation for this specialization becomes secondary. But the first two years provide the only possible place for some kind of general education to balance the specialized education to come. So the lower division has become a battleground between general education requirements and major requirements. For the undergraduate it seems only a miscellaneous collection of hurdles obstructing the specialized nirvana of choice. That is where we are now.

The digitization of information, however, changes fundamentally the relationship of the disciplines. To revert again to the world of arts and letters from which I come, having a common digital base for art, music, and literature and a common expressive mode—digital multimedia rather than the printed book—seems to mean that the disciplinary separations we are accustomed to and the departmental structure upon which they are based will dissolve. Consider the new digital-based art forms now emerging—music videos, interactive fictions, interactive digital films, museum displays, motion-based theme park rides, the multimedia editions of Beethoven, Mozart, and Stravinsky pieces that Robert Winter has done for the Voyager Company, the new Voyager CD-ROM edition of *Macbeth*. They all mix words, sounds, and images in new ways, and they don't fit into current disciplinary and departmental structures.

Our students will feel the power of this shift even if we do not. When they look for multimedia modes in the university curriculum, perhaps they will find them in the *non-specialized* part rather than in the major. Although I am not qualified to speak about the sciences, I wonder whether a similar convergence is taking place there. The future felt center of education may lie not in hierarchical disciplinary orders but in some kind of hypertextual interconnection. As an analogy consider distributed computing and single-processor computing or the current management debate between top-down and bottom-up management.

If the center of gravity of the undergraduate curriculum reverses itself, then the nondisciplinary curriculum will constitute the felt center of experience, and once again general education is emerging—but through a technological door rather than a conceptual one. If you contemplate such a reversal—a curricular coherence established by a digital network of interlocking informational bases—you really have a new way to think about general education itself. It has always sought coherence in a central body of knowledge, in a common curriculum pursued in an often mindlessly standardized fashion, and in a definition of itself as in opposition to specialization. But as Alfred North Whitehead made clear long ago, education always strives for an oscillation between these two poles. The general education debate has always been about how we can orchestrate this oscillation. Hasn't the nature of digital information offered us a new, and much better, way to do this?

I've just bet a lot of university money on an emergent field of inquiry called *artificial life,* which explores the digital replication of evolutionary growth in silicon rather than in carbon, as life on earth has up to now been. It also is working on a new, evolutionary way of thinking—a genuine alternative to top-down propositional planning and thought.

Solutions are not imposed or even arrived at through the eureka method but are allowed to evolve from a small group of variables. I'll ask you to look there for wisdom in how to "plan by not planning" a new digital-based curriculum and for stochastic guidance in letting a new series of curricular foci evolve. This could be a really new way to think of the general part of general education.

How Will the Library Constitute a Gateway to the Informational World in Its Charge in this New Curriculum?

Here is a suggestion for how you might think about a new curriculum and a new library within the same intellectual frame. Considered on the largest scale, the undergraduate curriculum is an attention structure. It allocates a scarce commodity—student attention—in what we hope is an optimal way. The real subject of that gateways conference that the library just sponsored was the same thing: "the gateway" as an attempt to allocate scarce student attention in an optimal way.

In an industrial society, the scarce resources are goods and services. In an information society, the scarce commodity is not information—we are choking on that—but the human attention required to make sense of it. Human attention structures work differently from goods and services and will require a new kind of economics and a new kind of economist. The economists have not realized this yet, but then neither have the rest of us. If, in a digital-based information society, a library no longer just collects books but constructs a particular set of attention structures— gateways to information—the librarian and, to personify the problem, the library will be the new "economists."

Libraries have always been in the information business. In the industrial world, though, information came in the form of physical, manufactured, units—books, reports, journals—and thus fit nicely into the dominant quantitative pattern of an industrial society. To see how well you were doing, you need only count your units. If, in such an economy, the person with the most toys wins, by the same logic the library with the most books is the best. Great libraries were made primarily by great collections—of units. Dispensing these units to the end users was a secondary, if often complex, task. I do not mean by this that librarians did not take this task seriously; quite the contrary: the skill and care of reference librarians has always constituted, to my mind, the most dependable excellence in university life. Bibliographers have tried with great skill to anticipate demands in burgeoning fields. But—speaking as an outsider, the library has always seemed to be basically a dispenser of information as required—an information service that aims to have what the user requires.

In a digitized information society, these primary and secondary functions change places. Digitized information is immanent and not physically placed and, unlike the book, can be given away and kept at the same time. In a world of databases, the library with the most units no longer wins. At the same time, the dispensing of information—the new economics of human attention—becomes central. In an information-rich world where human attention is the scarce commodity, the library's business is orchestrating human attention structures. This is an active, not a passive, function, but the design of library shelves has never lent itself to much variation, and the design of human attention structures demands a great deal of it. Essential choices are involved about what is important and what is not. "Architects of great skill" (to borrow a phrase from an eloquent Council on Library Resources pamphlet of several years ago) and with a new kind of training will be required for this kind of design. Where will they come from?

Efficient use of time was not important under the old regime. Leisure was, in fact, the trademark of the university world; efficiency came from the sordid world of commerce. No one thought of faculty time in terms of productivity (a convention still observed in university meetings), and certainly no one thought of student productivity at all. The great pastoral illusion moved in just the opposite direction—a student wandering lost but enrapt in the library stacks of learning.

All of that has changed and will change much more under the twin pressures of financial dearth and information glut. As the library begins to reinvent itself around the metaphor of the gateway, it seems that this gateway must be an active, imaginative creation that is integrally related to the processes of instruction in a fundamentally different way from a collection of books awaiting the student's call slip. The new economics of human attention works very differently from the old economics of book purchase and loan.

The digital curriculum will require profound systems designers—not narrow computer jocks but people aware of the whole intellectual landscape. Someone will have to teach navigational skills of a high order to the students, to create digital networks of student information and publication, to reconfigure knowledge from book-length packets into new forms. Whoever performs all these tasks—creates and manages an undergraduate publishing universe—will play a *central,* not a peripheral or support, role in our new undergraduate curriculum, whatever it looks like. The central informational task in a digital-expressive universe where print and electronic materials must work together is no longer strictly an indexical storage and dissemination task but something quite different.

Is there any pattern for how this new task might be undertaken, or for the library's role in it, in the current convergence of commercial media companies and services? A recent newspaper article, ("Digital Media Business" 1993) analyzed the current merger-prone communications enterprises into their three basic areas of concentration:

· The *content* of digital transmissions, such as databanks, consumer services, music, books, and movies;
· The *delivery* of information over telephone lines, cable television, satellites, and other wireless networks; and
· The *manipulation* of information with operating software, personal computers, hand-held communicators, television controllers, and the like to let consumers filter and customize the flood of data to fit their needs.

If a similar convergence is about to happen within the university, we should be thinking about the organizations on our campus that logically might converge in the same way. I have suggested two—the library and the university press—and there may be others that together can be reincarnated into a new organizational form that might be called a library but which would in truth be a new kind of organization. If so, we will need to train people to run it, and we must train them somewhere. Now that we have abolished the library school, where should that be?

Conclusion

The task that I have laid upon you is a crucial one. We in the administration have been diligent firefighters, trying to extinguish the current fiscal fires, deploying our water buckets with whatever dispatch a cantankerous faculty permits. But all of these efforts have been piecemeal responses to much stronger technological and financial forces. These same forces have fundamentally altered every large corporate enterprise in America that is not a protected monopoly. Our turn is next. There is no point in objecting that "we are not a business" because we are. The proper response is to ponder these forces and the changes they will bring in a properly *academic* context. The context I have asked you to consider is the undergraduate instructional one, and there are others—graduate and professional instruction and the whole domain of organized research. But for an educational institution, the final context in which we consider change must be the curriculum—what we teach, how we teach it, and to whom.

No one can predict the educational patterns that will emerge from changing circumstances of the modern digital world. If I have imposed my own views in any way in my charge to you, perhaps it has been in my feeling that the library may be the place where technology's effect on learning should be addressed. That would require a great change in institutional culture and a lot of money.

Please report back before the sun cools down. And please remember that general education—the student's whole educational experience through time—is the screen on which we must project all our designs and hopes.

References

"Digital Media Business Takes Form as a Battle of Complex Alliances." *Wall Street Journal,* July 14, 1993. p. A1.

Hardison, O. B., Jr. (1989). *Disappearing through the Skylight: Culture and Technology in the Twentieth Century.* New York: Viking Penguin.

Harvard University. (1945). *General Education in a Free Society.* Cambridge, MA: Harvard University. Also known as the *Harvard Red Book.*

12

Information Processing and the Making of Meaning

Karen Price

On my flight back to Boston after a trip out to Apple Computer in California, the pilot said over the intercom: "Good morning, ladies and gentlemen. This is your pilot speaking. We have now reached a cruising altitude of 35,000 feet and are on our way after a considerable ground delay. The good news is that we are making excellent time. The bad news is that we are trying to figure out where we're going."

In a way, this story could be describing how we sometimes plunge into incorporating technology in education. While there appears to be agreement that the gateway library will improve access to information and that it will play an important role in creating a better environment for learning, we need to examine what the gateway endeavor tells us about our beliefs in how people acquire information and develop knowledge.

A well-educated tenth-century monk could never have imagined owning more books than he could read, and even Chaucer, with a library of sixty volumes (Clark 1974), owned more books than anyone else in Europe at the time. It is now estimated that 80 percent of written language already exists in digital form. Today, we strive to make *all* information available to *anyone, anywhere*. Millions of people subscribe to online services that provide access to an abundance of information. Will this information promote the development of knowledge? Even though students may have access to it, learners continue to be biologically finite in what they can attend to meaningfully.

Until the invention of the telegraph, information could be transmitted only at the rate of the speed of a train—35 miles per hour. Today we have increased the speed of information transmission to the point where new technology enables "the Oxford English dictionary and the Bible to be downloaded in seconds." Will speedy transmission promote the development of knowledge?

President Rudenstine (1993, p. 5) has written that Harvard University plans to "invest in new technologies that increase access to the vast information resources and communication networks that exist at Harvard and beyond." Of course, a world-class university must enable its faculty and students to access information, but will this access promote the development of knowledge?

Anyone who receives mail knows that we are inundated with information. Some of us might think that we receive more than our share of the 60 billion (Postman 1992, p. 69) pieces of junk mail the post office delivers to mailboxes each year. With 12,000 periodicals, a quarter of a million billboards, and hundreds of discussion groups on the Internet, people now are being referred to as information processors and the world as information to be processed.

The Russian neurologist Aleksandr Luria (1968) recounts a relevant case history in his book *The Mind of a Mnemonist*. His patient remembered every piece of information and every experience exactly as he had experienced it, and every piece of information and every memory were as clear as every other and were equal in importance to every other. His dilemma illustrates that when the quantity of information is no longer controllable, people have no way of finding meaning in their experience.

While we may sometimes suffer from a lack of information, the quantum increase in both information and interactions is problematic. We spend hours sorting through and replying to e-mail, answering machines at home, and voice mail at the office. We spend hours sifting through periodicals, mail, and faxes. We have seen a dramatic change in the number of personal interactions in which we are involved each day.

But what impact does all this information actually have? Sociologist Neil Postman (1992, p. 60) takes the provocative and somewhat cynical view that "there are very few political, social, and especially personal problems that arise because of insufficient information. . . . Is it lack of information about how to grow food that keeps millions at starvation levels?"

When is access to more information related to the subsequent development of more knowledge? More information is available to us now than ever before, yet this access to information doesn't necessarily make us more knowledgeable. For instance, Buckminster Fuller (1962, pp. 9–10, 20–23) reminds us that even though we have the relevant information, people still speak of the sun setting rather than the earth revolving around the sun. In other words, knowledge is information that makes a difference in the way other information is perceived (Bateson 1972, pp. 457–459).

There is an important distinction between information and knowledge, and the two are not necessarily related. When Einstein wrote that, "Nothing interferes so much with education as schooling," perhaps he was thinking of the misguided emphasis on the rote regurgitation of information that is often mistaken for knowledge. We see this in Eliot Hirsch's best-selling list of (sometimes inaccurate) facts that comprise what the author calls the guide to "cultural literacy" and "what every American needs to know," in *Monarch Notes,* or in their sixteenth-century precursor Ramus, who nimbly reduced all intellectual content to tree diagrams and skeletal outlines. I was astonished to hear Secretary of Education William Bennett, at one of the early meetings of Harvard President Bok's Committee on Assessment, insist that, "Instructors must not teach anything they cannot test. . . . It is better to teach thirteen facts about Napoleon than to spend time in the classroom discussing values clarification."

A discovery made in 1901 by sponge divers off a Greek island also illustrates how information and knowledge sometimes remain unrelated. While looking for sponges, the divers rescued an odd device from the ocean floor. It turned out to be an astronomical computer made by the ancient Greeks (Price 1959, p. 62): "Consisting of a box with dials on the outside and a very complex assembly of gear wheels mounted within, it must have resembled a well-made 18th-century clock. . . . At least twenty gear wheels of the mechanism have been preserved, including a very sophisticated assembly of gears that were mounted eccentrically on a turntable and probably functioned as a sort of epicyclic or differential gear system." Why didn't this ancient computer, a highly sophisticated source of information, add to the Greeks' knowledge base? Because, as Arthur Clarke (1973, p. 116) points out, it "merely *described* the planets' movements; it did not help to *explain* them." The explanation was given hundreds of years later by Galileo, using inclined planes, pendulums, and falling weights.

A New Environment for Learning

With the implementation of the gateway, will the library be the same library we have always known, with the addition of more information and layers of new electronic tools, or will the gateway actually change the reality of the library in more profound ways?

For centuries, every good cook has known that, in order to double the quantity of a dish, she can't just double the quantities of each ingredient without running the risk of concocting a foul-tasting mess. Similarly, Galileo put forth the square-cube law, which says that changing the quantity of something will change its quality. As something doubles in size, its volume will triple and its shape will change. Therefore, enormously huge buildings or ships cannot be built of the same materials *and* maintain the same proportions as the original or they will collapse under their own weight. Either the original proportions have to change, or the materials have to change.

Just as buildings that double in size need significant design changes, the library with the electronic gateway will, in my view, become a new environment for learning. A change of this magnitude in the scale of the library actually will create a change in the institution.

Changes in the storage and distribution of information change the culture and the way that people express themselves. "Is Achilles possible when powder and shot have been invented?" Karl Marx asked (Postman 1992, p. 21). "And is the *Iliad* possible at all when the printing press and even printing machines exist? Is it not inevitable that with the emergence of the press, the singing and the telling and the muse cease; that is, the conditions for epic poetry disappear?"

New technology changes the way we express ourselves as well as the way we learn. The print culture reinforced literacy, and now the oral tradition and long oral recitations of musical poems have, for the most part, been lost. Similarly, automated cash registers increase a reliance on electronic computing, and now, young clerks have difficulty making change without machines. The gateway will change the environment for learning: technology changes our learning environment whether we want it to or not.

First, the source of the learner's information changes. With access to the electronic gateway, the learner no longer relies on the teacher as the sole expert. This shift in the source of information has important implications:

· Learners will be expected to take more responsibility for information gathering through exploring information resources and communication networks.
· The role of the teacher will change to helping the learner sift through, interact with, and make meaning from vast amounts of information.
· Teachers can no longer assume that all students are focusing on the same information at the same time.

Second, the unit of information shifts from books to bits of information. In other words, students will focus on searching through information resources and databases rather than through books on the subject. The Los Angeles County Public Library, the largest circulating library in the country, reports that it receives more requests for information than for books.

Third, the way we search for and locate information changes. The way we search for information influences and sometimes even determines how we develop knowledge, and the way the information is organized obviously defines what we find. I remember how exasperated I was once when I finally found "abortion" listed under "mother and child" in a database. Boolean search logic is very different from traditional browsing in a library. The latter often gives rise to serendipitous discoveries that may make us reformulate our original questions. With an abundance of information, will the searching become so important that we lose the opportunity for the serendipitous associations we used to make when prowling the library's miles of stacks?

Fourth, the model of information distribution changes. As more and more information is electronically stored, our traditional paradigm of information distribution changes. Information that was once stored and distributed (textbooks) is now distributed and stored, as when we search the Internet for information, download, and store relevant information in printouts or on our hard disk. We have evolved from a store-and-distribute paradigm to a distribute-and-store paradigm.

Fifth, the medium of interaction for the learner shifts. Changes in knowledge storage change the mediums of interaction. For Socrates and Plato, the medium of instruction was oral. Learning in an oral medium, when it is not just monologue, results in group work and interpersonal interactions. Learning in a print medium shifts interactions in the direction of more individualized learning.

Technology changes the way we interact with information by changing the media in which we learn. Medical school training illustrates this dramatically. We can trace significant changes in the way medical students have learned and interacted with medical information over the centuries. Initially, doctors dealt directly with the patient's experience and verbal descriptions of their ailments. Later, with more knowledge about the body's systems, doctors began to rely less on the patients' verbal descriptions of their ailments and more on direct observation of the patient's body. Today, with the incorporation of technology in medicine, doctors typically focus most on test results and information obtained through technology. What the patient knows is regarded as untrustworthy; only what the machine knows is considered reliable. It's interesting, however, that doctors who seem even minimally interested in the patient's experience are highly rated by patients. This change in the media of interaction has caused medical educators to debate whether medicine is about the disease or about the patient.

Oliver Wendell Holmes's opposition to the stethoscope may not have been so ridiculous after all. He feared that "interposing an instrument between patient and doctor would transform the practice of medicine" and that, relying more on machinery than on their own experience and insight, "doctors would lose their ability to conduct skillful examinations" (Postman 1992, p. 99). New media change the way we acquire information and, as with medical study, even the focus of the content.

Critics predict that increased computer use will encourage private learning to the detriment of oral skills and group interactions. But any assessment of the computer's role in learning must acknowledge that we can choose to use the same tool in different ways. While print has been emphasized by teachers for the past four centuries, it has not usurped the use of oral instruction and group problem solving. The same can be said for technology.

Several years ago, I began incorporating computer software in my classroom teaching at Harvard using a personal computer with a large-screen display. Although some of the software in the early 1980s was uninspired by current standards, something unexpected took place. The computer display, which all of the students could see and discuss together, served as a marvelous stimulus for student discussion—like a medicine that fails to cure anything but has interesting side effects. My subsequent research showed that more student discussion was generated when information was displayed on the large, shared computer display than when the same information was printed on individual sheets and given to each student. Other researchers have demonstrated repeatedly in a variety of settings how much more students learn when they are working together at a computer terminal than alone.

Finally, the learner becomes more and more responsible for figuring out the context of the information. When information is distributed in small bits rather than in larger contexts such as books, for example, the information may be "context-free." With a statement such as "Researchers today reported that drinking red wine prevents heart attacks," the learner has to determine the context to make meaning of this information. How much red wine? Who were the subjects? How large was the sample size? What was the context in which the red wine was imbibed?

Information Is Not Knowledge

In traditional publishing, information is presented in a very biased way. The learner is shown the editor's views on the relative importance of each piece of information through such attributes as the use of larger and smaller fonts or boxes containing an especially important line or two from the text. Because these typographical clues are typically lacking in the information available on the Internet and other communication networks, learners will have to work harder to construct meaning from that information.

One of the effects of having such an abundance of raw information is that it somehow legitimates that information. Consider a study on how learners acquire information. In 1922, Joseph Weber claimed that his research demonstrated that learners acquire more information through sight than through any other type of experience. By asking students to trace, through introspection, the origin of their knowledge of 250 words back to the "type of experience" through which each was learned, he concluded that half of a learner's knowledge is acquired through visual experience. Similar figures were cited by Ellis and Thornborough in 1923 and by A. P. Hollis in 1928. In 1968 similar statistics were reported by Ted C. Cobun, in 1973 James Kinder quoted Cobun's figures, and in 1976 Randhawa cited similar figures again. The same bit of information has been picked up, restated, and legitimated over and over again, and few scholars—even those involved in multimedia today—realize that these familiar and ubiquitous figures were probably based on one highly questionable experiment that took place more than fifty years ago.

This is a wonderful example of how information is mistaken for knowledge and how we become preoccupied with information and then lose our ability to question or recognize the wisdom behind the knowledge.

In Plato's *Phaedrus* (Postman 1992, p. 4) Theuth shows his invention—writing—to King Thamus, claiming that it will "improve both the wisdom and memory of the Egyptians . . . a sure receipt for memory and wisdom." But in a provocative and thoughtful rebuttal, the king replies, "Your pupils will have the reputation for [wisdom] without the reality; they will receive a quantity of information without proper instruction, and in consequence be thought very knowledgeable when they are for the most part quite ignorant. And because they are filled with the conceit of wisdom instead of real wisdom they will be a burden to society."

Now that we can store and distribute information on a vast scale, we are sometimes overtaken by a sense of wonder, as in a magic show when our attention is directed to the wrong place. Figures are repeated over and over: "Laserdiscs hold 54,000 frames!" "The new Sony MD format will hold 140 megabytes of information!" These are not irrelevant facts, but we need to ask *why* we want to store and generate more information than ever before and *how* we can interact with all that information to develop knowledge.

How can the learner develop knowledge from information? Consider a Harvard pilot study that was sponsored by the Office of Information Technology, Kodak, and McGraw-Hill. Picking and choosing from an online database of copyright-cleared materials provided by McGraw-Hill, English as a second language instructors created customized textbooks and handouts that could be printed as needed here on campus. Instructors incorporated excerpts from authors such as Robert Frost, Russell Baker, Joyce Carol Oates, and Studs Terkel, from articles in the *New York Times, Business Week,* and *Harper's,* and from existing ESL textbooks, along with their own handouts.

I then electronically scanned in hundreds of pages of these materials to make a machine-readable database that instructors could search for readings, articles, and poems that have high-frequency occurrences of the particular grammar, idiomatic, or lexical items they were trying to teach. An instructor teaching conjunctions, for example, can use a software concordancer I wrote to show additional instances of the use of *however* in the literature pages of their customized textbook, and students can use hard-copy indexes to find the pages where particular points of grammar occur in their customized textbooks.

This pilot demonstrates how information can be transformed from a static document to a dynamic, multipurpose learning tool. It also demonstrates the shift from the store-and-distribute paradigm that produced traditional text materials to the distribute-and-store paradigm in which articles are downloaded from a database to create customized textbooks. We are not just transporting information to a new medium; we are transforming learning.

These "new and improved" technological approaches sometimes mislead us into thinking that they have no connection with the past and that traditional methods are inherently inadequate. However, the gateway embodies many pedagogical values from the past—John Dewey's concern that schooling not be separate from the curriculum; Quintilian's suggestion in the first century A.D. that learners be motivated and helped to develop skills at finding information so they can be self-directed learners;

and Comenius's seventeenth-century suggestion that information and knowledge be related to people's needs. Comenius even conceived of a world university where scholars would pool knowledge to solve problems. The gateway must, as Larry Dowler (1993, p. 8) writes, be a center for learning as much as an access to resources. We must develop interfaces—both human and technological—that help learners select information and interact with it meaningfully in order to develop knowledge.

Whether the gateway actually helps create a better environment for learning depends as much on our goals as on the tools provided. A marketing executive "once noted that people do not buy quarter-inch drills because they want quarter-inch drills. They buy quarter-inch drills because they want quarter-inch holes" (Perelman 1992, p. 24). As enthusiastic proponents of technology, let us remember to clarify our goals as we continue to identify and evaluate ways in which our use of the gateway may contribute to a better environment for learning.

References

Bateson, Gregory. 1972. *Steps to an Ecology of Mind*. New York: Ballantine.

Clarke, Arthur. 1973. "Technology and the Limits of Knowledge." In *Technology and the Frontiers of Knowledge: The Frank Nelson Doubleday Lectures at the Smithsonian*. New York: Doubleday.

———. 1974. "Aladdin's Lamp." In *Dimensions of the Future*, edited by Maxwell H. Norman. New York: Holt, Rhinehart and Winston.

Cobun, Ted C. 1968. *Instructional Process and Media Innovation*. Edited by Robert A. Weisgerber. Chicago: Rand McNally.

Dowler, Lawrence. 1993. "The Gateway." Discussion paper presented at the "Gateways to Knowledge" conference held at Harvard University, November 5–6.

Ellis, D. C., and L. Thornborough. 1923. *Motion Pictures in Education*. New York: Crowell.

Hollis, A. P. 1928. *Motion Pictures for Instruction*. New York: Century-Crofts.

Kinder, J. S. 1965. *Using AV Materials in Education*. New York: American Book Co.

———. 1973. *Using Instructional Media*. New York: Van Nostrand.

Lamberski, Richard, ed. 1976. *Association for Educational Communications and Technology, Research and Theory Division, Newsletter 5*, no. 3 (November): 14.

Luria, Aleksandr. 1968. *The Mind of a Mnemonist*. New York: Basic Books.

Perelman, Lewis J. 1992. *School's Out: Hyperlearning, the New Technology, and the End of Education.* New York: Morrow.

Postman, Neil. 1992. *Technopoly: The Surrender of Culture to Technology.* New York: Knopf.

Price, Derek J. de Solla. 1959. "An Ancient Greek Computer." *Scientific American* 200, no. 6 (June): 62.

Pulliam, John D., and Jim R. Bowman. 1974. *Educational Futurism: In Pursuance of Survival.* Norman: University of Oklahoma Press.

Randhawa, Bikkar S. and William E. Coffman, eds. 1976. *Visual Learning, Thinking, and Communication.* New York: Academic Press.

Rudenstine, Neil. 1993. "Open Letter from the President." *Harvard Gazette* LXXXIX, no. 8 (October 15): 1, 9–10.

Weber, Joseph J. 1922. "Relation of Experience to Learning. *Educational Screen* 1 (November–December): 315–317.

13

Homesteading on the Electronic Frontier: Technology, Libraries, and Learning

James Wilkinson

What are university libraries for? This complex question used to have a simple answer. Like the institutions they served, university libraries fulfilled the double role of preserving knowledge and promoting discovery. They acquired and preserved books and periodicals, artifacts and archives and, at the same time, made these treasures available to a community of users as a resource for scholarship. In the minds of library users (though perhaps not of librarians), libraries did not exist as ends in themselves. Rather, they provided means required for *other* ends—study, learning, and research—by preserving the written word. In this sense they resembled their great predecessor, the library of the Museum of Alexandria, created two millennia ago to house the learning of the Hellenistic world.

Lately, however, the double function of university libraries has begun to change. For a variety of interconnected reasons, our definition of *information* itself has broadened, and so have information and preservation methods. In addition to books, periodicals, maps, and archives—information encoded chiefly as written language—libraries increasingly house phonograph records, audiotapes, compact discs, photographs, videotapes, and, most recently, electronically stored computer data. This shift toward the visual end of the spectrum mirrors the changing needs of users. Students raised in an age of television and professors who once were content to consult written archives exclusively now desire access to a broad variety of resources—audio, visual, and material. An additional incentive for change is the financial cost of accumulating and storing print materials in the old way. Librarians cannot afford (in the most literal sense) to cling to accustomed ways of discharging their responsibilities to the academic community.

Another force driving these changes is technology. Information technology has transformed data storage of all kinds. Crumbling books printed on aging, acidic paper can now be rescued as ASCII files through optical scanning, and contemporary periodicals can be stored in electronic archives. But preserving the written word is only a small part of what technology allows libraries to offer. Through digitized images students can voyage on a computer-simulated trip through Beijing's Forbidden City or study three-dimensional color models of complex proteins. The Perseus Project, initiated almost a decade ago by Harvard and Brown Universities, has made available a growing portion of the entire corpus of classical civilization—Greek texts, vase paintings, ground plans of temples—at the click of a mouse. Both texts and images can be linked for remote viewing. From the computer on which I am now writing, I can call up pictures of the Parthenon or stanzas by Sappho or an artist's reconstruction of the Museum at Alexandria.

One of the most powerful aspects of this revolution in information technology is the remote access it permits users who are physically separated from the library or computer mainframe on which this information is stored. We now have a growing virtual library of electronically encoded data that can be consulted from anywhere in the world. In addition to being physical repositories of material, libraries now increasingly serve as access points for the electronic network on which the virtual library resides. Hence the concept of library as gateway—not only a place to store research materials but also a portal through which electronic information can pass to the user.

As library functions broaden with the growth of technology, librarians are expanding their own role within colleges and universities and asserting the need and desirability to act as teachers as well as custodians of information. In part this move reflects the changing wishes of their clientele. Undergraduates now use research libraries such as Harvard's Widener Library as part of their normal studies—especially when conducting small research projects such as term papers. The concept of the "librarian as teacher" acknowledges that a great deal of learning occurs in libraries (as well as in the classroom) as a result of these student research activities and that librarians are in a good position to facilitate that learning. The emerging importance of technology within the library precincts also leads to the need for experts who can initiate library users into the *arcana imperii* of digital software. Just as teaching hospitals are attached to university medical schools, we can establish teaching libraries where students learn about research firsthand. Here librarians clearly have an important role to play.

But there is more. Librarians have sought to engage themselves more actively in teaching at the very time that teaching and learning themselves are being reexamined and redefined within the university as a whole. Since the early 1980s, public interest in improving and redefining teaching has sparked an ongoing reform movement within American education. Educators have focused in part on investigating how students actually learn. In the old model, teachers actively dispensed knowledge and students passively benefited from their wisdom, but the new model increasingly emphasizes partnership, problem solving, and active learning.

We have realized that traditional, top-down teaching often educates students only superficially. If teachers dispense knowledge without also focusing on how it is received and whether it is retained, they are almost guaranteed that it will be badly learned: memorized lecture notes have a short half-life and are quickly forgotten. Yet when students actively participate in the pursuit of knowledge—whether through discussing their readings in section or asking questions in lecture or exploring the real world in field trips or laboratory exercises—they generally absorb material better and retain it longer. Increasingly, teachers share the process of investigation, as well as sharing its results, with their students. The New Pathways curriculum at the Harvard Medical School represents just one of many examples of the growing commitment to problem-based learning on the university level.[1]

Thus in the current debate over university libraries and their future, three distinct movements converge. New forms of information, new financial constraints, and new technologies have transformed library holdings (whether actual or virtual) in dramatic ways. Librarians themselves now aspire to expand their traditional reference functions to include an active partnership in teaching. And teaching itself, which both libraries and technology attempt to serve, is being reconceived as a complex process of learner-centered teaching and active learning that is guided by a teacher who is no longer a distant authority but a concerned and committed guide.

Is there common ground and common purpose among these movements? If we imagine a Venn diagram of intersecting circles, do all three converge somewhere in comfortable superposition? In what follows, I argue that common ground does indeed exist and that a promising way to explore and exploit that common ground is through the strategic use of information technology. But I also argue that the very technology that makes possible a richer partnership among librarians and learners poses dangers as well. No innovation is without cost. Information technology creates problems for libraries as well as solves them; it can overwhelm as well as instruct, constrain as well as liberate. Some advocates of information technology argue for its use as if the possibilities it allows will cure any and all problems in academe. Yet if librarians are to play a truly useful role in the emerging electronic classroom, they will be the critics as well as advocates of information technology.

Traffic Jams on the Information Superhighway

Before the electronic age, historians observed (and even complained) that the challenge of writing about ancient history was that too little evidence had survived and that the challenges of writing about contemporary history was the reverse. But for today's classical scholars, the advent of the Perseus Project and the Internet means that information is no longer such a scarce commodity. Indeed, the problem of confronting too much rather than too little data has now become frustratingly familiar to scholars from many disciplines. Anyone wishing to write a biography of the late President Kennedy, for example, must resist the temptation to explore more than just a portion of the Kennedy papers. It would take years of continuous reading to exhaust the holdings of the John F. Kennedy Library in Boston alone. How many journal articles and books on the Kennedy White House should a researcher consult? The secondary literature is enough to cause serious scholarly indigestion before the main course has begun, and more is being published all the time.

Yet despite this information glut, much of the thinking about new college and university libraries has focused on the problem of information access. The assumption seems to be that scholars and students are primarily starved for evidence, desperate for another digitized document or a longer list of scholarly monographs in their field and that the more evidence put at their disposal, the better. Students and faculty can be assured of obtaining the maximum amount of information through electronic bibliographic aids such as Harvard's HOLLIS. And as software programs such as Motion Picture Experts Group (MPEG) become more sophisticated, library online offerings will increasingly include digitized videos of lectures, film clips, and science experiments, as well as the more traditional fare of text and still pictures. An art history student can use her computer to pull up images of all of the Sistine Chapel ceiling, both before and after the recent restorations of Michelangelo's frescoes. A government student can access transcripts of the latest congressional debates in Washington or view excerpts of debate coverage by C-Span. Desiderius Erasmus once dreamed of a library "with no limits other than the world itself." The virtual library is now making that possibility a reality.

But a question remains: Is all this information a good thing? Here I have my doubts. Unless they are sifted through and selected in a useful way, facts remain brute facts—lifeless, inert, like bricks piled in a brickyard waiting for a mason. Bits of information need first to be screened and sorted before they can be assembled into creative patterns. Without the ability to view information selectively, users experience an increase in volume as a liability rather than an advantage. Being swamped with "infojunk" does not necessarily satisfy the user's research needs.

What tools are available for someone who wishes to actively interact with the facts circulating along the electronic superhighway? The links available through Gopher, Mosaic, World Wide Web, and other search programs on the Internet are powerful and growing more so. But though their power has increased, the sheer volume of information available online has swelled even more rapidly. As of February 1995 there were over five million documents on the Web, a number that is expected to double every six months, and also 27,000 Web sites, a figure that now doubles every fifty-three days (*Business Week* 1995). There are, of course, reasons for this imbalance between information and access: it is far easier to create databases of raw data such as the 1990 United States Census results than it is to create links between *types* of information. Thus while the tools for facilitating access to information have improved, the proportion of data that is useful has decreased. In a sense, we remain far better at storing information in the virtual library than at extracting it with any degree of efficiency.

A major problem affecting the system that links components of the virtual library such as relational databases and hypertext is that it is horizontal and not vertical. In democratic fashion, it treats all data equally. Like is linked to like in a web of information where the primary question is not "How important is this?" but "What does this remind you of?" Thus we can navigate from California census data to information about highway use to data on air pollution, or from Sophocles to a picture of the Greek theater at Delphi to a digitized recording of the opening lines of the *Oresteia*. This is not a trivial achievement, and in practice the navigating certainly is not uninteresting. Browsers surfing the Internet or multimedia databases find it both stimulating and instructive. But the ordering of information on the Internet or in a keyword search (say, for articles dealing with AIDS) does not allow the user to discriminate between what is more and less important. The small traces of verticality that persist lie in the ability of hypertext to provide definitions of key terms or to offer users more information on the Emperor penguin's nesting habits when they double-click on the image of a bird. But this shallow verticality is not the same as an inductive chain that follows the logic of rational argument—first read A, then read B, and then read C—where the last can be understood only once you have absorbed the first two. Compared with this higher-order linking, the prevailing logic of electronic linking is primitive indeed.

The information superhighway, in other words, provides too much information and too little organization. Busy users—especially academic users—need a reliable system of triage that is not based on similarity alone. If I set out to write a history of postwar European immigration or a stylistic analysis of Henry James's *The Ambassadors*, I want to access essential data without being overwhelmed by hundreds of titles of learned articles whose quality I cannot test or control without reading them (and thereby defeating the purpose of triage). What I need is not more information but the *right* information. In some instances, this means only a very modest amount. The German literary scholar Erich Auerbach produced one of the great works of twentieth-century literary criticism, *Mimesis,* while in political exile in Istanbul during World War II and credited his success in part to the fact that Turkish libraries stocked so few Western scholarly journals. As he wrote in a now-famous afterword (Auerbach 1988, p. 518), "It is very likely that this book has seen the light thanks precisely to the absence of a large research library. Had I been able to inform myself about all that scholars have written on so many topics, I might never have gotten to the point of writing [my book] at all."

Who will perform the complex triage that separates what the researcher needs to know from the mass of the second- or third-order information that threatens to overwhelm her? How can we combine access with selectivity? Some traffic-watchers on the information superhighway, such as Danny Goodman (1994, pp. 126–128), have argued that programmable "agents" can do this work for us. Electronic instructions fed to the computer would allow it to identify those items we wish to retrieve from the mass of available information. But I think that a far better human agent is at hand—reference librarians. So far, much of the organization of the various databases available through the virtual library has been done by programmers rather than by people whose professional expertise lies in the area of research and the organization of research materials. If, as some have suggested, students will increasingly read custom-crafted sourcebooks created from electronically stored text, then reference librarians can play a major role in shaping course readings as well as access to research materials.

In order to discharge this role, librarians will need extensive computer training and ongoing technical support. But their most important responsibility will be to know what information technology is good for rather than simply how it works. Today the challenge in adapting technology to meet the needs of librarians and library users alike is not simply or even primarily technical: rather, it is conceptual. Existing technologies—not to mention those to be developed in coming years—far outstrip our ability to make use of them. It is a little like having an eight-cylinder

Ferrari for a five-mile daily commute; the tool is impressive, but its full power cannot be brought to bear on the task at hand. We need somehow to match educational goals with technological means when those means are changing rapidly and when we still have not fully exploited yesterday's, let alone today's, information technology for educational purposes.

The Challenge of Active Learning

What are our educational goals? This question should precede any thinking about university use of information technology, but in fact, it seems most often to be asked as an afterthought. Next I would ask, How does information technology enhance learning?[2] We should start with the conditions that promote learning and work back from there. Much of what we hear about information technology presents it as a solution, but what problems does it solve? The pedagogical issues that technology is supposed to resolve will remain vague until we define teaching and learning problems in a more concrete manner. Only then will we be able to tell whether this technology simply replaces existing teaching tools at greater cost or provides something genuinely new.

So how *do* students learn? A growing body of research on learning suggests that while different styles do exist, there are some common features to all learning that can be reproduced in new situations—that is, learning based on an understanding of concepts rather than on rote memorization alone. Many bright and even average students can produce a facsimile of learning that allows them to do well on examinations if those exams simply test memory. But what really counts is transferable knowledge—learning students can take out of the classroom and apply to other courses, to other problems, and to life. For this to happen, at least three conditions must be present. First, students must be motivated; they must experience a "need to know" derived from curiosity, ambition, or conscience. Second, students must actively engage in the learning process rather than passively absorb information like so many sponges. Active involvement means reading, discussing, and problem solving in the area of study—efforts that involve the analysis, deduction, and reproduction of learned material. Finally, students must be able to use what they have learned by taking it into an arena beyond the classroom, even if that arena is *another* classroom. Conceptual understanding and not simple mimicry should be the goal.[3]

Problem solving, as noted above, is a key element of this sort of learning, a lesson that has not been lost on faculty. In field after field, teaching has come more and more to resemble the practice of research. Teachers increasingly involve students in solving puzzles as well as memorizing facts. The facts, of course, form an essential foundation for successful research or problem solving, but they are not ends in themselves. My favorite example of this approach is the New Pathways curriculum at Harvard Medical School, where first-year students are given an actual case of forensic detection to begin their studies and in so doing briefly enter the world of international espionage. The case concerns Georgi Dimitrov, a Bulgarian dissident living in London during the 1970s, who one day experiences a sharp pain in his calf while waiting for a bus. A fellow passenger has just stabbed him in the leg with a pointed umbrella. The umbrella is poisoned, and within thirty-six hours poor Dimitrov is dead. But how was he murdered?

In order to solve this case, students must understand the circulatory system, the effect of poisons on muscle tissue, and the time it takes them to spread throughout the body. They have to research these aspects of anatomy and toxicology and determine how they apply to the case of Georgi Dimitrov. Just like Sherlock Holmes, who could recognize at a glance the soil types to be found within a twenty-mile radius of London, medical students master a set of highly specialized data in order to be able to solve concrete problems. The case of the Bulgarian dissident carries with it a pedagogical message: true learning means being able to use what you know in novel ways.

Most recent developments in information technology, however, seem to ignore the direction in which educational reform is moving. Courseware seems stuck in the old world of rote memorization and "learning as reproduction"—as if software developers and educational innovators live on separate planets instead of being connected by e-mail and the Internet. One problem inherent in much existing pedagogical software is that it does not focus on problem solving at all but rather functions as a sort of super encyclopedia, facilitating access to facts galore. Hypertext, that set of embedded footnotes, helps students to gather information about definitions of terms and allows them to find out more about Dickens's childhood. But it is just information. Addressing the problem of learning involves going beyond acquisition of information, even through horizontal links, to a creative interaction with that data. Rather than simply learn new definitions for the constituent parts of plant cells or view the ruins of Teotihuacán in digitized color, students would be challenged to do something that the software developers never even dreamed of. They need what some have termed an "intellectual sandbox," not just a photo album.

This limitation is especially vivid in the realm of testing and examination. A number of computer courseware companies offer so-called "self-paced" learning programs—drill on irregular French verbs or the periodic table of the elements—that students conduct at their own speed and repeat as many times as they like. Such programs help students to memorize difficult material, but the sort of testing that occurs in self-paced learning is often exclusively multiple choice. Multiple-choice tests are fine for reminding students of the forms of the present subjunctive for the verb *être*. They are far less appropriate for courseware that deals with, say, American history, where the mismatch between computer technology and current pedagogy is most apparent. Few teachers would argue that multiple-choice testing measures student learning in subjects where complex phenomena and multiple causality are the rule, yet cutting-edge technology in effect forces them to regress in their choice of testing instruments and make do with the exams of yesterday.

Current technology thus limits certain kinds of teaching and learning while facilitating others. Although it is now possible to take electronic field trips, exploring remote terrain without leaving the classroom and its video monitor, what information technology does best is to anticipate the expected. Interactive videodisks, for example, allow students to ask questions about what they see and receive answers—but only answers to those questions that the programmers have foreseen. Similarly, a bibliographic search conducted through the use of keywords depends on a close match between user interest and librarian choice to be effective. An article filed under "French nationalism" will not help me if I look it up under the subject heading "de Gaulle" and vice versa. For technology that is not directed at conversations in the present, such as e-mail and teleconferencing, it is almost impossible to anticipate all the quirks of viewer response. A classroom presentation heavily dependent on such technology is difficult for faculty to adapt to the whims and queries of the class. I remember one lecturer, armed with an impressive array of computer-controlled slides and video clips, who eventually told his class to stop asking him questions because they interfered with his carefully crafted presentation and threw him off stride. He could have taught better with no computer at all.

Perhaps the most potentially useful computer courseware programs allow students to visualize the results of laboratory experiments or to simulate changes in a controlled environment through computer modeling. Sim City, a commercially available program on urban design, allows students to play with various urban plans but also requires them to provide adequate power and city services to city residents and balance the city budget. An interactive videodisk developed at Harvard Law School provides another sort of simulation—a dramatic chase of a narcotics suspect that ends in a conviction—provided that the student requests a judge to provide a new search warrant at a crucial juncture. If the student fails to do so, the case is dismissed. Such programs hint at ways in which computer technology can expand student horizons rather than limit them, especially by inviting students to play and experiment in the electronic sandbox. But so far these programs remain rare.[4] Even the best of them only supplement—albeit compellingly—more traditional instruction.

Libraries Old and New

Librarians can provide the missing link between technology and learning by understanding both. Libraries have always been involved in the problem-solving game. Their materials exist to facilitate research. They acquire books, tapes, and artifacts not because they know for certain how they will be used but "just in case," because they believe that they may be useful in some manner as yet unknown. Acquisitions policy involves faith in the future on a grand scale, and we should extend to our students that faith in the capacity of exploring minds. The ideal would therefore be a library that enables the students to solve problems better: that, after all, is the very heart of research and learning.

A point of entry for libraries to aid learning through technology lies first in aiding students and faculty to maneuver onto the information superhighway. Just as librarians used to walk students through the mysteries of the card catalog, now they explain how to use an electronic listing of library holdings such as Harvard University's HOLLIS. They also help students and faculty learn how to navigate on the Internet. By linking information to research needs, libraries may even be able to perform triage for their clients—that crucial editorial function that has so far been all too rare. A literature search in HOLLIS or ERIC could yield a list of the most often requested items or even a "librarians' choice" list similar to that found in some local bookstores. Since libraries provide information about how to access other information, they can offer useful filters to students and faculty in need of them—a version of the information superhighway where not all the lanes of traffic drive along at equal speed. Clearly, this filtering must be done intelligently and not capriciously. But who better suited to the task than those who understand *both* the available resources and the needs of the client—the librarians?

Given the rapidly changing computer environment, libraries are needed to keep users informed of the latest research tools as well. One clear advantage that libraries possess over individuals in the burgeoning new world of multimedia is efficient use of resources. Because computers and their software are expensive, libraries can afford newer and better models than all but the wealthiest individuals and more important, can provide experts to help clients use them effectively. Wasted user time should not be one of the hidden costs of new technology. On the contrary, in order to amortize their share of the information superhighway, universities need to make it available even to the technologically challenged. As William Geoghegan (1994) recently noted, instructional technology has yet to be broadly adopted in part because the technology fraternity that created it is by definition a minority and one that has trouble understanding the fears and concerns of the rest of us. Thus in order to gain access to the latest and best hardware and software, students and faculty may come to rely on college libraries every bit as much as on media centers or computer labs.

Some of this library teaching can be direct and face to face, but a good deal also can occur online. As custodian of an electronic archive, the university library might host or facilitate electronic discussions concerning the material available at the virtual library—interest-group conversations similar to those that now occur on the Internet. Librarians also can offer research advice online. For example, a user group focused on Latin American history could post questions about library holdings to the library expert in charge of Spanish or Latin American acquisitions and receive replies. Suggestions for acquisitions could be solicited in this way, as could general comments about the quality of library services. Electronic mail, as we are beginning to discover, is an excellent vehicle for feedback. So is conferencing—the use of computer-based communications to supplement in-class discussions.

Information technology facilitates assessment. Faculty comments on student papers, student questions about faculty lectures, midsemester and postsemester course evaluations—all flow with greater ease across a campus that has an electronic information network. Such a network can exist independently of the university library, but since the library will be tied directly into the network through its catalog and various online services, an extension of its role in order to promote evaluation seems only natural. Just as librarians advise about reference holdings, they also could offer advice on evaluation, especially if they have been trained in the arts of electronic triage. They even could benefit from more frequent user evaluations of their own performance. Conferencing is a powerful tool that libraries can adopt to spark ongoing debate about their aims, client wishes, and possible new services. Thus technology can bring librarians closer to the people whose scholarly and educational needs they are pledged to meet.

Does all this mean that the library as a physical space has become obsolete? I would argue that, on the contrary, its usefulness as a teaching space remains unimpaired and may even increase. A great deal of teaching still requires direct contact to be truly effective. In general, students continue to express a wish for more interaction with faculty and with one another and not less. Just as some of the research formerly done in libraries is now done in faculty offices or student dorm rooms—with a personal computer serving as a study carrel—so can some of the group learning that formerly occurred exclusively in classrooms now take place in libraries. This is especially true for teaching that makes use of specialized technology that would be expensive to duplicate in every classroom. Experimental teaching areas with a heavy computer and AV presence are now almost exclusively the province of those working in university computer services, and they know a great deal about the hardware but often little about how to adapt it for teaching needs. Here it seems to me that libraries could usefully supplement or even take the lead in providing a learning environment where information technology is made available with some thought to how learning really occurs.

Indeed, most learning—even with a strong element of technological assistance—will in the future continue to integrate old and new methodologies. Videotaped scenes of past historical events will help to spark classroom discussions conducted in the traditional way. Group research results can be shared with other research teams thousands of miles away through teleconferencing, but then work in the individual laboratory will go on as before. Conferencing through information technology networks can enhance collaborative learning but cannot replace the warmth and support of student-teacher contact, just as a telephone conversation cannot completely supplant face-to-face dialog. Were this so, there would be no need for diplomatic summit meetings, sessions of the United States Congress, or business lunches, and human beings would communicate exclusively by phone, fax, or e-mail. Some of our learning in the future may indeed resemble NASA mission control in Houston, where telecommunications feeds information to a group assembled in the same space, and where deliberations among that group are improved by the quality of the information received. But most will continue to require the warmth and wealth of cues that are possible only when we confront one another directly. The task is therefore to find the educational uses for which computers are best suited—a task in which librarians, once again, can play an essential role.

Technology may even help to increase direct human contact in the classroom. Over the past four years, the Derek Bok Center and Dr.

Marlies Mueller of the Harvard Romance Languages Department have jointly been developing an interactive videodisk for instructors in elementary French. The videodisk itself contains classroom scenes—some positive, some negative—while the computer program asks apprentice teachers to respond to what they see. Part of their response involves answering questions, which (because of the limits of technology) are inevitably multiple-choice. But another part consists of entering comments in a notebook. Here the unexpected result of the interactive videodisk training has been to promote group discussion as trainees jointly craft and edit a response. Was the teacher on the screen explaining her point clearly? If not, why not? What would have been better? It is difficult to imagine that the discussion would be so lively without the inspiration of a classroom scene viewed on laser disk; but neither would it be so spirited without the group itself—real people arguing in a real space in real time.

What changes will be created by the meeting of technology, libraries, and learning? Many future developments remain hidden behind bends in the information superhighway. Future technologies will doubtless become more flexible than their current prototypes; perhaps we will even get beyond multiple-choice questions in our software. Libraries will continue to interpret the brave new world of information technology to their clients and continue to serve as repositories for nonelectronic treasures such as books, prints, and artifacts. But the convergence between research and learning suggests that librarians can also play an increasingly useful role in doing what I have tried to do in this article—point out some of the pitfalls of technology in the classroom as well as its merits and think about how best to integrate old teaching methods with the new.

What are libraries for? To their two traditional roles as custodians of knowledge and hosts for creative research, I would suggest that we add a third role—as locus and advocate for electronic teaching. This role will mean creating new partnerships among librarians, faculty, and students and pursuing an ongoing effort to master technologies subject to constant change. The alternative is for virtual libraries to become the only real game in town, which would be a great and irreparable loss. As Richard Lanham (see chapter 11) has argued, in an information-rich world, "the scarce commodity is . . . the human attention." Dispensing information in a way that increases the human attention paid to our students and faculty and that enhances learning and research is a challenge for which the university library is ideally suited.

Acknowledgments

The author wishes to thank Daniel Goroff for his suggestions and help in the preparation of this chapter.

Notes

1. For a discussion of both the strengths and weaknesses of this approach to teaching, see Patel, Groen, and Norman (1991) and Tostesen (1990).

2. Information technology also may hold down staff and administrative costs, but that should not be its *primary* use in a university library system.

3. On the premises of active learning, see Bruer (1993).

4. On the pedagogical promise and pitfalls of computer technology in the classroom, see Boettcher (1994).

References

Auerbach, Erich. 1988. *Mimesis: Dargestellte Wirklichkeit in der abendländischen Literatur.* Bern: Franke Verlag.

Boettcher, Judith V., et al. 1994. *One Hundred One Success Stories of Information Technology in Higher Education: The Joe Wyatt Challenge.* New York: McGraw-Hill.

Bruer, John T. 1993. *Schools for Thought: A Science of Learning in the Classroom.* Cambridge, MA: MIT Press.

Cortese, Amy, John Veritz, Russell Mitchell, and Richard Brandt. 1995. "Cyberspace." *Business Week* (27 February): 78–86.

Geoghegan, William. 1994. "What Ever Happened to Instructional Technology?" Paper presented at the "Twenty-second Conference of the International Business Schools Computing Association" held at Baltimore, MD, 17–20 July.

Goodman, Danny. 1994. *Living at Light Speed.* New York: Random House.

Patel, Vimla L., Guy J. Groen, and Geoffrey R. Norman. 1991. "Effects of Conventional and Problem-Based Medical Curricula on Problem Solving." *Academic Medicine* 66, no. 7 (July): 380–389.

Tostesen, Daniel C. 1990. "New Pathways in General Medical Education." *New England Journal of Medicine* 322, no. 4: 234–238.

VI

Tools for Learning

The two chapters in this part could easily have been included elsewhere. Anita Lowry's discussion of the Information Arcade at the University of Iowa reflects some of the same practical considerations of the gateway expressed by other librarians presented here; the Information Arcade is an example of a library in transition. Roy Rosenzweig and Steve Brier describe a software program, a computer textbook, but are most concerned about demonstrating the benefits of their application for learning and might easily have been included in that part. In fact, both chapters provide insights into some of the specific advantages and benefits of technology for both students and teachers; they come together, I think, in finding solutions to pedagogical issues by developing appropriate technological tools. What also unites their presentations is their emphasis on the importance of primary sources and the role technology plays in making them more accessible. Seeing primary sources from which a text or document has been created permits a student to begin the process of analysis that many believe is the essential ingredient in education and learning. From this perspective, technology is not just something the library must accommodate or respond to but an opportunity to improve the quality of education and redirect library support to teaching and learning.

14

Gateways to the Classroom

Anita Lowry

In the spring semester of 1993, Brooks Landon, a professor in the English Department at the University of Iowa, taught a course entitled "Literature and Culture of Twentieth Century America," which focused on how technology has affected literary culture in the twentieth century (Landon 1993b). A central concern of this course was the meaning and implications of the 1893 World's Columbian Exposition in Chicago, a great cultural event that served to officially introduce Americans to the twentieth century.

It was not the first time that he had taught this course, but it *was* the first time that he had taught it in an electronic classroom. With the special facilities of this classroom, Professor Landon was able to use The White City, an ambitious hypertext database that he is creating about the Columbian Exposition, to guide his students through a multimedia tour of documents, images, and interpretations of the fair. Instead of writing term papers, the students in the class researched and prepared their own hypertext mini-database on topics relating to the exposition and thus made their own contributions to the ongoing development of The White City database.

In discussing the course with a colleague, Professor Landon (1993a) expressed great pleasure with the quality of the work done by the students in the class. He considered one of the most impressive indicators of the success of this electronic course and its unorthodox assignment to be that students in this class had done much more research and made greater use of primary source materials than undergraduate students usually do. They sought out a wide range of contemporary source materials on turn-of-the-century America from the library's stacks and special collections in order to analyze, digitize, and incorporate them into their multimedia projects.

Primary sources—whether the creative works of the human imagination or the documentary records of human affairs or the experimental and empirical data of the human and natural sciences—do not yield their secrets readily. They do not come to students with their multiple layers of meaning predigested and transparent or their contradictions and paradoxes smoothed away. They may reflect a time or place far removed from the student's experience and learning or provide evidence of a world inaccessible to the student's senses. Teaching students about the nature and use of primary source materials and teaching them the special analytical skills that these sources demand are among the challenges that faculty face in both graduate and undergraduate courses. Just getting undergraduates interested in primary sources may be the first and greatest hurdle.

While I would not argue that electronic resources are a panacea for teaching students to appreciate primary sources, I *would* argue that they can be an invaluable tool for this purpose. Electronic texts with text analysis programs, numeric databases and statistical or mapping software, digital images and image analysis software, hypermedia databases linking primary sources with commentary and reference sources—all these resources present source materials to students in completely new ways. They make source materials both more accessible to students and less accessible, and it is by virtue of both of these seemingly contradictory characteristics that they make such excellent teaching tools.

On the one hand, electronic databases can bring together materials from a great variety of sources, many of them obscure or difficult to locate, and put them literally at the fingertips of scholars and students. While both librarians and faculty are accustomed to thinking of this kind of accessibility as an aid to research or independent learning, it can just as certainly be a boon to lecturing and discussion in the classroom. At Stanford University, in an undergraduate English course nicknamed "Electronic Chaucer," Professor Mary Wack and her students used a large collection of images in an online database, the Stanford Humanities Image Archive, to explore manuscripts, art works, maps, and other documents of medieval culture. In this database each image can be accompanied by up to thirty-five pages of information, commentary, and bibliography, and the images and text may rapidly be retrieved, displayed, juxtaposed, and examined, inside or outside of the classroom. Here is how Professor Wack (1993, p. 9) describes one of the ways her class has profited from this database in the classroom:

When my class informed me that they really didn't understand the concept of "ordinatio" after our first session on it, I was able to show them a page from Ellesmere juxtaposed with pages from both the Kelmscott Chaucer and an Ovid MS. On the spur of the moment I could illustrate by comparison and contrast how the elements of page design contribute to a reader's interpretation of the text. . . . . The quality and flexibility in the reproduction of the images goes far toward reducing the logistical problems of access to the sorts of objects that medievalists often study (manuscripts, objects in European collections). . . . it opens students to the many possibilities for concentrated engagement with medieval objects more typical heretofore of graduate work.

At the same time, however, texts or data in electronic source databases are not laid out neatly on a page or prearranged clearly in a chart or graph for browsing or casual perusal. The software that accesses the source materials contained in a database requires the user to formulate a question or series of questions in order to retrieve information from the source and organize it in a meaningful way; this makes explicit the close attention and questioning stance that must be brought to bear on primary source materials. With these electronic resources an instructor can give students vivid and dynamic lessons in the interrogation and interpretation of primary source materials.

For example, students in Columbia University's renowned Contemporary Civilization course must come to grips with seminal works of the Western intellectual tradition from Plato to Freud—no mean feat for undergraduates. In his Contemporary Civilization class, Professor W. D. Van Horn has used a full-text database containing key works by Jean-Jacques Rousseau (1990) to teach his students strategies for examining some of the difficult paradoxes in Rousseau's thought by searching through the database for pairs of opposing concepts, such as nature and society or freedom and obligation. Not only does this full-text database enable students quickly to locate relevant sections of the texts for closer study, but the process of identifying concepts, of selecting words and combinations of words to define them, and of further refining those definitions as a result of searching the database helps students to focus closely on the words and structure of the texts and to recreate for themselves the terms of Rousseau's arguments (Van Horn 1991).

Last but not least, with the advent of increasingly capable but easy-to-use software for scanning and optical character recognition, text analysis, image analysis, information management, statistical analysis, visualization and simulation, and multimedia presentation and authoring, more and more scholars and students are eager to create their own electronic versions of primary source materials for teaching, as well as research. The Electronic Text Center (ETC) at the University of Virginia maintains a large, networked database of electronic texts in the humanities, with sophisticated analytical software. Faculty and students use the facilities and resources of the Electronic Text Center not only to explore the existing electronic texts but also to create their own. The following examples are drawn from the experiences of those who have used the Electronic Text Center (1992):

[A]n undergraduate survey course used [ETC] holdings in the 19th century novel and added Frances Brooke's *Lady Julia Mandeville,* an 18th century Canadian novel to the [ETC's] collection of on-line texts; a Shakespeare survey course created a teaching tool using text, images, and digitized sound from different productions of *The Merchant of Venice* to run alongside the on-line collections of Shakespeare's works; an English composition class used [ETC] services to gather Bush/Clinton position papers from the Presidential campaigns; [and] graduate bibliography students used collating software, image scanning, and digitized sound while preparing and presenting editing projects.

What do all of these exemplary teaching projects have in common? First of all, they require undergraduate students actively to engage primary sources. Second, they bring electronic primary source databases into the classroom, where the instructor can teach the processes of analysis and engagement and where the students can learn from and reinforce one another in the experience of confronting difficult or elusive source materials. Finally, in at least three cases they depend for their success, indeed for their very existence, on the library: Professor Landon's course met exclusively in the electronic classroom of the Information Arcade in the Main Library at the University of Iowa, and his students did most of their research and the preparation of their hypertext databases in the library and the Arcade; Professor Van Horn's class met in the Electronic

Text Service in Butler Library at Columbia University when they examined the electronic edition of Rousseau's works; and the various classes at the University of Virginia used the Electronic Text Center in the Alderman Library and its online database of electronic texts and text analysis software, which is accessible over the campus network.

These courses and class assignments, and the pioneering library facilities and support that make them possible, are not unique nor are they yet widely emulated. They require a new configuration of library resources and services that will vary in extent and focus from institution to institution but that share certain characteristics and certain basic assumptions about the library of the future. In the remainder of this chapter, I outline what I see as some of the most fundamental elements in the library's evolving role of supporting the use of electronic primary sources for teaching and research.

First of all, the library must be very aggressive in its efforts to provide access to high-quality electronic source materials that are held locally as well as available over campus and national and international networks. Several years ago, arguing that libraries should acquire textual databases like the works of Shakespeare, a member of the HUMANIST online discussion group (Whittaker 1989) posed the following provocative but presumably rhetorical question: "Is the library a place where one can actually do research, or is it only a place where one can look up the research that others have done?"

In other words, will libraries continue to provide access primarily to indexes and other bibliographic works in electronic formats, or will they also make available textual, numeric, visual, and aural primary source materials in electronic formats? I think that many if not most academic libraries have committed themselves, at least in theory, to the latter, but they are moving cautiously and are still trying to fit these resources into familiar reference paradigms of "looking things up."

Instead, I would argue that libraries must recognize that successful use of electronic primary source materials goes beyond information retrieval. By their very nature, electronic primary source materials give users the ability to accomplish unprecedented kinds of manipulation, reorganization, and recreation in the pursuit of knowledge and understanding. Computer-aided research and teaching no longer mean simply searching through a database, bibliographic or nonbibliographic, and printing out or downloading the results. Increasingly, faculty and students need and expect access to tool software for complex textual or statistical or image analysis, to scanners along with image manipulation or optical character recognition software for transforming paper documents into digital ones, to multimedia presentation and authoring programs that enable them to create their own hypermedia works of analysis and imagination, and to simulation and visualization software for "virtual" experiments with primary data.

Way back in 1986, David Crawford (1986, p. 569), a musicologist at the University of Michigan, addressed what he saw as a new teaching role for librarians, saying, "Your role as curators of knowledge seems to be taking on a new dimension. Now part of that knowledge . . . is technology itself, and you will find yourselves teaching others how to use it."

These words are even truer today, with the proliferation of sophisti- cated electronic resources and analytical tools. In this teaching role we will find ourselves working in close collaboration with scholars, comput- ing professionals, and graduate student assistants. For example, the Elec- tronic Text Service at Columbia University, the Electronic Text Center at the University of Virginia, and the Information Arcade at the University of Iowa all use graduate students, chosen for their subject knowledge as much as for their technological expertise, to help provide reference and instructional services. I am convinced, however, that the library is a natural venue for teaching people to use electronic primary source ma- terials for research and teaching and that we must prepare to take the lead in teaching ourselves and others what is possible and how to do it (Lowry 1990).

According to David Seaman, director of the Electronic Text Center at Virginia (Electronic Text Center 1992), "A principal aim of the Electronic Text Center is to help create a new broad-based user community within the humanities at Virginia. We work daily with individual users to intro- duce them to new working methods, new teaching possibilities, and new types of equipment. The Library was adamant from the earliest stages of this enterprise that these new services had to be introduced and taught through ongoing workshops and demonstrations."

Let us return now, for a moment, to the electronic classroom in the Information Arcade, where Professor Landon teaches, using a variety of print, media, and electronic resources, and where his students use the same equipment to share their hypermedia explorations with him and with their fellow students. The classroom has twenty-four student Macintosh microcomputers and two microcomputers (one Macintosh and one IBM-compatible) at the instructor's station, along with various pieces of equipment to provide access to electronic information sources on CD-ROM, laserdisc, magnetic disc, read-write optical disc, compact discs, and videotape. Of course, they are all networked to the Information Arcade's file server and to the campus backbone and Internet, and the instructor's equipment is connected to the classroom's Sony projection system. The classroom is an integral part of the Information Arcade, both physically and conceptually. One wall of the classroom is floor-to-ceiling glass that can be made opaque (to shut out distractions from the rest of the Arcade) or clear (to allow staff to observe the users of the machines when no class is in session). But beyond the practical reasons for this glass wall, not to mention its obvious "gee-whiz" effect, the glass is a most appropriate symbol for the Information Arcade's electronic classroom. To me, a classroom with glass walls is an evocative metaphor for the close two-way relationship between the formal teaching and learning that takes place within a library's electronic classroom and the research and independent learning activities going on all around it in the rest of the library. An electronic classroom in the library, for the use of both librarians and faculty, is a vital gateway to the successful and widespread use of electronic source materials for teaching and research. In recognition of that fact, more and more libraries are including such classrooms in their renovation and building plans. At the same time, we in the library, the computing center, and the university must also plan and build for the delivery of electronic resources to classrooms outside the library via the campus network. The library without walls is another metaphor, a familiar one evoking the idea of a library that is electronically linked to diverse sources of information outside its physical boundaries and that electronically delivers information to people and places beyond its walls. We must embrace and extend both these metaphors and create not only classrooms with glass walls but also classrooms without walls that will truly integrate electronic source materials into undergraduate and graduate teaching.

Note

An earlier version of this chapter, entitled "Electronic texts and multimedia in the academic library: A view from the front line," appears in B. Sutton (ed.), *Literary Texts in an Electronic Age: Scholarly Implications and Library Services,* Champaign, IL: Graduate School of Library and Information Science, University of Illinois, 1994, pp. 57–66. Reprinted by permission of The Board of Trustees of the University of Illinois.

References

Crawford, David. 1986. "Meeting Scholarly Information Needs in an Automated Environment: A Humanist's Perspective." *College and Research Libraries* 47 (November): 569.

Electronic Text Center. 1992. "The Electronic Text Center, Alderman Library, University of Virginia—Users: Fall 1992." Information sheet.

Landon, Brooks. 1993a. Interview with Dr. Joan Huntley, Research and Development Project Leader, Second Look Computing, Weeg Computing Center, spring.

Landon, Brooks. 1993b. "Literature and Culture of Twentieth Century America." Course description, University of Iowa, January.

Lowry, Anita. 1990. "Beyond BI: Information Literacy in the Electronic Age." *Research Strategies* 8, no. 1 (Winter): 22–27.

Rousseau, Jean-Jacques. 1990. *Discourse on the Origin of Inequality* and *On the Social Contract in Political Philosophy: Machiavelli to Mill* [computer file]. Pittsboro, NC: InteLex. *Past Masters.*

Van Horn, W. D. 1991. Class notes and conversation with the author, Columbia University, October.

Wack, Mary. 1993. "Electronic Chaucer." *Computers and Texts* 5 (April): 9.

Whittaker, Brian. 1989. "Oxford Electronic Shakespeare, etc. cont." Electronic message on HUMANIST List [a network Listserv discussion group], vol. 2, no. 740 (18 March).

15

Historians and Hypertext: Is It More Than Hype?

Roy Rosenzweig and Steve Brier

"In ten years or so," D. H. Jonassen (1982, p. 379) predicted more than ten years ago in *The Technology of Text*, "the book as we know it will be as obsolete as is movable type today." Jonassen is hardly the only technoenthusiast to be carried away by the potential of electronic media to reshape the way we consume and read information. More than thirty years ago, Ted Nelson (1981), who coined the term *hypertext,* was arguing that print books would be obsolete in just five years (see also Landow 1992; McKnight, Dillon, and Richardson 1991; Conklin 1987).

Nelson may be an imprecise prophet, but he has a flair for inventing words. The 1980s did not see the withering away of the print book, but they did mark the emergence of a vast literature (most of it, ironically, in print form) on hypertext. In Nelson's words (1981, p. 2), hypertext is "nonsequential writing—text that branches and allows choices, best read at an interactive screen . . . a series of text chunks connected by links which offer the reader different pathways." In its most general meaning—chunks of linked information—there is nothing very new or extraordinary about hypertext. Works as diverse as the Talmud and a footnoted scholarly article are built from pieces of interlinked information that can be read nonsequentially.

What is new, however, is using computers and electronic storage media to rapidly link together vast quantities of information. Back in 1945 Vannevar Bush, the first director of the federal government's Office of Scientific Research and Development, proposed the "memex," a device "in which the individual stores his books, records, and communications, and which is mechanized so that it may be consulted with exceeding speed and flexibility." Bush's vision was only that; the technology of his

day was inadequate to his ambition. (His solution to the storage problem—microfilm—is guaranteed to make any historian groan.) But by
1961, when the even more ambitious Nelson was a sociology graduate
student looking for a way to organize his research notes, the computer
had appeared as the obvious solution to the problem of storing and
linking enormous quantities of information. For the past three decades,
therefore, Nelson has been promoting what he calls his Xanadu project—
an effort to build a "docuverse" in which all the world's literature is tied
into "a universal instantaneous hypertext publishing network" (Nelson
1981, ch. 1, sec. 4).

Nelson's Xanadu—like the Xanadu of *Citizen Kane,* a film by one of
Nelson's heroes, Orson Welles—remains uncompleted. Still, the failure
of hypertext or electronic books to live up to the promises and prophecies
of their hyperenthusiasts should not lead us to dismiss out of hand the
possibilities of using computers and digital media to present the past.
Even considering the existing technology, electronic history books do
have a place on our shelves even if it is not yet time to toss our trusty
paperbacks into the dustbin of history (books). In this chapter, we report
on our own effort at electronic publishing as a way of suggesting some
of the advantages and a few of the limitations of this new medium.

Briefly summarized, our electronic history book, *Who Built America?
From the Centennial Celebration of 1876 to the Great War of 1914*
(Rosenzweig and Brier 1993), was published by the Voyager Company
and developed by us in collaboration with Josh Brown and other colleagues at Hunter College's American Social History Project (ASHP) and
at George Mason University. It provides an interactive, multimedia introduction to American history of the late nineteenth and early twentieth
centuries on a single CD-ROM disc for Macintosh computers. The core
of this computer book is a basic survey of American history from 1876
to 1914 that is drawn from the second volume of ASHP's book, *Who
Built America?* published by Pantheon Books in 1992. To this textual
survey we add nearly 200 "excursions" that branch off from the main
body of the text—and, in the process, transform it. Those excursions
contain about 700 source documents in various media that allow students
as well as interested general readers to go beyond (and behind) the printed
page and immerse themselves in the primary and secondary sources that

professional historians use to make sense of the past. In addition to about 5,000 pages of textual documents, there are about four and a half hours of audio documents (oral histories, recorded speeches, and musical performances), 40 minutes of films, more than 700 photographic quality pictures, and about 75 charts, graphs, and maps.

The advantages of the computer and CD-ROM for presenting the turn of the century to students are easily summarized. One advantage is the vast storage capacity offered by the CD-ROM, which can hold 640 megabytes of data—the equivalent of more than 300,000 typed pages. Whereas the print version of the four chapters of *Who Built America?* could only include 40 primary documents of 250 to 750 words each, the CD-ROM includes not only many more documents but also much longer ones. For example, we have dozens of letters written home by Swedish, English, and Polish immigrants rather than just one or two. Indeed, the educational version of the disc includes six full-length books, including Upton Sinclair's *The Jungle* and Booker T. Washington's *Up From Slavery.* (The large capacity of the CD-ROM also encouraged us to incorporate some less serious excursions that might not find their way into a conventional book. One excursion explores the origin of the custom of answering the phone with "hello" and includes an early vaudeville routine of the immigrant "Cohen on the Telephone." Another allows users to complete the world's first crossword puzzle, which appeared in a New York newspaper in 1913.)

The second key advantage of this medium is its ability to locate and keep track of vast quantities of information very efficiently. If we asked you to find the 117 instances of the word *work* in the first four chapters of the printed volume, it would take you a couple of days and you would probably miss some of them. In the electronic version, the same task would take only about 11 seconds. In just a few more seconds, we even could locate the 406 instances of the same word in all the thousands of pages of primary documents, the excursion introductions, the captions, and the time line and then provide a list of all the instances in context. The computer also tracks which instances you look at and keeps markers for the ones that you want to return to later. Moreover, you can search in more extensive and complex ways: you can be taken only to the instances of *working class* or *working-class politics* or even pages where the word *class* appears anywhere near the word *women*. The program also offers many other ways to locate and link things quickly. A resource index, for example, provides users with rapid access to all 700 primary documents whether organized by topic (from American Indians to women) or by type of document (film, audio, photographs and images, puzzles and games, maps and graphs, text). By using the find feature and the resource index those who want to can learn about American history in a decidedly nonlinear fashion.

A related advantage of the computer's ability to access and keep track of information is simultaneity or the ability to move very quickly from one body of information to another—to shift from reading African-American Congressman Robert Smalls denouncing the disenfranchisement of black voters, to studying statistics on the effects of the secret ballot on voting, to examining the text of the Louisiana grandfather clause, to considering the historical debate between C. Vann Woodward and Howard Rabinowitz on the origins of Jim Crow, to listening to a recording of Booker T. Washington offering his famous "Atlanta Compromise." In effect, readers can instantly move behind the page to see the primary source materials out of which the basic text has been crafted. In addition, they can quickly locate information that will help them understand what they are reading. You can, for example, hold down the mouse on any place name in the text and be shown that place's location on a U.S. map. If you are lost temporally rather than spatially, you can switch to any of seven categories in a detailed timeline that spans the 1876 through 1914 period.

The third key advantage provided by the electronic book is its multimedia elements. For historians, the advantages of multimedia are obvious. The past occurred in more than one medium, so why not present it in multiple dimensions? The four and a half hours of audio "documents" are particularly valuable in making the past immediate and vivid. Thirty-five different oral history witnesses—Miriam Allen DeFord on her introduction to birth control in 1914, George Kills in Sight on the death of Crazy Horse, Pauline Newman on organizing the "Uprising of the 20,000" in 1909, Eubie Blake on the origins of ragtime music, Vaseline Usher on the 1906 Atlanta race riot, Luther Addington on religion in rural Appalachia—tell their stories in their own words.

These reminiscences are supplemented by sixteen contemporary sound clips of famous Americans, including William Jennings Bryan delivering the "Cross of Gold" speech, Woodrow Wilson campaigning for the presidency, William Howard Taft appealing to labor voters, Andrew Carnegie touting the "Gospel of Wealth," Russell Conwell looking for "Acres of Diamonds," and Weber and Fields doing one of their popular vaudeville routines. Twenty-five songs present the musical diversity of the nation, including Mexican corridos, Sousa marches, Italian-American Christmas music, Tin Pan Alley tunes, African-American work songs, and coal miner laments.

When we first started work on this project in 1990, the only way to present film electronically was to put it on an additional laserdisc to be played on a separate laserdisc player and television monitor. But the appearance in 1991 of QuickTime software, which allows the display of films directly on the computer screen, has enabled us to incorporate twenty early film clips as well. Thus, the excursion on the 1912 election includes film footage of all three major party candidates. Other film footage includes Edwin Porter's "documentary" of the sinking of the *Maine,* women suffragists marching down New York City's Fifth Avenue in 1915, a 1904 view of the interior of the giant Westinghouse factory, black soldiers marching in the Philippines, heavyweight champ Jim Corbett knocking out Peter Courtney, and a street car view of Boston in 1906. We also have drawn on the earliest fiction films: the excursion on the railroad allows you to see the film classic *The Great Train Robbery* in its entirety, and the excursion on temperance includes a satirical view of Carry Nation in *The Kansas Saloon Smashers.*

The advantages of enormous capacity and multimedia bring with them some dangers, however. There is no doubt, for example, that 640 megabytes offers exciting new possibilities that are simply not possible to duplicate in 640 book pages. But as we know from print books, length does not equal quality. The old warning from computer programming— "garbage in, garbage out"—applies equally to CD-ROMs. (Some of the earliest history CD-ROMS have won the derisive but accurate label of "shovelware.") Moreover, although sound and film are terrific additions to history teaching, these media can turn history into television commercials in which the media glitz overwhelms sustained contact with difficult ideas. We need to be wary of justifying multimedia with the usual refrain: that because students no longer read and are visually oriented, we need to respond to that shift in learning style with multimedia. We certainly should respond, for example, by drawing on and then developing skills of visual literacy. But there is no reason to give up reading simply because it is somehow old fashioned or out of fashion. We heartily embrace the slogan that our collaborators at Voyager have coined and even have printed on their tee shirts: "Text: The Next Frontier." Thus, despite the unconventional nature of this electronic book, we have retained some of the traditional features of a printed book. It looks much like a printed book on screen with two columns of type and frequent pictures. The reader can page through the book briskly using the arrow keys. To make quick paging possible, the pictures are not immediately presented in full, eight-bit photographic quality, which takes a few seconds to load into the computer's memory. But the higher-quality image, including a de-tailed caption and source information, is only a click of the mouse away.

Other traditional book features are also retained. Users can, for exam-ple, take notes in the margin or in a separate notebook. (Less tradition-ally, a resource collector serves as a sort of multimedia notebook in which readers can assemble their own compilation of specific sound and film clips and pictures as well as text.) If students prefer to highlight electroni-cally, they can select and boldface or underline any text. Electronic highlighting has an advantage over the printed book: it can be erased in an instant. You even can electronically fold over the corner of a page so that the computer will rapidly locate that marked page for you.

Just as *Who Built America?* on CD-ROM retains many of the tradi-tional features of a print book, so too the process of writing it was quite traditional in many respects. Most of our work involved the customary tasks that are familiar to all historians: selection, analysis, and synthesis. Our CD-ROM contains many more primary documents than any print book, but those documents still represent only a small selection from the vast historical record. That selection is rooted in our best historical judgment. Similarly, the documents cannot readily stand on their own. Every document is explained and contextualized; we spent hundreds of hours researching the backgrounds for each document and synthesizing the latest scholarship on a myriad of topics from sharecropping in the

South to Indian education at the Carlisle School to Asian immigrants at Angel Island to Coxey's Army in Washington to the Armory Show in New York. The new electronic media certainly are not going to displace historians. A more realistic worry is that the vast space of the CD-ROM will challenge the energy and ingenuity of historians to fill those discs in creative and intelligent ways.

New electronic media also will challenge our creativity as teachers if we are going to use them to democratize education and empower students. At its best, interactive technology makes exciting materials available to a broad audience; it gives students and others direct access to primary documents that might be available at the Library of Congress but not their local library. In addition, computer technology can allow students and other readers to have more control over their learning, to move at their own pace, and to make decisions about the direction they want to go in and the byways they want to investigate. New technology also may free up teachers from some of the most repetitive and least edifying aspects of teaching and allow them to spend time working directly and creatively with students.

We need to monitor the opposite tendencies that are at least implicit— that expensive new technologies may wind up being available only at affluent institutions and that technology can be exploited to make education more constraining and move students at an even more rigid lockstep through material. At least to some, the new technology is seen as a cheap and quick fix to the problems of American education. Chris Whittle and his business and education allies, for example, are promoting technology as a way to increase teacher productivity and (not coincidentally) turn education into a private and profit-making venture.

Our own view, however, is that we are a long way from the days when students will telecommute to Digital U. Even the seemingly simple and straightforward task of getting faculty and students to learn and make use of new computer technologies is far from simple or straightforward. Moreover, at least for the next few years our struggles with incompatible formats and platforms will remind us why the adoption of standard railroad track gauges was an important breakthrough of the late nineteenth century. We doubt that teaching will be as readily subject to automation as some believe or hope. Still, the future is far from determined. Any new technology carries within it repressive as well as liberating possibilities. Although a Luddite resistance to technological change may seem appealing at times, we argue instead that engaging with these new technologies will ensure that they indeed become badly needed tools of empowerment, enlightenment, and excitement. We may still be a long way from the death of the print book or the birth of the hypertextual docuverse, but the rapid emergence of new electronic media for reading, storing, and linking information means that even those of us who spend much of our time studying the past will need to play close attention, as well, to the future.

References

American Social History Project. 1992. *Who Built America?* New York: Pantheon Books.

Bush, Vannevar. 1945. "As We May Think," *Atlantic Monthly* (July): 101–108.

Conklin, Jeff. 1987. "Hypertext: An Introduction and Survey." *Computer* (September): 17–41.

Jonassen, D. H. 1982. *The Technology of Text.* vol. 1. Englewood Cliffs, NJ: Educational Technology Publications.

Landow, George P. 1992. *Hypertext: The Convergence of Contemporary Critical Theory and Technology.* Baltimore: Johns Hopkins University Press.

McKnight, Cliff, Andrew Dillon, and John Richardson. 1991. *Hypertext in Context.* Cambridge: Cambridge University Press.

Nelson, Theodore H. 1981. *Literary Machines.* Swathmore, PA: the author.

Rosenzweig, Roy, and Steve Brier. 1993. *Who Built America? From the Centennial Celebration of 1876 to the Great War of 1914* [CD-ROM]. Voyager Company, 1 Bridge, St., Irvington, NY 10533, 1–800–446–2001.

Postscript

Lawrence Dowler

Society needs to engage in a serious, prolonged conversation about what it wants higher education to achieve in a world of networked information. Such a conversation will have profound implications for research libraries. In this postscript I hope to help promote such a conversation by considering how information technology is influencing the mission and goals of research libraries and, in particular, by viewing these technological changes from the larger perspective of higher education. In thinking about these issues, I attempt not to summarize the preceding chapters but to draw on and be instructed by them. Many of my coauthors will no doubt disagree with some, if not all, of my conclusions, but neither my observations nor theirs will be the last word on this subject. Scholars, with the benefit of hindsight, will one day write those chapters. For now, it is enough to let the conversation begin.

Information Technology: Two Views of Libraries and Learning

Information technology, especially rapid developments in communications and distributed computing, is having an enormous impact on libraries. Indeed, distributing information over networks is the primary impetus for rethinking libraries—not just to think again but to think anew about the role of libraries in universities. Distributed computing is here and growing, and as it continues to grow it will change the parameters and institutional structures that currently support teaching, learning, and research. Many of the chapters presented in this book grapple with various aspects of this change, and, indeed, the several conceptions of the gateway are really attempts to bridge the gap between the traditional library and the incipient electronic library of the not too distant future.

A fundamental change is occurring here. If we think of the information revolutions that have occurred in history—writing, printing, microprocessors, computers, and networked communications—the last two have occurred in less than a quarter of a century. We scarcely grasped the implications of computers before we confronted an even more far-reaching development in distributed computing and networked information. The problem is how to respond to these changes and negotiate the uneven organizational terrain in which they are embedded within universities and libraries.

Information technology is perhaps the principal and defining trend of our time. David Ward (1994, p. 23), chancellor at the University of Wisconsin–Madison, has observed "a critical interdependence between the way higher education is organized and the way information technology is deployed. What's important about information technology is not its hardware or software but its disrespect for boundaries—all boundaries, including academic boundaries." The library is the battleground on which tradition most visibly encounters the verge created by information technology. Our creativity is found not so much within our institutions but on their borders, and the creative tension between the traditional role of the librarian as the custodian of our nation's intellectual heritage and the library as a place for studying it and the emerging role of the librarian as teacher and the library as a classroom. This tension has inspired the concept of a gateway that helps the library to make the transition from the comfort of familiar forms toward different organizational structures and new modes of learning.

Those who are optimistic about the possibilities for information technology to improve education and research hold two predominant attitudes: some are interested in how technology dramatically increases access to information and transforms scholarly communication, and others are more concerned with how digital technology affects how and what people learn. These are not mutually exclusive categories, but many writers tend to focus on one theme or the other depending on their primary interests. The systems lens focuses on process to support access to information and communication; the cognitive lens examines teaching and learning in the new environment.[1] One perspective views technology as a system and a process; the other views the human constructs for communication itself as a technology. From this perspective, any change in the conditions of communication alters what can be learned. Viewed as a system, on the other hand, networked information appears to undermine existing institutional agendas and organizational structures for providing information. By questioning the qualities and characteristics of digital information, the operative issue will become the definition and meaning of literacy itself. These two views about the meaning of information technology converge over the need for librarians to add value to information—that is, to provide filters and expert systems to help people locate and use information. But even on matters of apparent agreement, there are differences. Disciples of information as system want to know how librarians can make the system more efficient; adherents of the cognitive view wonder how to turn information into knowledge and thus make it more effective.

Perhaps nothing illustrates our understanding of information technology and the particular lens through which we view it better than our answer to this question: Is the gateway a place or a process? This question informs virtually every discussion about the future role of libraries in a digital environment. "The library as an idea," observes Jay David Bolter (1991, pp. 103–104), "will become as ephemeral as electronic technology itself; it will no longer be a building or even a fixed conceptual structure, but instead a constantly evolving network of elements." Thus, if one fully embraces technology and a system of distributed computing and networked information, logic suggests there will be no need for the library as a physical entity in the future. From this perspective, librarians who insist on the continuation of the library as a place seem nostalgic and needlessly romantic. But promoting a false dichotomy between electronic information and the physical environment obscures the synchrony between the use of information in learning and its milieu.

The loss of sense of place created by networked information and distributed computing may profoundly affect how people learn or even do research. All media, after all, affects social behavior, not through the power of the messages but by reorganizing the social settings in which people interact (Meyrowitz 1985). In the twentieth-century West, we have tended to look inward rather than to the external environment to locate the clues to human behavior. Freudian theory's emphasis on internal psychological processes and neurochemistry's focus on chemical processes and the nervous system are seen as the keys to interpreting human behavior. But a growing body of evidence recasts the relationship between behavior and the physical context in which they occur (Gallagher 1993, pp. 13–17, 132–134, 171–176). We must not ignore this relationship in learning. It is no accident that most scholars and writers have a preferred place in which to work and that for many that space is to be found in monumental research libraries. Can we reliably assume that the physical environment for learning will play a lesser role in the future just because one can now obtain most information from a screen?

Finally, the argument over network or place, really a debate about the delivery and use of information, begs a fundamental question for libraries. The question is not about which pipelines to use to deliver information or where to locate the equipment for using it. Rather, the question is, How will the shift from a culture of print to a culture of digital technology affect literacy and learning? For five centuries print has defined how we organize and present knowledge. In the words of one observer (Bolter 1991, p. 2), "This shift from print to the computer does not mean the end of literacy. What will be lost is not literacy itself, but the literacy of print, for electronic technology offers us a new kind of book and new ways to write and read." The challenge for libraries is to devise new strategies and tools for organizing and presenting knowledge that are consistent with the digital world and to create new educational and writing spaces as well. This is what the gateway library aims to do.

The Mission of the Gateway Library

Three attributes of the gateway define its mission. First, the gateway is a teaching library that aims to help people at all levels learn how to identify the information they need from the growing morass of information and cultural evidence in electronic and other forms. Second, the gateway is a place for learning how to evaluate and assess information and turn it into knowledge. As a center for learning, the gateway is an agora that invites discussion and interaction among individuals and small groups and is part of an ongoing process of discovery. Third, the gateway is predicated on the idea that access to information is not enough, that librarians will be obliged to become editors, and that they will need to create filters to help learners select the information they need from the ocean of information now available to them.

Teaching in the Gateway Library

Teaching is the core of the gateway library. Librarians have discovered that technology and electronic information bring students and faculty into the library looking for assistance and that every new database and electronic information source seems to generate more demand for instructional support. The challenge for libraries is to see this kind of teaching and instruction as central to its mission and to allocate staff resources for this purpose. The library must take seriously its growing role in teaching. Just as there are teaching hospitals, Jim Wilkinson (chapter 13) recommends teaching libraries; this is what the gateway library aspires to become.

As the definition of *information* has broadened over the past twenty or thirty years, students and scholars require more assistance in locating the information they need. In addition to books and periodicals, libraries house videotapes, audiotapes, manuscripts, maps, archives, computer data, photographs, and a variety of artifacts that document our cultural life.[2] Increasingly, scholars must use sources from sometimes unfamiliar disciplines outside of their field of expertise. For researchers the problem is how to locate needed information in a library cataloging system that is based primarily on describing publications; for librarians, the challenge is how to locate sources that may be housed in separate institutions such as archives, historical societies, and museums.[3] These changes require more mediation and instruction in learning how to locate needed sources. The question is not so much one of technology, although this may be an issue for some, but a matter of understanding the content and possible uses of these multiple sources.

Billy E. Frye (chapter 1) contends that the increasing importance of research and scholarship and the emergence of new academic disciplines have resulted in many highly desirable changes. "Perhaps most significantly," he says, "the tie between teaching and scholarship became less the established canon around which intellectual life was centered and more the very process of search for objective knowledge. It is this, I believe, that has contributed most to the success of modern universities, not only because it created a great expansion of knowledge but because it has engendered a spirit of inquiry in place of dogma." The problem for the library, however, is that collections, classification and cataloging schemes—indeed, the very structure of the library as an organization—are based on the nineteenth-century academic structure of the university, a structure that appears increasingly at odds with the new academic disciplines and forms of scholarship. The challenge for the library is to find a way to effectively respond to these changes in teaching and research by adding value to information and providing the expertise that these emerging academic interests require.

Technology alters the way we interact with information by changing the media in which we learn. Print encouraged the shift from the oral tradition to individual learning; today the growing importance of visual images in communication is another shift. Electronic information, especially multimedia, represents a radical transformation in the way we interact with information and hence the way we learn.[4] This transition already has changed teaching, which has moved from instruction by reading and lecturing to learner-centered instruction that uses technology to manipulate and query data in new ways.

Perhaps most important and least understood is the problem of how to teach students to think critically about information in various forms. In the past, liberal education focused primarily on a critical reading of texts. But in an environment in which multiple forms of media—visual, audio, artifacts, and data—are important sources for research and learning, students need to understand the uses and limits of each medium and to evaluate critically the appropriate uses of each medium for various purposes.[5] "Critical thinking about information," says Peter Lyman (chapter 10), "requires that each of the senses be taught to make a critical reading of each of the media that present information." These skills are important for current coursework but are critical for life-long learning.

The Gateway in Learning

How do students learn, and what is the role of the library in supporting learning? There appears to be a growing recognition that even college students learn best when they are actively involved in the learning process through problem solving and discovery and when what they learn can be applied, even if only in another class. This paradigm shift from memorizing facts to discovering the information needed to solve a problem allies learning with research and therefore teaching with research.[6] Software applications and database developments do not often take advantage of these elements of learning, and it may be up to the librarians who evaluate and acquire these tools and products to also assess their value for learning. Computer simulations, for example, can model the behavior of complex systems to show the effect of individual variables or the interactions of multiple variables, an idea that is difficult to convey by lecture. We must aim therefore not just to automate current teaching practices, as many virtual classrooms do, but to seek out and select, develop, and employ technologies that stimulate and aid learning.

Electronic information significantly changes the learner's perceptions and uses of information. For one thing, people extract bits and pieces of information from digital sources, and the learner, rather than the author of a text, must provide the context for that information.[7] One aspect of hypertext and hypermedia, for example, is its capacity to link sources in ways that disrupt the continuity of a narrative (Landow 1992, pp. 52–56, 71–87). A play or novel is no longer a text to be read through but a series of bits of information linked to other sources. The power of the media creates an archive of information that the learner dips into as he or she wishes. One reads in rather than through a document, and the author of the document merges imperceptibly with the reader who accesses it (Bolter 1991, pp. 153–159, 166–168). Moreover, the medium of interaction also shifts. Just as the oral tradition was oriented toward the group and print toward individual meditation, electronic interaction appears to shift the orientation again toward group learning.

The challenge for libraries, then, is to respond to these changes in teaching and learning and create an environment for problem solving and student-centered learning. The gateway library will supplement traditional library reading and study spaces with flexible areas for interaction among learners and with multimedia technologies.[8] This is not just an incremental addition of technology into existing library programs and space but a reorientation of the library to actively acquire and participate in the development of the tools used in learning.[9]

Expert Systems and Librarians as Experts

Access to information has been the principal focus of librarians in recent years. The principal problem for learners, however, is too much information. To filter out excess and identify the useful must now become our primary concerns. Information is expanding faster than anyone can process, store, retrieve, and use it. A kind of Gresham's law of information is operating in which not only does bad information threaten to drive out the good but the sheer volume of information threatens to overwhelm whatever might be useful. The defining problem for librarians is to create the tools that will enable learners to locate the information they need and deliver it in the form in which they need it.[10]

Part of the problem is that library cataloging and classification schemes are predicated on a knowable universe and a limited output of publications—a model that is inadequate in a digital world. Moreover, as the metaphorical web of information becomes reality, thus linking the bits and pieces of information, we are faced with our inability to evaluate and create hierarchical relations among data that reflect their relative importance.[11]

Knowledge is continually changing, and the individual researcher is unlikely to have an overview of the entire knowledge system. One of the challenges for gateway librarians will be to provide this overview by mapping the changing world of information and developing the navigational tools that will enable a learner to traverse an unruly informational landscape and then evaluate the bits and pieces of information they discover.[12] Librarians must shed the passive posture that views their work as essentially reactive to current trends in scholarship. The knowledge base must be deepened by librarians who trace the contours of fields of knowledge and design maps, templates, or filters for learners to discover what they need from the surfeit of information.[13] Traditional library cataloging schemes will not do. Instead, we will need to develop expert systems that incorporate the changing nature of inquiry *and* the sources that are discovered that pertain to it. But expert systems are only as good as the most recent design, and they require the attention of expert humans to keep them updated and mediate between their limits and the rising expectations for information.

Implications of Information Technology for Libraries and Universities

The gateway as a response to information technology and to the influence of digital information on teaching and learning has a number of implications for both libraries and higher education. How the two spheres interact and respond to these changes will profoundly affect the future of both. In this section, I briefly mention three implications of these changes on libraries and some implications for higher education.

Implications for Libraries

One implication of the dramatic growth in the quantity and variety of information is that librarians will become increasingly specialized. They will need expertise to manage the sheer volume of sources needed for research, the changing nature of inquiry, and the continued development of information technology. Although the need for library generalists will continue, specialized knowledge on the environment, for example, or on comparative literary and historical studies that cut across disciplines will require a greater depth of knowledge about sources and how they are used in research. Moreover, technology will impose its own demands for expertise. The volatility in technology involving images, data, multimedia, as well as text will demand constant attention and will affect the requirements and training for library positions.[14] The question is whether the library will maintain its role in supporting the information needs for research or whether academic departments will acquire their own information specialists and thereby further fragment knowledge and diminish the value of the library in the academy.

Despite the trend toward distributed computing, greater centralization of some library services is called for by the high cost of support for distributed computing and networked information (more than the cost of equipment). Indeed, more coordinated and even centralized library support for some information needs is one of the features of the gateway. One can argue that library services, especially reference and instruction, can also be distributed over the network. But until the systems for retrieving information become as powerful as our capacity to store it, it seems likely that teaching and instruction and even reference support will

still need to be conducted face-to-face in the library. Technology undoubtedly can improve discovery and enhance our ability to locate needed
information. After all, this is one of the aims of filters and expert information systems. But research and discovery are highly associative processes, and the changing nature of inquiry, even more than volatile
technology, will necessitate human intervention to satisfy information
needs for the foreseeable future.

As the information environment continues to change and becomes
increasingly specialized, it will require greater flexibility and even new
forms of institutional organization. An avalanche of breathless literature
talks about reengineering organizations, empowering people, eliminating
hierarchy, and the like, but most organizational change in libraries has
been as modest as it has been within universities. A gateway library that
emphasizes teaching, learning, and greater specialization among staff will
require a radically different structure. For one thing, the organizational
unit may often be a single instructor and a few students, with individuals
engaged in teaching drawn from staff spread throughout the organization. The institution needs to support the work of such units but also
keep the one-person department from becoming an independent island
with no vision of or allegiance to the commonweal. Most commonly
this dilemma is expressed in terms of ensuring accountability in an
organization composed of individuals or teams. But the real issue is
not accountability. Rather, the measure of success is achievement and
accomplishment. Flexibility, maintaining commitment to a common purpose and mission, preserving the individual's sense of competency in an
ever-changing environment, and providing a reward structure that honors
special skills and knowledge will become essential ingredients for libraries
that embrace the gateway concept.

Finally, the gateway library will centralize some activities but will
depend on the skills and contributions of individuals scattered throughout an entire institution. Traditionally, librarians have identified with a
single organization, most often characterized by a building; now they
must identify with a process or program that may be independent of one's
primary affiliation. Problems of identity and loyalty, as well as the coordination of functions, may become the principal challenge and will make

issues of organizational structure, management style, and leadership even more important in a gateway library.

Implications for Higher Education

The decline of the library as the center of the academic community is of greater moment to universities than it may at first appear. The old saying, practically a homily, that "the library is the heart of the university," was more than symbolic rhetoric. Prior to World War II, the curriculum drew together college and university faculty into a scholarly community, which the library's collections and schemes for classification and cataloging mirrored. The curriculum and the library were part of the same intellectual frame, and the library was the physical and intellectual commons shared by all members of the community. Over the past four decades, however, the growth and success of research has fragmented knowledge and created ever more specialized areas with their own literature and scholarly publications. Hence, even before serial prices began to rise, the enormous volume of published knowledge began to alter the basic purpose and functions of research libraries. In this already fragmented environment, the library is unlikely to provide a counterweight to the centripetal forces pulling at members of the university community.

The apparently diminished centrality of the library within the university community has been exacerbated by technology. First, parts of the research community, especially in the sciences, have access to information and research sources that do not depend on the library. Second, distributed computing and networked information means nearly everyone can be less dependent on the library for at least some of their information needs. Finally, as Richard A. Lanham observes in chapter 11, both the university and the library are a reflection of the culture of print; academic departments and disciplines, classes of instruction, textbooks, and even the curriculum are responses to information and knowledge based on print. Thus, the structure and organization of universities and libraries are susceptible to the changes brought about when information is delivered by digital technology.

For all of these reasons, a battle has developed between those who wish to preserve the traditional substance and forms of the academy and those who embrace technology, either to revivify what they see as a moribund enterprise or to increase academic efficiency and reign in rising operating costs. The library is a lightning rod for these competing views. The argument, however, is not about libraries in particular but, as many of the essays in this volume make clear, about the nature of teaching and learning.

A gateway library must think of itself as part of an international research community. No library can collect every print and primary source, let alone every piece of electronic information. The future of research will require cooperative arrangements for preserving the varied evidentiary sources now required by researchers. Because the gateway is a portal to these resources and coordinates the delivery of instructional services within the library, it is well positioned to take the lead in developing cooperative collection programs. The challenge will be to create institutional structures and incentives to sustain cooperative resource sharing and development among libraries, museums, archives, and historical societies on a national level (Dowler 1994).

Decisions about acquisitions, the methods of cataloging and providing access, and, ultimately, reference and library instruction will all be affected. Students and scholars will need to be provided with the methodological training that new curricula, new sources, and new intellectual interests demand. The authority of the text is giving way to new forms of information, and each form and genre must be evaluated by different criteria than those that apply to texts. Research universities have scarcely begun to consider how to meet these challenges, and few libraries, despite all their efforts involving automation and technology, have seriously considered the underlying intellectual problem of how to preserve or provide access to the range of sources now required for learning and research. Nor have they thought about new requirements that digital information will introduce.

The expanding definition of information and the importance of non-print sources for research test the limits of the traditional library, even as shrinking resources limit their ability to respond to these new conditions. Interdisciplinary and cross-cultural research also challenges the disciplinary framework that has served libraries and scholars for the past one hundred years. Study of the environment, for example, touches nearly every academic discipline; it connects disparate sciences, informs public policy, and enlists ethical and humane values in an intellectual discourse that touches our lives with power and immediacy. Here, then, are the conditions for reintegrating fractured knowledge and education by honoring ideals larger than ourselves, solving problems that matter to our continued existence, and drawing on multiple ways of knowing. Here, too, are the conditions for reconfiguring the curriculum and libraries as partners in the same intellectual enterprise.

Conclusion: Questions about Boundaries

In reading these essays, one is struck by how infrequently the fundamental issue under discussion is the technological or the budgetary deficiencies we generally blame for educational and library problems. More often, it appears, the most intractable problems, with the most promising potential solutions, direct us to changes in institutional and organizational structures, goals, and objectives. We may find, for example, that the educational goals of an institution are really more important to the quality of education than the methods and tools that they employ. Creating an organization, for example, that connects scholars, library, and technical staff may be more important to the effective use of technology within a university than acquiring a large quantity of technological tools. The relationship between print and electronic sources, the kind of instruction that helps students and faculty locate and use information, and strategies that promote collaboration among institutions to provide access to information are all organizational issues. Who should develop the navigational tools and create filters or expert systems that help people locate the sources they need? What kind of skills are needed to work in this new environment? Should the entrepreneurs who develop database and interactive applications for learning be librarians, other information experts within the university, or commercial agents? And, most important, what does literacy mean in a digital age, and who should teach it, and how should it be supported?

In their struggle to define the library of the future, librarians too often bolt new technology, programs, and services on to existing functions. The library must focus not only on how information may be packaged and disseminated in a networked environment but also on the nature and qualities of electronic information. We err when we assume that electronic information is essentially the same as print and that the role of the library will therefore remain the same or, alternatively, disappear. The question we must ask is, will the library respond to information technology by simply overlaying electronic tools and information on to the existing structure, or will the library fundamentally alter the environment for teaching and research and thereby the reality of learning? The disciplinary boundaries that govern academic study will be increasingly expanded by digital technology, and the university administrative structures that support them will follow. The gateway, by sponsoring systemic changes to the way in which libraries support teaching, learning, and research, provides a bridge to the future and to the inevitably evolving structures and mission of higher education.

Notes

1. This bimodal perspective is most clearly conveyed in this book in the chapters by Paul Ginsparg (chapter 4), Richard C. Rockwell (chapter 5), and John Unsworth (chapter 6), who tend to view information technology through the systems lens, and the chapters by Richard A. Lanham (chapter 11), Karen Price (chapter 12), and James Wilkinson (chapter 13), who focus principally on the effect of digital technology on cognition and the processes of knowing. Jan Olsen (chapter 9) appears to be in the systems camp but is constrained by the practical considerations of managing a library that is still in transition from a traditional to an electronic library. Although they also address the uses of technology in teaching and learning, Anita Lowry (chapter 14), Roy Rosenzweig (chapter 15) and Steve Brier (chapter 15) are concerned less with digital literacy and more with technology's potential to improve learning within the existing culture of print. Peter Lyman (chapter 10) oscillates between the two views, stressing the cognitive view when discussing teaching and learning and the systems view when addressing scholarly communication and the growth of networked information.

2. In chapter 2 Patrick Manning describes changes in the study of history and its implications for the discipline and the requirement for a variety of sources. Anthony Appiah (chapter 3) appeals for new sources from an interdisciplinary perspective but fears that their acquisition will be hindered by old agendas and traditional views about what is worth acquiring.

3. Richard C. Rockwell (chapter 5) argues that distinctions among kinds of information are breaking down and that this blurring of boundaries will necessitate rethinking the organizational structures that currently divide them.

4. The most thoughtful exploration of this topic is Lanham (1993).

5. Throughout chapter 11 Richard A. Lanham especially considers the implications of literacy for education in the age of the electronic word.

6. James Wilkinson, in particular, emphasizes in chapter 13 the changes in teaching that have occurred in recent years.

7. Karen Price's chapter 12 is especially good at explaining the differences in learning that occur in a digital environment.

8. The best descriptions of this are in the articles by Anita Lowry (chapter 14) and Jan Olsen (chapter 9).

9. Roy Rosenzweig and Steve Brier explore the advantages and some dangers of electronic media in chapter 15.

10. Paul Ginsparg (chapter 4) and John Unsworth (chapter 6) both stress the need to add value to information to make it useful. For Unsworth adding value is a matter of survival for the humanities. For Ginsparg, too, there is a question about which agency, commercial or academic, will ultimately develop the tools needed to improve the usefulness of information.

11. Wilkinson (chapter 13) is eloquent on this point.

12. Steve Fuller (1994) provides a perceptive analysis of expert systems and research.

13. Richard C. Rockwell (chapter 8), in particular, thinks librarians must address these concerns and take the lead in providing the tools and expertise that are needed to effectively use information.

14. Jan Olsen (chapter 9) is particularly good at describing the implications of the various electronic genres for library staff.

References

Bolter, Jay David. 1991. *Writing Space: The Computer, Hypertext and the History of Writing.* Hillsdale, NJ.: Erlbaum.

Dowler, Lawrence. 1994. "The Implications of Electronic Information for National Institutions." *Leonardo* 27: 171–178.

Fuller, Steve. 1994. "Why Post-Industrial Society Never Came." *Academe* (November–December): 22–28.

Gallagher, Winifred. 1993. *The Power of Place: How Our Surroundings Shape Our Thoughts, Emotions, and Actions.* New York: Poseidon Press.

Landow, George P. 1992. *Hypertext: The Convergence of Contemporary Critical Theory and Technology.* Baltimore: Johns Hopkins University Press.

Lanham, Richard. 1993. *The Electronic Word: Democracy, Technology, and the Arts.* Chicago: University of Chicago Press.

Meyrowitz, Joshua. 1985. *No Sense of Place: The Impact of Electronic Media on Social Behavior.* New York: Oxford University Press.

Ward, David. 1994. "Technology and the Changing Boundaries of Higher Education." *Educom Review* 29, no. 1 (January–February): 23.

Index

Havelock, Eric, 154
Health services, 78
hep-th, 43, 47–48, 53, 57
Higher education, xiv, xvi, 1, 7, 151–
152, 215
changes in, 4, 225–227
High school, 157
Hirsch, Eliot, 171
Historians, 184
Historical demography, 21
History, 19–20, 23, 31n6, 97,
228n2. *See also various subfields*
as discipline, 29–30
and electronic research, 99–100
multimedia presentation of, 208–
213
at Northeastern University, 24–28
HOLLIS, 35, 39, 96, 100, 101, 102,
143, 185, 192
Hollis, A. P., 176
Holmes, Oliver Wendell, 174
Home Shopping Network, 81, 90
Houghton Library, 100
http. *See* Hypertext transfer protocols
Human attention, 164, 165, 195–196
Humanism, 87–89
HUMANIST, 203
Humanities, 6, 78, 97, 229n10
computer-mediated research in, 82–
85
copyrights and, 85–87
Hunter College, 208
Hypermedia, 85, 88, 104, 221
Hypertext, 85, 130, 156–157, 189–
190, 208, 221
classroom use of, 199–200
Hypertext documentation, 70–71
Hypertext transfer protocols (http),
54
Hypertextual connectedness, xiii

IATH-MOO, 88–89
IBM, 82
ICPSR. *See* Inter-university Consortium for Political and Social Research

Identity, 224
Image-enhancement technology, 78
Images, 38–39, 200–201
Immigration, 83
Indexing, indexes, 53–54, 56, 114,
116–117, 132, 210
CD-ROM, 101, 102
WAIS, 71, 72, 130
Inflation, 11
Information, 119, 173, 181, 201,
216, 229n10
abundance of, 3–4
access to, 67–68, 109–110, 112–
113, 222
adding value to, xvii
costs of, 141–142
electronic, vii, x, 99–100, 125–127,
145, 220, 221, 227–228
and knowledge, 144, 170–172, 175–
178
and learning, 189–190
nonprint, 15
organization of, 41, 112, 114
research and, 226–227
searching for, 173–174
social science, 60–65, 69–71, 77–80
transmission of, 169–170
Wal-Marts of, 117–118
Information Arcade (Iowa), xi, 197,
202, 204, 205–206
Information genres, 125–127
Information infrastructures, 81, 91,
109, 119, 120–121
Information literacy, xv, 140–141
Information management, 13, 37
Information revolution, 109
Information services, 13
Information superhighway, 45–46,
81, 116–117, 186–187
Institute for Advanced Technology in
the Humanities (U.Va.), 82
copyrights and, 85–87
projects of, 83–85
Institutional will, 1
Integration, 114
Intellectual property, 90, 91n1, 158